Bodyguard to the Packers

Beat Cops, Brett Favre, And Beating the Odds

Jerry Parins

*Former Director of Security
for the Green Bay Packers*

With Mike Dauplaise

Bodyguard to the Packers
Beat Cops, Brett Favre, and Beating Cancer

Copyright © 2008 Jerry Parins and Mike Dauplaise

TitleTown Publishing, LLC
PO Box 12093
Green Bay, WI 54307-12093
920-737-8051
www.titletownpublishing.com

Book production by Cypress House
Cover and book design by Burton Worms

Front cover photograph: Personal collection of Jerry Parins. Photographer unknown. Every effort has been made to trace the copyright holder of this photograph. The publisher apologizes for any errors or omissions and would be grateful if notified of any corrections that should be incorporated in future reprints or editions of this book.

Publisher's Cataloging-in-Publication Data

Parins, Jerry.
   Bodyguard to the Packers : beat cops, Brett Favre, and beating cancer / Jerry Parins ; with Mike Dauplaise. -- 1st ed. -- Green Bay, WI : TitleTown Publishing, c2008.

   ISBN: 978-0-9820009-1-5 (cloth) ; 978-0-9820009-0-8 (pbk.)
   1. Parins, Jerry--Biography. 2. Green Bay Packers (Football team)--Security measures. 3. Lambeau Field (Green Bay, Wis.)--Security measures. 4. Police, Private--Biography. I. Dauplaise, Mike. II. Title.
GV956.G7 P37 2008   2008906778
796.33264/06073 0809

Printed in the USA by Thomson-Shore

2   4   6   8   9   7   5   3   1

First edition

Printed on recycled paper

Contents

 # Prologue

MY DOUBLE LIFE AS A FAN of the Packers and an employee of the team began with a phone call from an irate Vince Lombardi to Police Chief Elmer Madson in the summer of 1965. Fans were walking onto the Oneida Street practice field while Coach Lombardi's team was working out, and he wanted some uniformed officers to keep them off.

I was one of those officers, and that's how my working relationship with the Green Bay Packers began. It continues to this day in my semi-retirement.

I'm just a regular guy — a former beat cop and detective from a disadvantaged childhood — who happened to see and experience some interesting and exciting events. You may have heard about some of them, but I've included behind-the-scenes perspectives that you won't read anywhere else.

The idea of writing down my experiences actually came from Ron Dauplaise, a longtime acquaintance of mine who attended West High School in Green Bay a couple of years ahead of me. Ron's dad was our principal, and Ron's wife, Ellen, was in my class. Ron loves stories, and he's one of a dedicated group of guys who dig up interesting tales to share as Lambeau Field tour guides.

Ron approached me at the stadium one day early in the summer of 2004 and said, "Jerry, I bet you have a bunch of great stories you could tell."

I agreed, but told him I wouldn't know where to start.

"I have a son who's a writer," he said. "Would you like to meet him?"

Ron hooked me up with his son, Mike, a former sportswriter who'd left the newspaper and corporate worlds behind to become a full-time freelance writer. Mike and I hit it off right away, and we immediately began a series of interviews aimed at pulling those old stories from my memory bank.

It was a long process, but a very fulfilling and humbling one. A lot of people have impacted my life and helped me through some difficult times. When you're a cop, a detective, or the security director for the Green Bay Packers, there are many instances when family time has to take a back seat to your job duties. I'd like to thank my wife, Sandy, and the rest of my family for all their patience in putting up with my various careers.

I hope you'll enjoy my story.

Jerry

Chapter 1
Growing Up in Titletown, USA

IT'S NOT SURPRISING THAT I ENDED UP with a job protecting an organization like the Green Bay Packers. After all, I spent my whole life taking care of people, first at home with my family and then as a police officer and detective. It's a position where I feel a sense of comfort and responsibility.

Life wasn't easy for me as a kid; in fact, it was pretty tough. My family consisted of my father, Jerry, my mother, Florence, and my brother, Roy, who's nine years younger than I am. A lot of responsibility fell on my shoulders to care for the house, my parents, and my brother.

The town of Green Bay is divided by the Fox River. When I was growing up, people generally stayed on one side of the river or the other, as if there were a big wall keeping them apart. It's still that way to some extent. Until I was in fifth grade we lived on a street that dead-ended at a railroad yard, then we moved to a slightly better area in the middle of the west side. I've been a west-sider my whole life.

I never knew my dad to be healthy. He had awful tremors from Parkinson's disease, which probably was caused by a combination of encephalitis and the malaria he caught in the service. He served in the Philippines, and I don't think my mother knew he was sick when they got married. His hands would shake uncontrollably, and he couldn't control his eyes, so we'd help him lie down and then cover his eyes so he could rest comfortably. Dad would stare at a particular object

1

or person for long periods of time, and that made me really uncomfortable. He also had a lot of phlegm, almost like someone with CP, except he could control his neck muscles. People had to know my dad pretty well to understand his speech.

We didn't have a car, so Dad and I would take a cab downtown to Benz's Barbershop on Main Street, on the east side, just south of the bridge. I think the guys there knew my dad from the days when he was in better health. I was embarrassed because he would drool and stare at people when they came in. I shouldn't have been so embarrassed, but I was only about ten, and naturally self-conscious at that age. I hate myself for my embarrassment—I should've been so proud of that man. After the haircut, we'd go into a nearby bar. Dad would get a highball of brandy or whiskey along with a beer, and we'd wait there for the cab to come back and pick us up.

My mother was a great woman. She cleaned office buildings for fifteen cents an hour from four in the afternoon to midnight. I was left with my dad a lot. I really don't know how we made it on so little money. I used to walk to Van's Bakery for our best meal. Dad and I would get a dozen sweet rolls for about fifty cents. They were fresh and really good, and that was our food for a day or two.

Even my mom couldn't cope with the challenges of taking care of my father and trying to make ends meet. When I was eight years old, she had a nervous breakdown and was placed in the Winnebago Mental Health Center, which was about an hour away. She was treated for depression and "nerves." Since Judge Robert Parins (the future Packers president) was an attorney and a member of the family, he helped us make decisions regarding her care. We were also close with my uncle, Frank Parins, who was my dad's brother and the judge's dad. My father came from a big, close family, and some of my cousins would come over to our house to help out.

Occasionally, we visited my mom in the hospital, but it was tough leaving her there when we went home. I got to walk outside with her on one visit—it might have been on Mother's Day—and the experience really had an impact on me. Those visits gave me an awful feeling about what mental health treatment was, like something out of Ken Kesey's *One Flew Over the Cuckoo's Nest.* It was the Dark Ages for mental health, almost like prison. Those were very trying years.

My mom got better, though, and my brother, Roy, came along. Once he was born, Mom's attention was focused on taking care of him. Meanwhile, Dad was slowly getting worse. He couldn't use a bathroom, and we had to give him showers.

The year after we moved, I started attending Annunciation Catholic School. It was probably the toughest year of school I ever had. My father was from a strict Catholic family, and Mom was Methodist. We had that split religion thing going on, and my parents would argue about it. On the bright side, Annunciation was where I met some of the kids who'd be friends of mine all the way through high school.

Msgr. Kiernan came to the house once a month to do confession and communion with Dad, but he wouldn't talk to my mom. The Sisters taught that it was a sin for my mother, a non-Catholic, to go into the church. That was really hard on me, and it hurt. I saw my mother as a saint. Was I supposed to look down on her?

My parents let me attend Lincoln Elementary for sixth grade, and that's when life changed for the better. School became much more enjoyable, and the kids from Annunciation stayed friends once we all got to Franklin Junior High and West High School.

I really didn't have an adult male role model, so my friends and their dads were very important to me. I didn't realize it at the time, but people were looking out for me, taking me under their wings because they knew I was really struggling at home. A couple of families in particular helped me out a lot during that time. Tom Kornowski and his parents were very good to me. I knew I could always go over to their house and have something to eat. Gary VanEnkenvort and his parents, Francis and Irene, would take me out to the fairgrounds to watch the car races. Just riding in a car was a treat for me. Gary went on to become a deputy with the Brown County Sheriff's Department.

Sports became more important to me when I got to high school, but I couldn't devote much time to them because I had responsibilities at home all the time. Mom still worked at night, so I had to take care of my dad while she was gone. Dad had to be fed because he couldn't even lift a spoon to his mouth. Television was just becoming common in the early 1950s, and since Dad spent his life sitting in a chair, watching TV was something he could really enjoy. That was the only time I remember him laughing a lot. I've still got that old TV set in my garage. It doesn't work anymore, but I won't part with it.

When we finally put Dad in a nursing home, he accepted it well. He wasn't a complainer, and he knew he needed to be taken care of. His body was turning to stone. He walked like his legs were stilts, because he had no movement in his knees, and he couldn't hold on to anything. His mind was sharp—he could remember roads he hadn't seen in twenty-five years—but disease was destroying his body. He lived in nursing homes for twelve years before finally dying in 1982.

My First Packers Games

A highlight of my early teens was sneaking into Packers games. Prior to 1957, the Packers played at City Stadium behind East High School. It was almost a three-mile walk from our house, and sometimes I'd walk the whole way alone. That worried my mother, who was very protective of me.

I had to sneak in around the rear of the stadium where there was a slot broken out of the fence. The big kids would lift me up, and then I'd have to slide and slither my way down or jump about eight feet. The guards would chase us and try to hit us with their clubs, but we'd run like hell, and we were a lot faster than they were. Once I got into the crowd and onto the cinder track around the field, I could stay in as long as I was alone. If two or three of us were together, we were a pack and became easier for the guards to spot. We had to keep walking around so we wouldn't get caught.

The field was surrounded by a railing to keep fans from walking onto the playing area. I'd tuck myself in under that railing and watch the game, usually on the visitor's side of the field. I remember watching one game against the Detroit Lions. I was so close to their bench area that I could hear them talking. Leon Hart was one of my favorite Detroit players.

Going to those games was something special because football and the Packers were important to me. When I was in ninth grade, our English teacher had us write about what we wanted to be when we grew up. I didn't know, so I wrote that I wanted to be a professional football player. Here's this little runt of a kid dreaming so big, but the teacher was very kind. I've never forgotten that. I didn't make it as a player, but I've worked with and met some of the greatest players in the game, so I almost fulfilled that goal. How lucky I've been....

High School Sports

Uncle Frank, who sold real estate, helped my family buy a nicer house when I was in ninth grade. I had a growing interest in girls then, too, so life was really changing. We had some great sports teams at West in the mid-'50s, and I played football as a junior and senior. At one point, West had a thirty-seven-game winning streak, and I was on the team that lost to Manitowoc 6-0 to end that run. As a senior, I played halfback on offense, and was a defensive back along with my close friend Jim Nuthals. Our quarterback, Clark LaChappelle, was a really good athlete and weighed more than Tom LaTour and I did as 145-pound running backs. Larry LeMere, a three-time state champion in the hundred-yard dash, was our fullback.

Fred Scheffen was a great player until he was stricken with multiple sclerosis. He was in very poor health for fifty years until his death in 2005. Throughout those years, several classmates continued to visit him, including Grant Turner, who now heads our crew of Lambeau Field tour guides. I think it's great that so many people cared about Fred for so long.

West also was a state power in track. We won the Class A (large school) state championship in 1954, were second in 1956, my junior year, and again in '58. Bill Andersen was someone I admired as one of West's top athletes. In addition to being a great halfback, he won the state 440-yard dash championship in track. Bill's brother, Larry, became my brother-in-law when he married my wife Sandy's sister Kathy. They're better known as Spike and Queenie.

I was a frail kid, but I was fast. As a senior, I was fortunate to go to the state track meet in Madison in the 880-yard (4 × 220) relay. Tom LaTour ran leadoff, I ran second, Ken Wolf was third, and Larry LeMere was the anchor. We didn't place, but it was a great experience. The Milwaukee kids had longer legs than we had and they kicked our butts. Lee Remmel, a writer for the *Green Bay Press-Gazette* at the time, followed us down in a car to cover the team. Lee later became the Packers' public-relations director for many years, and retired as the team's historian following the 2007 season.

I enjoyed my high school years, but I wish I'd been a better student.

Sandy and I

I met Sandy King when we were teenagers. She also has a sad story, which might partially explain what drew us together. Sandy was the fourth of five very pretty girls. They had a younger brother too. Everyone knew the King family, and we boys were all afraid of Mr. King.

Within a two-year span, Sandy lost both of her parents under tragic circumstances, beginning with her father's death when she was thirteen. I was playing in a basketball tournament for Annunciation Church on March 13, 1956, when word came that Sandy's father had been killed in a railroad accident in Tomahawk, a small lumber town in northern Wisconsin.

Not long afterward, Sandy's mom married a man named Norman Stiller, whose first wife had died during childbirth. Stiller treated Sandy's mom terribly, and on the day she filed for divorce in 1958 she disappeared. She never would have abandoned her family, and authorities never found her body. Stiller committed suicide right before he was scheduled to take a polygraph test, and the disappearance of Sandy's mom was never officially solved.

Sandy was only fifteen at the time and immediately took on the role of mother to her younger brother Robert (Corky). The kids continued living in the family's apartment by themselves for a time thanks to financial assistance from the older sisters. Sandy and Corky soon moved in with their sister, Sharon, and her husband, Dick Vanden Heuvel, who ran a farm on Lime Kiln Road in Bellevue, just east of the city. The move took Sandy away from her friends, who were like gold to her, and thrust her into the new Preble High School. Sandy hated everything about that arrangement.

I knew Sandy a little from school, but she was younger than I was and we didn't know each other very well. I was already out of school when her mom disappeared, and I actually dated her older sister, Judy, at one point. Sandy and I really met for the first time at one of the Wednesday night dances they held in the pavilion at Bay Beach, the local amusement park. In those days, you never went out alone. The girls and the guys were always in groups, and we paired off as the night went on. I borrowed my friend Don Carter's car to take her home that night, and we've been together ever since.

I didn't have the wheels to go see Sandy often, since very few kids had their own cars then. Families had only one car, so it was a big deal to get the use of your dad's car for the night. Sandy and I started doing things together with our groups of friends, and our relationship began to grow. Everybody walked to places like Dehn's Ice Cream, which was kind of like Arnold's on *Happy Days,* and dances at the schools, the YWCA, and the churches. Sandy walked all the way from Preble to the west side to be with me and her West High friends. She was so beautiful that she even made "court" in her senior year at Preble, but it was difficult for her to get a dress for the occasion because the family didn't have extra money for things like that.

After graduating from West in 1957, I got my first job—at Krueger Metal. I was thrilled to get that job, figuring that I'd be able to help out my parents. It was a pretty decent job, and I paid them room and board from the $1.37 per hour I earned working the day shift in the steel room.

Sandy was with me when I bought my first car, a new 1960 Chevrolet, for $2,600 from Broadway Chevrolet. That was a lot of money for me, but it was the missing link for a lot of things in my life. Now I had transportation for us to see each other more often and go places together, and it allowed me to start working a second job at a teenage bar on the northeast side of town.

When Sandy and I decided to get married, she had to take classes at Annunciation to become Catholic. Fr. James Putman, who taught the classes, tried to convince Sandy that she should become a nun instead. That wasn't going to happen, and we were married on April 15, 1961. Sandy and I began our life together in a small apartment on the west side. In November 1962 I saw a newspaper ad that would change our lives forever.

Chapter 2
Pulling Hooks & Walking a Beat

GREEN BAY POLICE OFFICER Tom Waldorf impressed me. I knew him from his work as a beat cop and had played some basketball against him. Playing ball usually included going out to the bars and then to a pizza place. Tom and I got talking about that newspaper ad for police recruits. Since I wanted to work outdoors, and associated police work with being outside, I decided to apply.

The police department was located on North Jefferson Street in a remodeled grocery store across from the YMCA. I filled out an application and waited for a call. There were no education requirements beyond high school, but you had to be at least five foot eight, weigh 150 pounds, and have 20/20 vision without glasses. I had to take a written test at the old vocational school on Broadway. There were maybe twenty-five people in the room, including two women.

A short time later I got a call from someone at the department telling me to come downtown for an interview. Officer Harold Compton and another officer showed me around, and I was very impressed. He explained that they were doing a background check on me and wanted to know why I wanted to be a policeman. I told them I wanted outside work. Harold taught all areas of law enforcement at the department, and officers referred to his training as "Compton College."

The next thing I had to do was see a doctor, an older man the City had hired to do these exams. He checked my eyes and they were good.

9

Then it came time to check my height and weight. I don't know if I actually hit five-eight, but I know the scale read 149¼ pounds when I stood on it. Since 150 was the minimum, I was scared for a moment that I was out. But the doctor said, "I see you're a little under 150. Maybe it's the scale." Then he pulled down on my back pocket to get me over 150. That kind man gave me the chance to be a police officer. Had he not cut me a break, I might have worked at Krueger Metal the rest of my life.

Pulling Hooks

The Green Bay Police Department Class of 1962 had a dozen guys and one woman. I officially started with the department on January 14, 1963. We were sworn in at city hall. I didn't even have a uniform yet—but they gave me a gun.

Back then we had more officers walking beats than riding in squad cars. We pulled a lot of doors in those days to make sure businesses were locked at night. The city was divided into different zones, and each of us was responsible for a particular zone. We were just starting to get radios and didn't have walkie-talkies, so we communicated with headquarters by "pulling hooks," red boxes attached to telephone poles, with phones inside. We had a special key to open them, and every hour and a half we had to ring in and tell headquarters our location. If you didn't, they'd send a squad car to your zone to look for you.

I started by walking the beat on North Broadway, the first major street west of the Fox River and an area known for its taverns and rough characters. Green Bay has a law dating back to the 1800s that outlaws alcohol sales west of Broadway. That set Broadway up as a popular place to own a bar—and made it the roughest street in town.

The first hour on the midnight to 8:00 a.m. shift consisted mainly of closing down the bars. I'd make an appearance in every bar, walk in and say hi to get to know the people, and more important, give them a chance to know me. Neighborhood policing is like that now, too. We'd make sure the bars were cleared out by closing time and then start pulling doors.

I walked a beat from Hubbard Street north to Mather Street, east a couple blocks to the river, and west a couple blocks to Maple Street, where a hook was located. There were twenty-three bars to watch in that small area. My dad's sister, Aunt Mae Parins Binion, ran a bar and rooming house on my beat. She'd leave food out to help me get through the night.

The railroads were huge then, and the major passenger depot on the west side was in my zone. The last passenger train came in at 1:00 a.m., unleashing a wave of new people into the Broadway district. The crew would usually catch a short nap in the depot, and a few hours later the train would head back south again. The freight system was very active then, too. A lot of blue-collar people hung out on Broadway, especially the workers at Larsen Canning Co.

We had a lot of homeless people, but at that time we called them winos. There weren't any shelters, so they often slept on freight trains and would panhandle a bit. Sometimes they'd scare you at night. The closest thing we had to a homeless shelter was a place the locals referred to as the stump farm, located in Oneida, just west of the city. It was called the stump farm because the residents had to cut their own wood, shovel snow in the winter, and do other little projects. We would arrest people for drunkenness, and the stump farm became a catchall place to send this type of minor offender. It became such a famous place that we'd have people come into town from all over northern Wisconsin during the winter because they knew they'd be sent there. At least the stump farm was a place they could go to dry out, have a warm cot to sleep on, and get three square meals a day.

That first winter walking the beat was a really cold one. About the only times I was inside for work was to attend in-services. We didn't study at a police academy in those days; they held classes at city hall where the city council meets now. And since there wasn't an indoor police shooting range, we used the range in the basement of the Army Reserve building to learn how to shoot. I'd never shot a gun in my life, having not had a father who could teach me.

Ray and Big Ray

In the 1960s, the King's X was a popular tavern and eating establishment on North Broadway. It was owned by brothers Jesse and Frank Whittington and managed by Boots Baker. It was the nicest place on Broadway and a popular hangout for the Packers. By the time I started working for the city, Vince Lombardi was already the Packers' coach and the team was really good.

One warm, beautiful night I was walking my beat and came up the alley behind North Broadway from the south. I was talking with some of the people sitting on the decks above the bars as I approached the King's X when I noticed a guy urinating outside. He was a pretty big guy and was wearing shorts. I knew all these people were watching me, and here's this guy urinating in the alley.

I said, "Hey, fella, find a different place to go to the bathroom." When the guy turned around, I saw it was Ray Nitschke, the Packers' middle linebacker. Ray would later become a Hall of Fame player, but he already had a reputation for being a hard hitter on and off the field. Here I was, at 150 pounds, telling him to stop taking a leak in the alley. I didn't have a radio and I only had a small club, but I had a badge and a uniform.

He came up on me, looked down at me, and I looked up at him. Ray was drunk, and the first thing he said in his intimidating, gravelly voice was, "What the f--- did you say?"

I'm standing next to someone I worshipped, and the guy's being nasty to me. I stood there for a moment and said again, "Why don't you find a different place to go." "What are you going to do about it?" he demanded. "Why don't you get the f--- out of here and go chase some criminals."

I stood my ground with Ray and I thought he was going to hit me. Ray was a very physical guy and challenged a lot of people to fights in the bars. The only person I ever heard of that got the best of Nitschke was a big guy from West Virginia named Ray Grimmett. Big Ray weighed at least 350 pounds and started at the police department at the same time I did. He was warm, friendly, and quite easygoing. He had a wife and two small kids, worked on boats in the summertime, and had a taste for moonshine whisky. He lived on North Broadway and would tell me some great stories. One day Nitschke picked a fight with Ray Grimmett, and big Ray just kicked his butt.

I didn't know what to do with Nitschke, and I guess I was scared, but if I learned anything from my police job, it's that if you back down while wearing that uniform you're going to get nowhere. The honor of that job is going to back you up. Without that knowledge, I probably would've backed down.

Just then, two people came out of the King's X and saw what was going on. One of them ran back inside to get Jesse, and he came outside and got all over Ray. "This is Jerry!" he yelled. By this time there were several people around us. Ray's penis was still hanging out of his pants. He was very inebriated, but Jesse was able to get him calmed down and back inside. That incident became a big story as far as my credibility on the beat was concerned, because I had challenged Ray Nitschke.

Some time later, I asked an advanced training instructor what I could've done if Ray had hit me. Would I have been justified in shooting him? "Absolutely," the instructor said. "Ray's hands are weapons." I liked Ray a lot, and he was one of the greatest Green Bay Packers ever, but sometimes I wonder if he'd have gotten into the Pro Football Hall of Fame had that incident gone down differently.

I had a tough act to follow on the Broadway beat. Frank Guarascio had walked it before me. He was a tough, good-looking Italian who had worked in the prison system. When word got out about the Nitschke story, Frank told me, "Jerry, you did good." That meant a lot to me.

A few months later, during the 1963 football season, I had an altercation with a player named Urban Henry, a defensive end whom Lombardi had gotten in a trade with the Los Angeles Rams. Henry was even bigger than Nitschke. I stopped in the King's X around closing time to make sure everyone was getting out, since the bar sometimes fudged on the 1:00 a.m. rule if there were players inside. Urban, who didn't know me yet, challenged me at the door. He was drunk and said to me, "It just might be *me* that throws *you* out of this place."

"I've got six in this gun," I said, "and I'll put six in your belly."

Urban looked at me and never said a word. He turned around as the lights went on and that was the end of it. I didn't stick around. You have to be careful in a situation like that, and only talk tough as a last resort. It would've taken a good ass kicking by someone before I would've drawn my weapon. We didn't carry Mace or Tasers, so we had to be able to talk and wait for help. Talking was the best way to cool down a tense situation, but I got into a few scrapes in which other Broadway people came out to help until other officers arrived. If you'd earned the people's respect, you got to know how many friends you had.

The people I encountered on the beat made it a rewarding job at times, though dealing with people who've had too much to drink is challenging. As I was about to leave for work on Christmas Eve 1964, one of the people who'd given me a particularly hard time stopped by our house. His name was Justin Wied, and he'd brought a bottle of booze as a gift.

"I had an issue with you on Broadway recently and I was totally out of line," he said. "I just want to apologize and wish you a merry Christmas."

Thirty years later, Justin Wied's grandson married my daughter, Missy, and Jason Wied is now the Packers' vice president of administration and corporate counsel. Green Bay can be a very small town.

Make Room for Family

I spent time in a squad car more often after that first year. Stan Keckhaver and I were riding together one night in 1965 when Sandy started having problems with her pregnancy about a month before her due date. The station called over the radio about 12:45 a.m. to tell me to stop at my 89—police code for home. Sandy was tough as nails. She thought she had a bladder infection, and since she had no family we could ask to take care of her, I dropped her off at the hospital and went back to work. I'm embarrassed to say I just dropped her off. The doctors tried to stop her labor, but the next afternoon she gave birth to Shelley, our first daughter. Our other girls, Toni and Missy, were born in 1968 and 1971.

Born with a hole in her heart, Shelley was a sickly child. Seven years later, the doctors decided she should undergo open-heart surgery, and the people of Broadway and the police department really stepped up to help. Ray Nitschke, along with more than a hundred people who didn't even know me well, signed up to donate blood for the surgery. That meant so much to me. One officer told me, "Jerry, I want to donate blood, but when I was in the service I got VD and now I can't give."

We had to get Shelley healthy enough for the surgery, which was scheduled to take place at University Hospital in Madison. We drove down to see the doctors, but civil unrest was a big problem at that time in the state capital. In fact, there was a bombing on campus, and the student body was protesting. The police wouldn't let us get to the hospital no matter how I pleaded with them. It's a good thing I didn't have a gun with me or I might have used it.

15

We were forced to turn around and drive all the way back to Green Bay. Our doctors at home then got us into Children's Hospital in Milwaukee, and we were able to get the surgery done there. Ironically, the only major bill I got was for blood, even though those hundred people had donated for us. Eventually, we got that bill thrown out, but it left a bad taste in my mouth for the Red Cross.

Prison Riots

With a population of fewer than 80,000 residents — mostly white — during the 1960s, Green Bay didn't have the demonstrations and rioting that the big cities had, but there were some problems nonetheless. Twice I was part of a large group of officers that had to go out to the Wisconsin State Reformatory (now the Green Bay Correctional Institution) for prison riots.

The first incident involved a standoff between inmates and the prison staff. It was a warm day, and a group of inmates had dismantled the recreation area to make weapons. They took apart the bleachers and everything. They didn't take any hostages, but they were now armed and demanded a meeting with the warden to discuss their grievances.

We were the first outside agency to arrive. Along with officers from the State Patrol and Brown County Sheriff's Department, we were there to support the guards as they tried to regain control. However, the warden didn't allow us to go in with guns, and Sheriff Norb Froelich wouldn't send his guys in there unarmed, so there was a standoff between the sheriff and the warden as well as between the inmates and the correctional officers.

We stood there, kind of like cowboys and Indians in the old days, maybe a hundred inmates on one side of the recreation area, and the officers lined up on the other side. As a very young, newly married officer, I remember wondering if I'd get out of there alive.

While the warden and other people tried to negotiate, the inmates shouted at us, waving their homemade weapons. To see if we were armed, they tested by sending an inmate running along the inside of the wall. One of the guards, who had a shotgun, fired a round in the air. The inmate hit the ground, turned around, and went back to the group. If this were a war, we probably would've lost, but that shot was enough to prevent any further incidents. Eventually, we were able to bring the situation to a peaceful conclusion.

The second incident was more physical and even scarier. The local fire department responded after some inmates set mattresses on fire. Things got out of hand, and the firefighters had to pull out when inmates started throwing debris at them. With gas masks on, our units had to go cell to cell to regain control of the population while walking through water and thick smoke. Again without weapons, we grabbed inmates out of their cells and handed them back to other officers to be handcuffed. We gradually regained control by taking down the prison one cell at a time.

I don't think I'd ever worn a gas mask before, which added to my anxiety. The city had bought the masks for us as a result of the Vietnam War riots happening around the country. We were facing more of these potentially violent situations, and there was even one at the University of Wisconsin-Green Bay campus. As police officers, we represented the establishment and were easy targets for various political groups. Each officer had his own thoughts about it, so there was a mix of opinions among the people in uniform.

I was working nights at the time, so all I got out of this extra stress was time on the books. If you worked four extra hours, they gave you six hours you could take as off time. When you accumulated eight hours of time, you could take another day off work. There was no overtime in those days, so there was no financial reward—when they set a budget, that expense total was it.

Not Much of a Promotion

Three years into my career, Chief Madson selected me to be part of a special traffic enforcement squad. He took two officers from the night shift, two from the p.m. shift, and two from the day shift for what he described as an elite traffic squad. We would work with radar and enforce areas that were known for frequent traffic violations. The chief asked if I could ride a motorcycle. I told him I could, then made my way through the training course, and passed the test. This got me off the night shift, but took me away from the Broadway beat where I was starting to build some friendships. I worked traffic for about a year, but I was one of the officers who had trouble making arrests. I just didn't enjoy giving out traffic tickets. Everybody speeds, so I concentrated on drivers who were really excessive. It was good duty for a while, but it got tough on me before long. The worst thing was working the Sunday morning shift. Sometimes we arrested people who were trying to get to church on time, and I really had a hard time doing that.

I finally got out of the traffic enforcement squad and they put me back on the beat working nights. That was hard because I'd become used to working days by then. Before long, however, I was able to return to squad-car duty with a partner. Later on, I moved to the detective division and eventually retired as captain of internal affairs.

On my final day with the police department, April 4, 1992, I walked my old beat all day, one last time. Even though the neighborhood has changed a lot, the bars and the people of Broadway remain a memorable part of my career.

Chapter 3
Front Row at the Ice Bowl

CHIEF MADSON, who was on the Packers' board of directors, sent three other officers and me over to the Oneida Street practice field in the summer of 1965 to help out Coach Lombardi. Coach, who was irate that fans kept walking onto the field and interfering with practice, was swearing up a storm on the phone, so the Chief sent Ed Wirtz, Howie Erickson, Ron Waise, and me over there right away. This turned out to be one of the most important calls of my life, as it provided my professional introduction to the Green Bay Packers.

Of course, I was thrilled to do anything with the Packers. I'd finish my night shift, sleep a little, and be at the practice field by 8:00 a.m. The chief used two of us, dressed in full uniform, at each practice. I would've worked there for nothing, and we almost did. Even though the pay was very low — $1.50 cash for about three hours' work — it was still a welcome addition since I wasn't making much more on the force than the $335 per month I started at.

There wasn't much of a fence separating the fans from the players at the practice field. It was more of a hurdle, really. The barrier was a series of two-by-six pieces of wood about two feet high, set between posts along the South Oneida Street side of the field, and though it was very long, it was easy to just step over. Back in those days, you'd put up a fence like that and most people would know they weren't supposed to go on the other side. Well, obviously that wasn't working, since fans were trying to get close to the players to ask for autographs.

We had some fans watching practices then, but numbers weren't a problem, and traffic wasn't anywhere near as heavy as it is today.

Fan photo days were easy from a security standpoint. Players would spread out around the practice field, and a relatively small number of fans — many of them with children — would walk around the field and have their pictures taken with the players. Once the team started winning in the 1990s, that event expanded to the point where it actually became dangerous to the players and fans, and we had to introduce more controls.

The area around the practice fields today is filled with streets, businesses, and parking lots, but in the mid-1960s it was fairly rural. The Brown County Veterans Memorial Arena opened in 1957, the same year as the new City Stadium (later renamed Lambeau Field), and framed the north end of the practice area. There was an open field on the south end, and the Packers had a couple of green buildings there with overhead doors and a few blocking dummies.

For resistance training the players used a machine that had a heavy railroad tie attached. We didn't yet understand the benefits of weight training and how it could help an athlete. The big weight machines didn't come into play until the 1970s. Compared to today's players, the players of the 1960s were a lot smaller at every position and relied on their natural strength. Today the guys are so big and fast it's amazing, but they work a lot harder in the weight room than the guys years ago ever did. Players these days lift two or three times a week throughout the season just to keep their strength up. The game is a lot faster, and there's really no comparison with what it was like in the '60s.

Near the equipment shed on the south end was a gated driveway that came in from South Oneida Street. Coach Lombardi's car was the only vehicle allowed there. The assistants parked across the street in the stadium lot. When we saw Coach's car coming from the stadium office building, we'd stop traffic so he could cross the street and pull into the driveway. Lombardi received the utmost courtesy from us, almost like that reserved for a judge. It was nearly military.

Those of us on the security detail didn't even go up to the office building at that time; we just went right to work at the practice field. I knew every player so well that I didn't even have to look at their numbers. Sandy and I were big football fans, and we sat together in section 37 for the games. After eleven years without a winning season, the 1960s were great times for Packer fans. The Packers' 7-5 record in 1959 started the momentum toward what we now call The Glory Years. Lombardi's teams were beginning to pile up NFL championships (1961 and 1962), and excitement was high about the chances that the 1965 team would be a contender. In fact, the Packers won the next three championships, beating the Cleveland Browns 23-12 at Lambeau Field for the 1965 title, followed by victories in the first two Super Bowls.

Sandy had worked up until Shelley's birth in 1965, so this was her first summer home as a full-time mother. Since policemen and firefighters didn't make much money then, I began working some extra jobs to make ends meet. Part-time work was always available for us because we were respected as officers, and I was very proud to wear that uniform. I worked as many as three part-time jobs in addition to being a policeman.

The Packers were always my first call, but there were a couple of other jobs that were regulars for me. Along with a number of other officers, I began working for Snider Daanen Furniture. I worked in the warehouse and did some deliveries, and the job was kind of fun. I worked for Schneider Allied in the moving business, too. Company president Al Schneider was on the police and fire commission. The work was hard, but they paid us more, so it was a popular part-time job for a lot of policemen. Some of the guys even worked as drivers for Schneider, which has since grown to become the nation's largest freight carrier. The company's orange trucks can be seen nationwide today.

Along with the little bit of security work for the Packers, I helped out with some gofer work and other small tasks for Dad Braisher, the team's equipment manager, and his assistant, Bob Noel, along with head trainer Bud Jorgensen and his assistant Dominic Gentile. There weren't as many people taking care of the team then as there are today. The players were my heroes, and I would do anything to be involved, including scraping the mud off their cleats after practice. Practices were very basic, so we didn't have much to set up.

I worked the games for the police department, but things gradually progressed to a point where, during the week, a few of us were doing more work directly for the Packers. I helped Bob Noel in the equipment room regularly, and eventually even made the Gatorade for practices—just doing whatever I could to help out. My job on the Mondays following games was to clean the players' shoes. Players weren't supplied with multiple pairs in those days, so if the game conditions were muddy, we'd dry out the shoes, brush off the dirt and grass, and replace any worn-out laces in time for Wednesday's practice. We'd also clean out the cleats, or replace them if necessary, a very time-consuming task compared to today, when equipment maintenance people use high-speed drills like NASCAR pit crews.

I had full access to the equipment area, but the training room was another matter. That was a private sanctuary for the players and trainers, and strictly off limits to anyone else. Even the media, which at that time had pretty free access to the locker room, wasn't allowed in the training room. One day, someone asked me to do something that required going into the training room for the first time.

"Jerry, we have rules," Dominic Gentile said. "This room is off limits unless it's your work area."

That was the last time I went into the training room for quite some time.

Even though I was still in my police uniform, I started helping out in more football-related areas such as getting the balls ready for practice and working on the equipment side a little more. I even learned how to tape the players' feet and ankles. When I first started with the Packers, if a player got hurt, we'd just put him in a car and drive him up the hill to the main building and the training room. Then things began to change, and we did more taping right at the practice field. Dad Braisher was getting older, so Bob Noel would even have his nephews and some of the coaches' kids helping out. It was only natural for me to step up, and I was happy to do it.

The Ice Bowl

Perhaps the most famous game in Green Bay Packers history—maybe even NFL history—was the NFL Championship in 1967 leading up to Super Bowl II. Better known as the Ice Bowl, this game reinforced Green Bay's reputation as one of the coldest places on earth. That's not really the case, but on this New Year's Eve day, December 31, 1967, it must've been close. The air temperature was 13 below zero with wind chill as low as 46 below. It was so cold that the Packers Band that entertained on the sidelines couldn't even play their instruments.

I was assigned to work the field that day in my role as a police officer, and I felt very lucky to be there. At most of the other home games, I had to ride my motorcycle outside the stadium, so this was very exciting for me. What a great job I had!

That day was so cold that it became a test of survival. It seemed to get colder as the day wore on. Usually, the tougher the weather, the more our fans seem to like it. You have to remember that in those days people didn't dress as warmly as they do today. Going to a game was more of a social event in the 1960s. People came to the game dressed up, and some of the women even wore dresses. We hadn't expected the weather to be so bad. A cold front had come in overnight, but the fever of the game overtook the weather.

I managed to get through the Ice Bowl because I kept moving. Our uniforms included a dark navy overcoat that was about waist length. They were very heavy and warm, and I wore a knit cap underneath my uniform hat. The key to survival was keeping clothing as close to your body as possible. I had long underwear on, but didn't know about putting petroleum jelly on my skin to keep it moist and insulated against the freezing wind. I remember talking to the television people, and the camera guys were very concerned about their equipment working properly.

Sgt. Loyal Nelson was in charge of the officers on the field. A young man just out of the Marine Corps, he was a tough officer. Crowd control wasn't much of an issue that day, so we were able to watch the game while moving around to stay warm. The people in the seats shared body warmth to keep each other warm, but we didn't have that on the field. People who were survivors that day looked out for each other. Drinking alcohol really isn't a good thing when it's cold out, but we didn't realize it then. I walked into the end zone at halftime. In the front row was a guy with blackberry brandy. I took a slug of it right out of the bottle and in front of thousands of people. Sgt. Nelson took a slug, too. We broke the rules of our profession, but we didn't care.

The hardest job in those days was working the traffic outside. Being at the games was a delight. You had the best seat in the house and you got paid for it. Today, police officers will tell you the toughest part of working a game is dealing with the crowd, not the traffic.

About the only thing I was concerned with that day was the blowers located along the player benches. We had straw piled up at the ends of the benches, and I was worried it could catch fire. It didn't, but I kept an eye on it just in case. They had tarps set up over the benches, like open-faced tents, and players came in and out of there as they tried to get a little warmer. The players didn't have the sports gloves they have today, and Bart Starr still has frostbite issues with his hands from playing quarterback that day.

The game itself was kind of boring, as neither team could really mount a drive. The Packers took an early lead before the Cowboys got back into it with an easy touchdown on a fumble recovery. The Packers led 14-10 at halftime, but couldn't get their offense going in the second half against a very strong Dallas defense. The Cowboys had a powerful team that year, led by future Hall of Famer Don Meredith at quarterback, and Olympic 100-meter dash champion Bob Hayes at wide receiver. It came out later that the Packers' defense could tell when a running play was coming because Hayes would have his hands tucked into the front of his pants.

In the fourth quarter the Cowboys used a trick play, a long option pass from Dan Reeves to Lance Rentzel, to take a 17-14 lead. I didn't think they'd try that type of play in such bad weather, and it caught the Packers by surprise.

The Packers had one last chance to mount a scoring drive at the end of the game. The electric heating grid under the middle of the field had stopped working. The field had long since frozen, and players were slipping and sliding all over the place. Bart threw a swing pass to Chuck Mercein, who was able to make yardage down the left side of the field in front of the Cowboys' bench to set up the winning touchdown.

Working the Packers' side of the field, I positioned myself at the side of the south end zone for the final sequence. After two unsuccessful running plays on which Packer running backs were unable to secure their footing, Bart convinced Coach Lombardi to let him try to win the game by running a quarterback sneak. Lombardi's famous response was "Run it, and let's get the hell out of here!"

I had a front-row seat for the most famous play in Packers history, and when Bart scored the winning touchdown, the Packers were NFL champions for the third straight time, 21-17. Still, one of my memories is how impressive the Cowboys' intensity was. They played one heck of a football game.

Afterward, my job was really easy. We didn't even try to keep the goalposts from being torn down. My assignment was to stand guard outside the two locker rooms, located near each other behind the north end zone. Between the two locker rooms was the kind of thin divider you'd see separating office cubicles today. It was warm inside, which felt great after being outside for several hours. I was struck by the deathly quiet of the Cowboys' side on my right, and the laughter and cheering coming from the Packers' side on my left.

Don Meredith eventually came out of the Cowboys' locker room. He had his jersey and pads off, and was wearing only a Cowboys T-shirt with a star on it and his silver jersey pants. Tears were streaming from his eyes. "I'm just going over there, officer, to congratulate Bart," he said in his Texas drawl. To a young officer, the difference between winning and losing was never more evident. My emotions were still running high, and Meredith's disappointment made me think *how can I celebrate?* His tears put me in my place and I never forgot that.

Meredith was a warrior. I'll always remember that he had a little blood on his arm, some tape, and those tears. He was one of my favorite Cowboys players ... if I had any.

Chapter 4
Between a Cop
And a Green Place

THE PACKERS DIDN'T EVEN HAVE a security director until former Detroit police officer Al Stevens was hired in 1982. Before that, the team would ask me to take care of those types of duties because I was out at the stadium all the time anyway. Even after Al was hired, they still came to me often because of my knowledge of the team and local law enforcement. The Packers were both a job and a passion of mine. Even though the extra hours on top of my police work tired me out, I just loved it.

When the police department complained that I wasn't writing enough speeding tickets on the traffic unit, one of the ways they punished me was by telling me I couldn't work Packer games, where I earned time and a half. I had tears in my eyes when they said that. I was heartbroken, but it ended up being the best thing that ever happened to me.

"They're not gonna let me work the games," I told Bob Noel. "Can I work for the Packers?"

"Sure," he said.

I became part of the game day crew and started working as a ball boy on the sidelines for a few bucks an hour. When Bart Starr became head coach in 1975, he started taking care of the players' families after the games, and that got me around the stadium a lot more. I'm fortunate that the job turned out so well for me in the long run, because I had no vision at that time of what it would turn out to be.

The Post-Lombardi Era

Coach Lombardi was a very structured individual, which carried over into every aspect of the Packers' daily routine. He was very strict and had rules for everybody. After Lombardi left the organization, things weren't the same around Lambeau. We had lost a powerful, dynamic kind of leader.

Phil Bengtson took over as head coach in 1968, and in his three seasons the Packers went 20-21-1. Bengtson was Lombardi's defensive coach and one of the very best at his job. He was a very important part of the Packers' dynasty of the 1960s, but he didn't have the leadership skills of a Lombardi. Of course, few did.

Late in 1969, Bengtson's second season as head coach, I was working afternoons and evenings for ;/// police department as a motorcycle officer when I was called down to headquarters. Bill Lindeman was the lieutenant on the desk, and a big sports fan, too.

"Jerry, I just got a call from Coach Bengtson. He asked if you were working today. He's going over to a bar where some of the players hang out, and he wants you to help him do a check of the place at eleven o'clock."

The coach's request wasn't an official police issue, so Bill and I talked about it behind a closed door. In those days, the police department did what it could for a Packers coach. Bengtson wanted to meet near My Brother's Place, a spot on Main Street where Sandy and I would sometimes stop by when I got a day off. I rode my cycle over there at about 10:30 p.m. and found Coach Bengtson and his wife sitting in their car. They looked as though they'd been out to dinner. I walked over and said hi, and he addressed me by name.

"Jerry, I set a curfew for eleven o'clock. I'm going to go in the bar, and I expect some of our players to be in there. I want you to assist me by telling me who these players are."

He planned to walk in through the front door, and if any players came out the back door, he wanted me to be a tattletale and name them for him. He mentioned that he planned to fine anyone who was in the bar after curfew.

This created a very uncomfortable situation for me. After all, I worshipped these players. I didn't work for the coach; he wasn't somebody I'd even have a cup of coffee with. I felt very nervous about what to do. I called back to headquarters to report that I was out of service, then parked around back. I recognized some of the players' cars, and I wondered if Coach had checked the cars out as well. I think he had taken a quick look, but that was about it.

At 11:00 p.m. Coach Bengtson walked into the bar. There were more than a couple of players in there, including a few starters. One of the players that came out the back door was Herb Adderley, the future Hall of Fame cornerback. To me, Herb was one of the greatest that ever played the game, and one of my favorite players. He'd been a star halfback at Michigan State before Lombardi drafted him number one in 1961 and changed him into a defensive back.

My relationship with the players very, different then compared to later in my career when I worked full-time for the team. There was even a time in the late 1970s when Officer Jerry Williams and I took a few of the offensive linemen over to the Chicago/Northwestern rail yard to do some pigeon hunting on a Saturday afternoon. Bill Hayhoe, Gale Gillingham, and Bill Lueck were in that group. We had permission to shoot the birds because they were after the grain in the rail cars and were a real nuisance.

I saw some of the players coming out the back door of the bar, and I didn't know what I was going to do. "Did you see the coach?" I asked them.

"Yeah."

"Maybe you'd better get out of here."

About fifteen minutes later, Coach Bengtson came around back and asked me if anyone had come out the back door.

"Well, yes, but it was really dark and there were a number of people coming out," I lied. "Some of them could've been players, but I'm not sure."

The truth is, Bengtson had had enough to drink himself. Back in those days, it was common for people to drink and then drive themselves home—there wasn't even any question. But regardless of whether Coach had been drinking, I understood that his job was all about his players, and they weren't supposed to be out after 11:00. Still, I didn't give him the name of any player who came out the back door. I lost a little respect for him that night, but I felt like I'd let him down.

The Packers started that season with six straight wins, so it was a safe bet they'd win the next day. I didn't hear another thing about that night until the following Tuesday, when I was helping Bob Noel clean the players' shoes. Herb Adderley came up to me and said, "Jerry, you got your vehicle here? I've got something for you."

We went out to my old blue pickup, and there on the front seat sat a football that Herb had asked a number of players to autograph. It was the first autographed ball I ever got, and it meant an awful lot to me. It was a thank you without much needing to be said. Down the line, some of the other guys thanked me as well.

Herb has always been special to me. His picture is among those on the hallway wall outside the locker room, along with all the other Packers in the Pro Football Hall of Fame. When I see Herb now at various events, he and I always laugh about that story.

My allegiance would be to the coach if I were presented with the same situation today. Working directly for the Packers put me in a very different position than where I was in 1969. At the time, though, I was just a part-time guy who was a cop and a fan first.

There were other times when I felt caught between my roles as a police officer and a part-timer with the Packers. Many people remember the 1982 strike year, when the regular season was reduced to nine games, and the 1987 strike year, when replacement players were used.

But not so many recall the brief strike during the 1974 preseason, when Bob Harlan was the Packers' contract negotiator and Dan Devine was head coach.

The team bused the rookies down to the practice field rather than make them walk through the picket line. The veteran players would stand right up to the buses with their picket signs, wearing T-shirts that read NFL PLAYERS ON STRIKE. I worked out there as a policeman and became kind of a liaison. It was just like mill workers going on strike, where the police have to be neutral and keep the strikers away from the people going to the job site. Most of the veterans knew me, which helped a lot, and because we had respect for each other, I could talk to them about what they could and couldn't do.

The event that brought the biggest conflict was a scrimmage between the Packers' rookies and the Bears' rookies at Lambeau Field. The veterans were told they couldn't come on the premises that evening, but they could demonstrate on the streets outside the Lambeau property. But the players decided they were going to make a point that night, and we ended up arresting a number of them at the south end of the stadium. The situation was a little scary, and the worst thing would have been to let it get out of hand. Most of the players had been drinking, and I was sweating bullets. We took a bunch of the strikers downtown and processed them just like we would anyone else. I remember that the Packers' Gale Gillingham and Clarence Williams were there, along with players from the Redskins, Rams, and Bears.

Once we got downtown, we let the guys sit on desks in a backroom of the detective division while we took their mug shots and their fingerprints. We went through the process without the situation escalating into anything more than it needed to be. It was an interesting position for me, because I was very loyal to the Packers, yet I had a job to do. I think the citations were for unlawful gathering or something like that, and the court ended up throwing them all out.

I don't think the players even had to post bond to be released. We made sure to keep the situation really calm or it could've developed into something wild. We bent over backward with the players, since of course we didn't want a physical confrontation to develop. We treated them with respect and gave them their phone calls. It took several hours to complete the whole process.

The media was locked out of the police station as we processed the players, but John Roemer of the *Green Bay Press-Gazette* took a photo of me through a window and it got beamed all over the country via the Associated Press wire. I have a copy of that picture, and several of the players even signed it for me.

After the court threw out all the tickets, I started to worry about whether I might get in trouble for issuing false arrests. I was following orders, but my name was on every slip for twenty-seven guys. Would the City protect me? Thankfully, nothing ever came of it. The players didn't have much leverage in that strike; several veterans soon crossed the picket lines, and the strike was settled before the season started.

As union president for the Green Bay Police Department, I was heavily involved with labor issues, and there was a general understanding that they'd used me for the players' case because I was in that union position. We were challenging Chief Madson, and had hired an attorney to bargain for us. Less than two years later, there was a changing of the guard in the police department. Madson lost his job on July 7, 1977, Don Cuene became the new chief, and I was promoted to detective. I went from being in uniform to detective sergeant, and I never went back to the uniform division again. I worked under the leadership of Captain Milt Steeno and Lieutenant Dick Rice. Dick was a hard-core policeman, really good at his job, and he and I had a very good relationship.

The 1982 football season was very tough on me, and not just because of the players' strike that shortened the season to nine games.

I lost my father in January, a month short of my forty-third birthday. That was one of the toughest things I've ever had to deal with. Dad's death really set me back. The department sent me out to the National Fire Academy that summer, and I was there over Father's Day. It was really hard not to be home for that. My dad had a big impact on me, and he still does.

Being a detective reduced the amount of time I could spend with the Packers. My mom got sick right after that, and football took a back seat to family and police work. When you lose your parents, or you have to make the hardest decisions about their future, it takes priority over everything else. I still kept my hours at the stadium with Bob Noel, which was a welcome escape from the pressures I felt.

I went nights as a sergeant, then bingo—everything changed in the blink of an eye. A terrible murder took place at the end of 1983, and it consumed most of my life for the next four years.

Chapter 5
Time Out for Murder

IN 1983 CHRISTMAS FELL on a Sunday, so Monday was still part of the holiday. Sandy and I were at a party that night and got to bed late. Around 3:00 a.m. on the 27th, I received a call from the station that a female body had been discovered on Lime Kiln Road on the far east side of Green Bay. Uniformed officers were already there by the time I arrived. I don't know if you can ever get hardened to the point that this wouldn't bother you, but this was one of the most gruesome scenes I'd ever seen. Any death is uncomfortable, but this one was different. What they did to her brought out all the guys' emotions to really go after this case.

The crime scene was ugly, with a woman's body on the roadside and bloodstains in the snow. We couldn't even see what she looked like at that point. Her throat had been cut from ear to ear, and a mass of blood and hair covered her face. The blood told us that the attack had occurred near a manure pit on the other side of the road, and somehow she had managed to stagger across the road before collapsing.

The murder had taken place outside the Packerland Packing complex, where livestock were brought for processing. Truckers used the manure pit to clean out their trailers. A driver bringing in a load for the next morning's kill was one of the first people to see the woman. He saw her stumble along the roadside and collapse. I don't know if it was because of the cold weather or her will to live, but she managed to get to her feet after the attack. The trucker told the guard at the Packerland entrance what he had just witnessed, then rushed back to check on the woman. He found her still alive, but bleeding profusely. The guard immediately called police, but the victim, whose name we later learned was Margaret Anderson, died from blood loss before EMTs arrived.

Before long, every available uniformed officer and detective was on the scene. Obviously, this was a major crime. Homicides are rare in Green Bay, much less one with this level of brutality. In all my years as a policeman, I don't think we ever had such a vicious murder. We've had people stabbed and shot, but this was different. This poor woman was a mess. She had been beaten badly before having her throat cut clear back to her spine. She was nearly decapitated, yet had remained at least semiconscious until the blood loss became too great.

We stayed out there collecting evidence for a long time. The fire department came out and we used a rescue squad as a place to warm up. We put all our skills to work, collecting blood from the initial attack site and photographing the tire tracks in the snow. It was so cold that nothing was melting, so we were able to cut chunks of blood right out of the snow and ice.

For more than twenty-four hours after the crime, we had no idea who Margaret was. There were almost a hundred bruises and marks on her battered body. Her nose and skull were fractured, two of her upper teeth had been jarred loose, a bone in her neck was broken, and three of her ribs were cracked. One other grisly detail was almost missed in the initial postmortem: a cue ball had been jammed so far up her vagina that it was initially mistaken for pelvic bone.

I hadn't slept much after the party, so I was running on adrenaline for the first couple days. The first hours after any crime are huge, but there was little for us to go on. We had no ID of the victim, no murder weapon, and no witnesses.

Finally, we got a call from Bob Anderson, Margaret's seventeen-year-old son, reporting his mother missing. We thought there was no way the woman could be this kid's mother; in fact, our first guess was that she was a teenage runaway. Dr. Darrell Skarphol, the pathologist at St. Vincent Hospital, looked at the victim's feet to estimate her age, and told us she was older than we thought. Margaret was actually thirty-five.

Once we were able to get a positive identification, we tried to piece together her story. We started by talking with the son, and the trail quickly brought us to a downtown-area biker bar called the Back Forty.

The Biker Subculture

Our department was well acquainted with several motorcycle clubs. They were major supporters of the porn and prostitution industries, and they liked to intimidate people — cops included.

A guy named Bill Evers owned a couple of questionable places in Green Bay that catered to the biker crowd, including a notorious spot called the Cheyenne Social Club. Biker groups provided the muscle for these types of operations, and we believed they transported women for prostitution and participated in drug trafficking. If we had pornography in Green Bay at that time, it wasn't much more than somebody taking her clothes off in a bar.

The bikers acted as unofficial employees for Evers, who paid them cash so there was no paper trail. When you deal with drugs and prostitution, you can imagine the potential problems that can come up, so Evers saw his association with the bikers as an insurance investment. Evers would buy the bikers beer and throw a party to thank them for their support.

I got tied into this network when I helped John Des Jardins, the assistant district attorney from neighboring Outagamie County, on the case against Evers. The friction between Evers and the police department was an ongoing issue that brought us in contact with the motorcycle clubs. They went so far as to burn squad cars as well as our own personal cars right at the department. Captain Bob Langan and I were threatened so often that the department had to install panic alarms in our houses. The bikers had some clout in their world of crime, and they liked to put that kind of fear in the back of your mind.

Two of the clubs involved in the Evers case were also involved in the Margaret Anderson murder: the DC Eagles, a club based out of the north side of Chicago, and the Drifters, a Green Bay-area club that probably held the number-one spot for challenging authority. These were fun-loving, free-riding guys, and the clubs were pretty much male oriented. The members of these clubs viewed themselves as 1-percenters—the 1 percent minority that fall outside of regular society. They were also white supremacists, anti-black and anti-Semitic.

A lot of that's changed today, and biker gangs aren't the problem they once were. In fact, they're more often in the news today for their charitable activities than for getting into trouble. Whoever came up with the idea that motorcycle clubs could change their image by doing things like fundraising rides and playing Santa at the hospitals is a genius. Now, the police deal more with youth gangs than with adult bikers. Harley-Davidson did a lot to change that bad-boy image over the years. During the Iraq and Afghanistan wars, bikers even provided unofficial security to protect funeral mourners from being harassed by antiwar groups. It's not that all bikers are model citizens, but they do a much better job of keeping their illegal activities out of the spotlight.

During the 1980s, the people in clubs like the DC Eagles and the Drifters were adult men, married, and fathers. An average guy gets a job, pays his taxes, and does what he does in life. The 1-percenters don't; they have their own subculture, and that's what we had to deal with. Biker clubs are very tightlipped networks and protect each other fiercely. They put the fear of God in their members to maintain confidentiality—a strictly "what you see here, stays here" code of ethics.

We learned a lot about them during the course of investigating this case from notes and letters that they sent each other. Their attitude toward women was especially bad. We heard some awful stories, but we couldn't know how true they were. Bikers had their own views on things, their own language, nicknames, and certain words they'd use only with each other. While executing a search warrant, we'd found a book that included a list of those words and what they meant. For instance, to most people, a derisive term for cops is "pigs." The bikers called us "bulls." They'd put you down while talking to your face. That's the character of these guys—they could sound as if they were being nice to you, but they really weren't. They had no respect for authority, the structure of our laws, or even basic civil rights. They felt they had the right to violate any of these as they saw fit.

During the course of our investigations, we learned a lot about how they networked, how they lived, and how they partied. The DC Eagles were a fairly large club, and their core area in northeastern Wisconsin was the Fox Valley, a group of cities a half-hour or so south of Green Bay. The Drifters were a pretty hardcore group in their own right.

Margaret's Last Hours

Raised in Montana, Margaret Copple married Robert Anderson Sr. and the couple moved to Wisconsin. They ended up in Green Bay, where Robert landed a job tending bar at the Central Bar on North Broadway. Margaret had no close family up here, so she didn't have a strong support system to lean on after she and Robert divorced. They were good people; they just had a different approach to life than what many people might consider the right path. Margaret was a working mother with two jobs, but I believe she had a relatively laid-back attitude. She wasn't in a motorcycle club, but frequented the biker bars.

We learned that Margaret and her boyfriend, Terry "Weasel" Apfel, who was a member of the Drifters, went out to a movie the night of the 26th. They did some bar hopping afterward and ended up at the Back Forty about 11:30 p.m. The Back Forty was owned by another Drifter named Mark "Shotgun" Lukensmeyer. Members of both the Drifters and DC Eagles were in the bar. By that time of night, most were intoxicated and high on pot or speed. Margaret was drunk as well—drinking tequilas with beer chasers as her beverage of choice—and she came out on the losing end of a fight with some Drifters women in the bar. Defense attorneys would later point to that fight as the reason for the multiple bruises on her body. There were a lot of biker girlfriends and wives in that bar, and Margaret didn't really fit in. She was drinking irresponsibly that night, and acted out of line. Apfel got her out of the Back Forty, but she went back in. He dragged her back out again.

The two fought in Apfel's car in the alley behind the bar around the 1:00 a.m. closing time. Apfel got out, yanked Margaret from the car by the hair, and then kicked her several times before pushing her toward Lukensmeyer and three other bikers who were standing there. Apfel suggested that they have their way with her. The three were Randolph "Gargoyle" Whiting, Mark "A.D." Hinton, and Denice "Bobber" Stumpner. They unlocked the bar door and took Margaret back inside as Apfel drove off.

That much we know for sure. The rest of the night's events depend on the version or combination of versions you choose to believe. Here's what we think happened:

A bartender witnessed the events in the alley as she helped close the bar. She testified that she yelled twice for the men to stop beating Margaret, but Lukensmeyer told her, "Get the hell out of here."

As she left, she saw him join the three others as they kicked Margaret repeatedly.

Once inside the bar again, Lukensmeyer poured some beers while Hinton had sex with Margaret on the pool table. Lukensmeyer then began beating her with a pool cue, swinging it so hard that he finally broke it. Shortly before 3:00 a.m., the four men and a severely beaten Margaret Anderson piled into Lukensmeyer's white Ford Torino. Lukensmeyer drove, Hinton rode shotgun, and Whiting and Stumpner were in the back seat on either side of Margaret.

After driving the few miles to Lime Kiln Road, Whiting got out of the car with Margaret, and a few minutes later he returned alone. We believe Whiting may have killed Margaret in an attempt to show he belonged with this crowd, since he was the youngest of the group and was only a club prospect at the time. One other interesting twist is that Hinton was dating Whiting's sister Barbara. That relationship would later play a role at Whiting's trial, when Hinton and Whiting tried to pin the murder on Lukensmeyer.

The next day, Whiting, Hinton, and Lukensmeyer went to the Back Forty in a brown Mercury Marquis. Stumpner had already skipped town. The three men removed some items from the bar in garbage bags, including a broken pool cue, and drove to a warehouse on the west side of town where Lukensmeyer's brother worked. They put the items in a Dumpster, then took two snow tires out of the Marquis, and put them on Lukensmeyer's Torino, which had been parked inside the warehouse. They changed the tires because they figured we had taken what impressions we could of tire marks from snow at the murder scene. At some point, Lukensmeyer also burned the white jacket he'd worn that night. During the trial, when asked directly about that and many other details, he repeatedly invoked his Fifth Amendment right to avoid self-incrimination.

We were able to find some evidence in the Dumpster behind the Back Forty, including parts of the cue stick. We also searched the bar itself and found a list of IOUs that Lukensmeyer kept with all his customers' nicknames. That was important because it jump-started our intelligence gathering on the bikers. We had to build that information from scratch because we didn't have much on the bikers at the time.

The volume of physical evidence also challenged us in this case. By the time the case was ready for trial, we had 280 pieces of evidence. We had an entire room set up at the police department to display evidence for defense teams during the discovery process. It took them two days to go through it all. The defense teams could contest the validity of some of it, but there was so much overwhelming evidence tying these guys to the case that it was our greatest asset.

Our police artist, Dick Buss, made drawings of the three different crime scenes: the Back Forty; the manure pit and the area along Lime Kiln Road; and the warehouse where they changed the tires and dumped the debris from the bar. We had to consider all of this evidence, yet we really never had a smoking gun—or in this case, a smoking knife. It's like putting a giant puzzle together, with every piece of physical evidence a critical part of the case you present to the jury.

One of the most important pieces was the broken cue stick we found in the Dumpster. During the autopsy, Dr. Skarphol noticed pieces of wood in Margaret's vagina. We brought in an expert in forest products, who testified that the wood was consistent with the type used to make cue sticks, called ramin. How it and the cue ball got there is a horrible thought, as Margaret was alive when they did that to her. The long, straight bruises showed that she'd been hit repeatedly with a cue stick. The state crime-lab team did a great job of removing any doubt about what had caused those bruises. They weren't all from the earlier catfight in the bar or from Apfel kicking her.

Sometimes we even found things that might have damaged our case. Much of what we discovered was hearsay evidence, so the questionable credibility of the bikers could actually hurt our own credibility. As a detective, you think more is better, and any evidence you get will be the piece that closes the door on a case. But if your source isn't believable, the defense can turn it around and use it against you.

This was a major case to everyone on the Green Bay Police Department, and we did everything we could to get these guys. The prosecuting attorney was Peter Naze, Brown County's district attorney and later a circuit court judge. He was proud of us because we were bulldogs, but he finally told us to stop digging. When we established that this wasn't a crime committed by just one person—that there were four people involved in the beatings and sexual assaults—it then became the police against the motorcycle gangs' 1-percenter attitude toward women—the part of this case that really bothered us.

To start the case we had to put together all the Ws—who, what, when, where, and why. Lukensmeyer was our number-one suspect to begin with. I remember dealing with his sister and family, decent people. We easily connected him to Hinton through the bar, and Hinton to Whiting because of Hinton's relationship with Whiting's sister. How Stumpner ended up there became part of the puzzle. Lukensmeyer was a very large man, and Hinton was a very powerful one.

Lukensmeyer and Hinton later came in voluntarily to give their versions of the night's events, but Whiting and Stumpner disappeared. Lukensmeyer's story led us into the DC Eagles organization. He painted himself as a bystander whose only role had been to drive the car. After we'd interviewed Lukensmeyer, Whiting became our number-one guy. We believed Whiting got out of the car with Margaret outside of Packerland Packing and threw her over the manure pit wall. The men might've thought she was already dead, but when they saw her move, Whiting got back out and cut her throat to make sure. After they drove off, the shock of the sow and the frigid night air may have stimulated Margaret to get up. We don't know how aware she was, but it's amazing she was able to walk as far as she did.

We were pretty sure that Whiting was the guy who'd killed Margaret Anderson, but now we had to prove it. We knew all four men were accessories to murder, yet we didn't know who did what that night. I credit Pete Naze and Tim Pedretti, an assistant DA, with working their tails off to put this case together.

At that point, everything we had came from Lukensmeyer, so we had to protect him as a material witness and get him out of the area for a while. The game plan was to take Whiting down first, then pick up the pieces around him, and charge the other three with lesser crimes.

Since I'd always liked motorcycling, I sort of admired bikers prior to this case. In my early days as a motorcycle cop, I'd learned that they weren't necessarily bad people just because they were in a motorcycle club. They just rode together, and "outlaw" was the image they liked to project.

Years earlier, I had known a guy named Bill Gelbke, an engineer and a fellow Green Bay West graduate, who'd built his own enormous motorcycle powered by a Buick engine. I'd be riding down the road on my shiny police department cycle, and Bill would pull up next to me, wearing a German-style helmet and dressed like one of the most hard-core bikers around. But he was a good guy, and I gave him respect. He never belonged to a motorcycle club, but he got into an armed confrontation with a police officer one day and ended up getting killed.

During the course of the Anderson investigation, I began to establish relationships with several members of the two motorcycle clubs and they started to trust me a little bit. Jack "Wolfie" Shavlik was one of these men. Jack had been president of the Drifters and was a Vietnam vet. His wife, Chris, was tending bar at the Back Forty the night of the murder, and was the person who later told us about Margaret's drop-off outside the bar. That was a huge help and a key part of our evidence. Chris was tough; she wasn't scared of anything. She and Jack had a little farm near Kewaunee, about forty-five minutes east of Green Bay, and I would meet with them at their house. I was more scared of his dogs than I was of Wolfie. We needed these people's help, and we slowly got a picture of what happened that night.

One of our young officers was from Chicago, and he went down there with us to gather intelligence on the DC Eagles. From working with the Chicago crime units, we knew the Eagles had a clubhouse down there. We needed to know how they operated and how they thought in order to find Whiting. Since he'd made himself scarce almost immediately after the murder, we now had a manhunt on our hands that lasted eight months. The media stayed on the case, and with the assistance we received from the FBI, it took on national prominence.

We thought we had a good lead from a policeman in Fort Myers, Florida. We knew bikers would go to that area and change their names and identities to hide amongst themselves. It's hard to infiltrate that kind of group, because their values are so different from mainstream society's. It's nearly impossible to fake that attitude believably. The Fort Myers detective had heard a biker talking about a case up in Green Bay, so we thought maybe Whiting was in Florida. We never could establish whether he was, though, even after spending hours on the phone trying to track down the lead. We later found out he had obtained a fake Social Security number, and he and his girlfriend were working carnivals. That might be how Whiting got down around Fort Myers. While on the run, carny work was the only job they held that amounted to anything. They'd even given blood to get some money.

Jerry Rogalski joined the case early on. We had a good working relationship, and he became a great partner. Like me, he knew this case inside and out. He had some good contacts, too, including knowledge of Bill Evers and that aspect of motorcycle club operations. Jerry knew a detective in Appleton (thirty minutes south of Green Bay) named

John Parker, who knew a guy named Frank "Frog" Seebantz. Parker worked for Seebantz as a gofer. I never fully trusted Parker, because I thought he was in too tight. I was always cautious with everyone I talked to, wondering what they knew and whom they knew. We had a Green Bay police officer who'd gotten too close with Evers, eventually tipping him off to what we were doing during the investigation. After all the time we'd put into the Anderson case, we didn't want to blow it with a similar problem.

Jerry was like a hurricane, tying pieces of information together from all directions. He was even able to get a membership list of the DC Eagles. Then we tried to learn about the home lives of every DC Eagle in the state. We found out that Seebantz had a trailer in Langlade County near Antigo, about two hours northwest of Green Bay, and there was another biker place near Crivitz about halfway in between. This part of Wisconsin is heavily wooded and rural, a very easy place to separate yourself from society. It was scary, but I took my own vehicle up there several times to nose around during our search for Whiting. I couldn't make any contacts there because I knew word would get out, so I'd stop at a bar and just listen to people talk. It was better to be a listener than a talker.

I ran all over the place for months, following up on virtually every lead. On August 20, 1984, I was up north with Stan Keckhaver, our department's photo identification guy. He and I had worked together as bartenders when we were younger. Our idea was to have Stan take photos of places while I drove. We disguised ourselves as fishermen, rented a wreck, and threw junk all over the back end to make it look believable. We had old clothes on, but we had our guns and badges with us. We'd stop at little bars and spend all day listening to conversations. We actually saw Whiting come out of Seebantz's trailer once, but at the time we didn't know it was him because he had changed his appearance dramatically. He'd shaved off his bushy beard, and cut his hair and colored it jet-black. One of his front teeth had been knocked out, which altered his look even more. We didn't want to be too aggressive; we'd been waiting nine months and didn't want to blow it by being careless.

I got permission to go up and meet a few officers from some northern jurisdictions, including Langlade, Lincoln, and Marathon counties, and the city of Merrill. I befriended these guys because I figured if anything came out of this north woods lead, we could share information with each other. On August 30, my relationship with officers from Langlade County paid off.

Ben Baker, one of the Langlade officers, stopped by a rummage sale at Seebantz's trailer and actually spoke with Whiting while pretending to shop. On Whiting's arm Ben noticed the DC Eagles tattoo, which matched the description of the one we knew he had. It was a warm day, and Whiting made the mistake of not covering up that tattoo. There was no way for us to identify him by looking at his face, but the tattoo sold it. Baker left the rummage sale and called Bob Langan at the Green Bay PD to tell him they had a fix on Whiting.

On top of dealing with this case, my personal life was filled with stress. My mom was battling cancer. Sandy and I had picked her up from the hospital that very morning and brought her to stay at our house. About an hour after we got her settled, Bob called from headquarters and said, "Jerry, I think we've got your man."

That set in motion a frantic flurry of phone calls to arrange to capture Whiting while we knew where he was. Everything just went crazy. How were we going to do this? We didn't have a search warrant, but we believed Ben Baker on his say-so. We went red light and siren all the way up to Antigo, the county seat of Langlade County. We set up a command center at a crossroads bar near Seebantz's trailer, and brought everyone we could to surround the place, including deputies from adjacent counties. We blocked off every road leading into the area, and even had to keep a school bus from going in there. Finally, it was getting close to 3:00 p.m. — time to make our move.

A female officer with a dog was positioned in the woods behind the house along with a few other armed officers in case Whiting tried to make a run for it. We saw Seebantz's girlfriend come out of the trailer and walk to the mailbox. She looked down the road and must have noticed the squad cars, because she ran back into the house. Bingo! Now we knew we probably had the real thing here. Still, we had to be extremely cautious because we didn't know who was in that trailer.

Luckily, Seebantz was out at the time and we got him on the roadway later. We knew there were others in the trailer, but didn't know who or how many. There was a lot of pressure on us to not only capture Whiting, but also make sure no one got hurt. After all this work, I thought *please, don't anybody shoot anybody.* We certainly didn't want an officer to get hurt.

Whiting immediately split out the back door and started running. He quickly saw the armed officers back there, then turned around and dove under the trailer. They sent the dog in after him and got him out, but he still wouldn't give up. Langlade County Deputy Denny Lutzow tackled Whiting and we finally got him secured. A few officers with rifles had Whiting scoped in, and if he'd done anything they would've taken him down.

It was a giant relief to get him. I remember media helicopters flying overhead. Tom Hinz and I had Whiting in the back seat of a squad car as we drove back to Antigo and the Langlade County Sheriff's Department. He didn't say a word to us the whole ride.

If the biker community had gotten Whiting out of the country, I don't know how this case would've gone. Would we have been able to go ahead with prosecuting the other three guys? I don't know. Whiting's capture was just the start. We had a case with a lot of physical evidence, but we still had to piece it all together. To make matters worse, Stumpner had fled and we had no idea where he was. He got into the biker network and they quickly moved him out of state.

The Trials

Beginning with Whiting's trial in March 1985, we took these guys down one at a time. The juries were selected from outside the area, mainly Milwaukee, because of all the publicity around Green Bay. The pressure to prepare for trial was extreme. Nobody wanted to make any mistakes since this was such a high-profile crime. Looking back, I think I felt a lot of that pressure because I wasn't an educated person. If I were a defense attorney reading police reports with poor grammar, I'd probably think this officer would be a piece of cake to cross-examine. Still, there are some basics when you're on the stand: be honest; look at the jury; and don't offer anything more than the answer to the question. The jury will believe you if you're sincere, so you don't have to be a polished speaker. Pete Naze told me, "Jerry, you're a believable person."

The jury can also read attorneys when they flip things around for their clients' benefit. Lukensmeyer was a key witness, and he played us. We ended up having to impeach him because he tried to change his story. He pled the Fifth frequently, and Pete finally ended up reading from the transcript of his pretrial deposition. The credibility of the bikers was a problem, and Tim Pedretti and Pete were very methodical in presenting the case.

I was prepared to testify, and Pete told me I did well. I remember getting some new clothes for the trial because I wanted to look good. Pete and Tim took turns asking the questions, going through every crime scene and all the circumstantial evidence.

If I had to do it again, I'd be much cooler on the stand. Life makes you better, and being involved in different cases gave me the experience and understanding of what the prosecution needs to win. I learned that circumstantial evidence can be very meaningful, even if that's all you have.

After Whiting was convicted of murder and sentenced to life, it took another year and a half to go through separate trials for Hinton and Lukensmeyer. We still didn't know where Stumpner was. Hinton's trial was in September 1985. He was like a mean bear that had been backed into a corner. To make sure he didn't do anything foolish, we had the judge ask the county officers in the courtroom to remove their guns during recesses. We wanted no chance that he could grab a weapon while they walked him out of the room.

We went down to the Milwaukee area to select the jury, and I did background checks on every potential juror. For instance, we didn't want to get any jurors who were Harley-Davidson employees, because they might be pro-biker. I learned a lot about the jury selection process during those trials.

I took Pete and Tim home after we returned to Green Bay from two days of jury selection. Then, as I crossed the Tillmann Bridge on my way home, I turned on my police radio and heard, "HQ to Jerry Parins."

"This is Jerry."

"Do you have the DA with you?"

"No."

It's a good thing I'd already dropped off Pete, because what I heard next was not good news. Hinton had managed to jump out of a moving squad car in the middle of Green Bay. He was handcuffed at the time, but not shackled, and luckily he hurt himself when he hit the road and was unable to run.

Great—one of the most dangerous men I've ever been around, and he escapes. I went back to Pete's house and told him what was up. That was one of the only times I ever saw him lose his cool. We didn't know all the details; only that Hinton had escaped and was now in the hospital.

What a kick in the teeth for us! The bikers had said they would try to get these guys out if we went ahead with the trials. We didn't know how they'd try it, but I sensed something was going to happen. It turned out Hinton wasn't badly hurt, and his escape attempt only delayed the case a day while he recuperated under guard in the hospital.

Hinton was eventually convicted of aiding and abetting aggravated assault, aiding and abetting kidnapping, and first-degree sexual assault. He was sentenced to fifty years in prison, but his mandatory release date with supervision was only twenty-two years. A month later, Lukensmeyer's trial followed Hinton's in what was a very stressful fall of 1985. Lukensmeyer was convicted of being party to the crimes of aggravated battery and kidnapping, and first-degree sexual assault. He received a fifty-year prison term with a similar mandatory release date.

We still didn't know where Stumpner was, and that continued to weigh on me. Forrest Gregg was the head coach of the Packers from 1984–87, but I was too busy with the case to be involved with the team as much as I would've liked. I did a little work when I could, while Jerry Rogalski and I made sure the case didn't die. We jumped on any valid leads that came in.

I paid visits to the Stumpner family in Berlin, a small town about ninety minutes southwest of Green Bay. They could've told me to get the hell out or slammed the door in my face, but they didn't. They let me in the house, and I asked them if they'd heard anything from their son. You've got to have compassion for people in situations like this, since one bad person doesn't mean his brother or sister or parents are bad. The Stumpners didn't like me because they didn't think Denice had done anything wrong, but they were civil. I made sure they knew we weren't going to quit until we found him.

Almost three years went by before we got our next big break. A TV show called *America's Most Wanted* had just come on the air. The results were just amazing: criminals featured on the show were being picked up, so we sent some feelers out to the show about Stumpner and our case, and they liked the story. The fact that a big article on it had run in *True Detective* magazine in April 1987 helped.

The show's producers came to Green Bay and put together a video reenactment of the murder. The show aired on Father's Day weekend, June 19, 1988. We met with John Walsh in Washington, D.C., and took calls late into the night after the show. We were there to answer any questions, and a number of calls rated follow-up.

A few days after the show, the FBI got a call from a girl who said she believed Stumpner was working on a horse ranch near Golden, Colorado, where her family kept a horse. She described Stumpner as a fantastic employee, good with horses and good with the families. I went to Colorado along with the FBI and Brown County Sheriff Leon Pieschek. While the FBI went to the ranch, Leon and I stayed behind in Denver. Sure enough, it was Stumpner. He was five feet six and a half inches tall, weighed 200-odd pounds, and had curly blond hair. Unlike Whiting, Stumpner hadn't changed his appearance at all, which made it easy for anyone who'd seen the TV show to recognize him. I sat with Stumpner handcuffed to me in the back of the airplane all the way to Green Bay. We had to change planes in Minneapolis, and we borrowed a private room for him to use the toilet.

After getting our prisoner back to Green Bay, Jerry and I were sent back to Colorado to find out what Stumpner had been doing while he was there. We discovered he'd worked installing drywall in Aspen. Most of the people there were uncooperative with us. At one point, Stumpner was arrested for drunk driving, but they didn't fingerprint him and he slipped through the cracks—one of the most wanted people in the country, and the authorities never knew it.

I visited Hinton in prison to see if he would testify against Stumpner. Hinton had been in prison three years already and was a big shot in the system. Trying to intimidate me, he came right up on me. I was mad at the guards for letting him get away with that. Predictably, Hinton refused to cooperate. In October 1988 Stumpner was convicted of aiding and abetting aggravated battery, being party to the crime of kidnapping, and first-degree sexual assault. He too received a fifty-year prison term His mandatory release date with supervision is January 2011.

The Aftermath

For policemen, many of the toughest cases involve domestic issues or crimes of passion. This case wasn't have either of those, and it didn't involve a serial killer. This was a case where people took advantage of a helpless individual and it got out of hand. I was so engulfed in the case that it took a toll on my personal life. At one point I worked about sixteen hours a day for nearly a month without a day off.

You don't realize what that kind of stress is doing to you when you're going through it. Looking back, I did two things that I now know were mistakes: I didn't sleep enough, and I drank too much. The only way I thought I could relax enough to get some sleep was to drink three or four beers. Wrong. I actually got less sleep, and it was hard on my body. My girls were teenagers then, and time went by fast while I was dealing with this case. Also, we were taking care of my mother before finally making the very difficult decision to place her in a nursing home. The cancer was in her throat, and I thank God she didn't live too long after that. She died in October 1985 — the same month as the Lukensmeyer trial.

This case was my life for close to four years, and it almost broke me. After we got Stumpner, there was a gap when everything slowed down. I had lost a lot of weight, and the emotional stress had taken a lot out of me. The doctors did a bunch of tests and at first they thought I had cancer, but I didn't. Finally, Dr. Chester Crawford said, "Jerry, we've got to get you out of this." He got me into running, and gradually my body and mind began to recover. The exercise brought me back to a level of stability.

The Stumpner conviction brought me closure, but it was a very difficult time in my professional life. I was out of the detective division by then, and had been promoted, but I couldn't handle returning to night duty. I gave up the promotion so I could go back to days, went through training, and ended up in Internal Affairs. This was also a very tough job. You take complaints about your fellow officers, and you might have to take away the badge and gun from a guy you work with.

To this day, I can't drive on Lime Kiln Road without thinking of that case. I thought about it even more as these guys' mandatory release dates began to come up. The first to get out of prison, on July 3, 2007 was Hinton, whom I consider the most dangerous man in that group. I wasn't looking forward to that date, especially since he reportedly made comments about seeking revenge when he got out. He was placed in a halfway house just a few blocks from our house. I was relieved when he was relocated to Central Wisconsin a short time later, but one of the most dangerous individuals I've ever encountered is free, and in my book that's not a good thing. Lukensmeyer was released on April 9, 2008, but I don't consider him as dangerous as Hinton. If that crime had been committed today, under the current sentencing laws, those guys would've never gotten out.

December 27 and August 30 are two dates I'll always remember: the day of the murder and the day we captured Whiting. I think of this crime and I still have the same passion for it after all these years. No one deserves to be brutalized like Margaret Anderson was. How can you do that to another human being?

Whiting was the only one convicted for Margaret's murder, but as far as I'm concerned they were all guilty because no one stopped it.

Chapter 6
Goodbye PD, Hello Lambeau

I WAS PHYSICALLY AND EMOTIONALLY spent after four years dealing with the various aspects of the Margaret Anderson case. Beginning with the investigation, continuing through the pursuit, and ending with the trials, the case had consumed my life, demanding most of my attention for much too long. Football became the catalyst for my return to reality.

Following the last game of the 1983 season, Bart Starr was fired, and Forrest Gregg was hired to replace him on December 24, 1983 — just three days before Margaret Anderson was murdered. Forrest was head coach for four turbulent seasons before resigning after a 5-9-1 season in 1987 to become head coach at Southern Methodist University, his alma mater. His time was marked by such thugs on the roster as defensive lineman Charles Martin, who body-slammed Bears quarterback Jim McMahon to the turf during an interception return. The James Lofton and Mossy Cade sexual assault cases also happened on Forrest's watch. His surly personality and the team's struggles on and off the field made for an unpleasant period in Packers history. Maybe God kept me busy during that time for a reason.

I had gone back to working nights when I became a detective in 1977, which freed up my days to work for the Packers. That was good news and bad news. While I enjoyed working with the team, the organization began to expect the world of me. After my shift for the Green Bay PD, I'd go over to Lambeau and work seven or eight hours. My "part-time" job became overwhelming.

Prior to the Anderson murder, I had worked regularly for Bob Noel in the equipment area. Along with some of the other part-time guys, I did the dirtiest jobs around the locker room, literally cleaning the grit and grout out of the showers. This connection was my way to come back into the building and say hi. It was important for me to maintain my connection with the organization despite all the time I was spending on the Margaret Anderson case. I really got after that crime, yet I always wanted to keep my job with Bob. As the case played out, it received a lot of publicity, and Bob was aware of that, so he cut me some slack regarding some of his expectations. I worked less for the Packers during those four years than at any point in my career, but I'd work for Bob whenever I had the chance, and I never missed the games.

Bob and I ran the daily practices from an equipment standpoint. I'd make the Gatorade, load up the carts for the various positions to use around the practice field, and handle much of the security work. We seemed to have more physical testing at that time, and the team would go over to the Ashwaubenon High School track for time trials. Every time the team did anything away from Lambeau, we'd have to move the drinks, the horns, the whistles, everything.

Today, the Packers have what amounts to four practice fields across from Lambeau Field. Two are outdoors and two are inside the 112,000-square-foot Don Hutson Center. Prior to the building's dedication in the summer of 1994, the Packers almost always practiced outside, and conditions could be miserable. Once in a while, when the weather became unbearable, the team would take buses out to the University of Wisconsin-Green Bay's Phoenix Sports Center or to St. Norbert College's Schuldes Sports Center for walk-through practices.

One Thanksgiving when Bart was coach, the team needed to practice on artificial turf for an upcoming game. The Oneida Street practice field only had a small section of turf, and practice that day was held in a snow/rain mix that was just horrible. I mixed up some chicken and beef bullion on electric burners, worried that the electrical outlets would get wet. There was nowhere to hide from the elements, and at the break, the whole team would come over and have a warm drink. Nowadays, the importance of hydration is much better understood. There are lots of people helping out with water and Gatorade and even hot chocolate during the course of practices and games. The Hutson Center was a major improvement, and it helped raise the Packers' image around the league as a first-rate organization.

We captured Stumpner and wrapped up the last of the Anderson murder trials in 1988, right as Lindy Infante was beginning his career here. I got back into working with the Packers at that point, and was very excited about the team's prospects with Lindy as head coach. Prior to being hired by the Packers, he was the Cleveland Browns' offensive coordinator, and before that he was offensive coordinator for Cincinnati when the Bengals went to the Super Bowl under Forrest Gregg.

One of the most respected football minds in the league, Lindy brought a fresh attitude to the team. He had a great personality, and we had a good relationship. About the only problem I recall during Lindy's four seasons was when one of his boys got arrested at the stadium late on the night of a game while trying to get into the restricted parking lot. I was working the games then, but my job didn't allow me much time to help Bob with equipment or practices. I was in an administrative position with the police department, meaning I worked days, Monday through Friday.

The Packers were at best just an average football team for most of Coach Infante's tenure. The team had a lot of challenges to get the ship straightened out. Tim Harris was a perfect example. An all-pro linebacker in 1989, his off-the-field issues led to his trade to the San Francisco 49ers after the 1990 season. Tim was out in a boat one night—he said he was duck hunting—and was reported missing on the bay. Eventually he was rescued, but questions remained about what exactly he was doing out there. Tom Braatz, the Packers' general manager, called me at the police department to see if we knew about any possible drug issues with Tim.

No matter how bad last year's team was, there's always excitement in Green Bay about next year. If you're a diehard fan like me, the next team is always going to be better. Getting a blue-chip player in the draft can really do something for your team and your attitude right away, and in 1988 Braatz drafted wide receiver Sterling Sharpe in the first round. Sterling set the team record that year for most receptions by a rookie, and would go on to become one of the greatest Packers wide receivers ever.

The Packers struggled through a 4-12 season in Lindy's first year, giving them the second overall pick in the 1989 draft. They could've had the first selection, but by beating the Vikings 27-7 in the meaningless final game of the season, they lost the first pick to Dallas.

The big question was whether the Packers would take UCLA quarterback Troy Aikman or Michigan State offensive tackle Tony Mandarich. Oklahoma State running back Barry Sanders, Alabama defensive end Derrick Thomas, and Florida State cornerback Deion Sanders were also available, but weren't as highly prized as those first two guys. Mandarich was hyped liked no any offensive lineman ever had been. He appeared shirtless on the cover of *Sports Illustrated* next to the headline THE INCREDIBLE BULK.

History shows that the Cowboys drafted Aikman and went on to become the dominant team of the early and mid-1990s, while the Packers had a few more years of bad football in front of them. Had the Packers been able to take Aikman, it might have changed the course of NFL history. Then again, we probably wouldn't have made the move to obtain Brett Favre prior to the 1992 season, so I suppose things happen for a reason.

Mandarich arrived with all the hoopla you would expect from the second overall draft pick. He was bigger than life in many regards, but he actually was a down-to-earth guy who loved the outdoors. I got to know him pretty well during his three seasons here. Tony was really likable. I've never run into an offensive lineman I didn't care for—even the nasty ones. Anyone you talk to in the game will tell you that the offensive linemen are the most practical people, and they're the blood and guts of a football team.

Tony got married at the Embassy Suites downtown on a Friday night. It was a private event, and he hired a few of us to protect his wedding. He was really interested in guns and loved to hunt, especially in his native Canada. An avid sportsman, he bought a house in a wooded area in Suamico, just north of Green Bay, where he lived with his wife and a couple of big rottweilers.

Stories about Tony's possible steroid use kept popping up; the Packers had even talked to the people at Michigan State about it prior to the draft. Of course, the school wasn't about to tell any NFL teams whether they knew anything about that, and Tony never admitted using steroids. The fact is he never tested positive for them, although the sophisticated tests used today weren't available back then. If the Packers could've sent me out to East Lansing, I think I would've found out within two weeks if Tony was or wasn't on steroids.

I didn't even know what steroids were at the time. They weren't prevalent, and few people really understood their effects. I liked Tony, though, and I thought he was a good person underneath all the hype. He came to me when his health began going downhill. He was losing his hair and couldn't maintain his weight. This was about the time when former Oakland Raiders defensive lineman Lyle Alzado was fighting brain cancer and died at age forty-two. It was later determined that steroids had played a role in Lyle's death.

After the Packers released Tony in 1991, his health kept him out of football for several years, but he resurfaced for a few seasons beginning in 1996 while Lindy was head coach of the Indianapolis Colts. As it turned out, Tony was never anything more than an average NFL player and a spectacular footnote in Packers history.

The Move to Full-time

By the time Lindy Infante was nearing the end of his tenure as head coach, I was putting in a lot of part-time hours for the Packers. Al Stevens had been security director since 1982, and I knew he wasn't going to stay much longer. Talking one day with team president Bob Harlan, I mentioned that if Al ever left, I'd appreciate the opportunity to apply for the job.

"Jerry," he said, "you'll get that from me."

That conversation took place in the fall of 1991 as the Packers were beginning what would become a 4-12 disaster of a season. In November, Bob suddenly fired Tom Braatz and hired Ron Wolf as general manager, and things really started to change. Bob called me into his office a few weeks later to tell me that Al would be leaving soon, and to ask if I'd I be interested in taking on the security director's job on a part-time basis.

Bob didn't think we needed a full-time person, but I was all fired up. Lindy was excited for me, too. I hadn't planned on leaving the police department just yet, and in fact things were changing downtown at the same time. I was working in Internal Affairs and had recently applied for the job of police chief. I didn't have the education for the position, but it was fun just to be interviewed. Instead, Bob Langan got the job, and he was going to promote me to head up the uniform division.

"I'm sorry, Bob, but I've got an opportunity to go to the Packers, and I'm taking it."

Between the time Al announced his plans to leave and my official hiring, I got my feet wet in the security role. I put in a lot more hours than I actually charged the Packers for, and I was still working full-time for the police department. I had an idea of what the security job was like, but it would've been nice to get more input from Al. As a part-time employee, I had gradually learned about the job responsibilities. I set up security people to help fans and players cross Oneida Street to the practice fields, had officers on hand to help protect the players, and established some security for training camp. They gave me a little office in the back of the old Lambeau administration building with a desk and a phone. It was hidden away, but still kind of neat.

Things happened very quickly as soon as the 1991 season ended. Ron Wolf fired Coach Infante after the last game, and I was afraid that my chance at getting more than twenty hours a week left with him. Ron hired Mike Holmgren as head coach on January 11, 1992, and it seemed like things within the organization were just flying. I officially retired from the police force on April 4, and took on my new job at the twenty-hour level. I was overwhelmed by the dedication of the people in the Packers' organization — not just the coaches, but the people behind the scenes. There are a lot of good people in this organization, and it's well respected throughout the NFL.

Right from the start the job was a lot more than twenty hours a week. I was just happy to leave the police department, even though it meant taking a pay cut and losing my benefits. I took $38,000 in unused vacation pay and put it into an account to cover our health insurance. When my extended City coverage ran out, the Packers picked up my insurance. That was a concern at the time, but when I look at the bigger picture of how my life changed, it all worked out well. The Packers have been very good to my family and me. I didn't take the job for the money, that's for sure, but it was something I wanted. Would I do it again? Of course I would.

Building the Security Team's Role

The first time I met Coach Holmgren was in May 1992. We talked about the upcoming training camp and I asked if I'd have the chance to travel with the team.

"That's not even a question," he said. "You're the security person. Of course you'll be traveling with us."

Coach Mike had been the offensive coordinator for the San Francisco 49ers, and security was a huge part of their operation. The Niners were one of the most successful road teams in the 1980s, and that was one of the main reasons Ron hired Mike. Before he arrived, the Packers were took a more conservative approach to travel and security, while the 49ers had made it a top-priority operation.

Part of my job early on was just learning to work within the Packers' structure, and then learn what Coach Holmgren specifically wanted from me and the security team. Ron eventually elevated the status of my position, and Mike Reinfeldt, the team's chief financial officer, called me in one day to say they wanted me to go full-time with benefits. The Packers knew the job had had become much more demanding than what was required under previous coaches.

Ron and Mike's perspective on what a security person is to an NFL team was very different from anything the Packers had done before. We didn't even have an attorney on staff when I started. I was able to observe a lot of changes both from the security and the football standpoints, and I think those guys' arrival was the best thing that's ever happened to this organization. Coach Holmgren gets a lot of credit, but I don't think he gets enough. It costs money to be proactive and have a full-time security department, and you've got to stay on top of things because people can be so irresponsible.

My real boss was Bob Harlan — Mr. H, as I call him. I worked for the Packers' administration, not the head coach. If the team fired everyone in football operations, I wouldn't lose my job. The security job has changed even more as the organization has grown. There's more money involved, more vendor contracts, and over 10,000 more people in the stadium now than there were in the 1990s. I also answered to the football side of the organization. The head coach was my boss at another level, and any of his requests became my responsibility as well.

When Ron and Mike were putting together their respective parts of the organization in '92, Coach came to me and said, "Jerry, we're going to set up a security program similar to what I knew with the 49ers."

Everything I did that first year or so was following Mike Holmgren's lead. If I had any questions, I went and asked him. I gradually started implementing some of my own procedures, developing the security program to where it stands today. I'm very proud of that, because there were things we were doing before 9/11 that many teams didn't start doing until afterward.

One of our public relations people gave me an article about the 49ers' great record on the road. That, and the win-loss records it produced, was one of the reasons they were so successful in getting home games for the playoffs. I knew Mike and Ron wanted to bring that same style here to Green Bay. Other than having skilled players on your team, it's those intangibles that set great teams apart.

There are always distractions surrounding an NFL team, especially when you're winning. Think of some of the stars the 49ers had in their glory years: people like Ronnie Lott, Joe Montana, and Jerry Rice. But the Niners had managed to limit the distractions, and we were determined to instill that into our program. I helped drive the 49ers around Green Bay during the '80s when they came to town for games. They came in buses to work out in our indoor facility, and I just watched how they operated. They had full-time security staff on each bus, and the team's movements were on a very detailed time schedule. It was entirely different from how the Packers operated, and I was very impressed with it.

"Jerry, you're part of the travel team," Coach Holmgren told me, "so your job is to keep distractions to a minimum."

Taking an organization the size of an NFL team on the road is a major task, one that I didn't really know how to do when I became security director. Moving a team involves charter flights, hotels, and buses. There are a lot of opportunities for things to go wrong, not to mention a bunch of young guys looking to have some fun. They have to understand that they're not on a business trip arranged for them to go party. The veteran players understand that, and they prepare themselves properly the night before a game.

There are a lot of temptations for players, and some of the guys don't feel as much responsibility to their teammates as others do. I learned real fast that when you come into a city, there are questionable ladies hanging around the hotel. I learned to attach myself to players who needed some extra guidance to stay out of trouble. The dangers associated with this lifestyle came to light in 1991, when Magic Johnson came out with his HIV admission. Having had different women in every city, he had really put himself at risk.

Coach Holmgren was great about giving me the flexibility to grow into the role, and I shared everything I learned about the players' activities with him. Those first two years, our security team created all the procedures for going on the road from scratch, and I'm very proud of that. Some of the measures we initiated became part of the league's recommendations following 9/11. Prior to that, most teams had hired security people from the host city to help out on away games, but when you think about it, it makes no sense to take a multimillion-dollar operation on the road and then trust someone else to protect it. And those hometown guys usually want the other team to win, too.

We started bringing three Green Bay police officers along with us on trips, and before long we increased that number to six. It costs more that way, but then we've got the best people on the job. Plus, our officers have better relationships with the players than anyone from a different city could have. The guys who travel with us want to be there; they cover the hotel floors after dark, and they do their jobs well. They make it possible for me to sleep at night. In the big picture, it's a lot safer this way because we know every person on that airplane—even the flight attendants.

With the extra screening procedures that TSA (Transportation Safety Administration) workers have to do at airports, it would take forever to get our group on a plane if we had to go through the normal process. Thankfully, we're usually able to go through a different part of the airport and get checked separately before boarding our Northwest Airlines charters. Doug Collins and I help check names off the manifest as people board the plane, and the process only takes about a half hour. Doug was my assistant before he took over as security director when I moved into semi-retirement in 2007.

As soon as I was hired, there were a few things I decided to make better. Since I didn't have a chance to learn the ropes from Al Stevens, I talked with Bob Noel and the equipment guys instead. From what they told me and what I already knew, I started to establish my own type of system. Of course, there were also things I needed to learn right off the bat. The process began with being involved in team meetings. I really enjoyed that, seeing how Coach dealt with the team after a loss or a win. I learned that when you win, you don't get on top of the ladder, and when you lose, you don't go all the way to the bottom. Controlling your emotions is hard to do, especially after a win on the road, which feels awesome.

After losing an overtime heartbreaker at home to the Minnesota Vikings in the 1992 regular-season opener, we went on our first road trip. The Tampa Bay Bucs had Vinny Testaverde as their quarterback, and the Packers had Don Majkowski. Both teams were bad, and the national media jokingly referred to the match-up as the Bay of Pigs game. We stayed at a hotel owned by New York Yankees owner George

Steinbrenner. It was right on the water, and very nice, but it was hotter than hell in Tampa the first weekend of September.

I was new at this travel thing, so I just packed my bags and went on the trip. I called the crime-prevention guy at the hotel and arranged to get some people on our floors. I was trying to implement some of the same security measures that I knew the 49ers had, even though I really didn't understand it myself.

We got to Tampa on a Friday night, and I was happy to see that there was security on our floor. However, there was a wedding going on in the hotel, and that stressed me a little. There were more than just Packers people on the floor, and in fact the wedding party occupied a room right across from mine. I wondered how in the world I'd be able to protect the team's privacy. An older gentleman was sitting in a chair, supposedly in a security role. I talked to him and he assured me he'd often worked the floor for visiting teams.

As the evening went on, I tried my best to relax, and even went out for a run. I helped with bed check at midnight; all the guys were in their rooms, and everything was good. A little later, I walked down to the main lobby and ran into assistant coaches Gil Haskell, Sherman Lewis, and John Johnson.

"Hey, Jerry, you want to go out and have a beer with us?" they asked.

"Sure!" I said, honored to go out with the coaches.

We jumped in a cab and ended up at a girly place. Sherm paid the ten bucks for me to get in, but they didn't serve any alcohol there, so I just drank a Coke. We had a fun time. I was laughing so hard I was crying. The girls would come dancing by us and Sherm would stick money in their garters. What an experience!

At 1:30 a.m. John and I cut out. It was about two miles back to the hotel, and eventually we were able to grab a cab. I went up to the team's floor and my so-called security guy was sound asleep in his chair. The people across the hall were pleasant, but they were drinking until about 2:30 in the morning. I was really upset about that guy falling asleep on the job, and stayed up all night worrying about the noise the wedding party was making. I was just annoyed with this whole arrangement.

The next morning, before the team left for a Saturday walk-through at the old Sombrero Stadium, I went upstairs and vented my frustration to John Johnson. I told him that I didn't like this hotel and that we had to do something different. "The team has to give me some leeway to hire someone else," I told him. I couldn't believe I was doing this so early in my new job.

It didn't take long for my complaint to get back to Coach Holmgren. He quickly called a meeting where I shared my concerns with him, with Dick Blasczyk, the team's finance director and travel coordinator, and with public relations director Lee Remmel.

"From now on," Coach said, "Jerry arranges for the security in hotels. This is how we always did it in San Francisco."

We all learned a lot right there about why the 49ers were so successful. I didn't really know what a distraction it was to be on the road, or the effect it could have on a team—even having someone get sick can be huge—but I was learning fast how disturbing it was to have fans around and how important it was to protect the floors properly. The Packers lost 31-3 to the Bucs the next day, and it was bad. Coach was furious after the game, and started making changes to get things better right away. Later on, we laughed about that trip, which was the type of disaster that had to happen for us to change job assignments so quickly. Eventually, I was also put in charge of securing escorts for the drive to and from the stadium, and more responsibilities kept coming my way.

Our next game was at home against the Cincinnati Bengals, and it turned out to be a historic day at Lambeau Field. Majkowski got hurt in the first quarter and was replaced by the very young Brett Favre. With thirteen seconds left, Brett hooked up with Kitrick Taylor on a thirty-five-yard touchdown pass to give the Packers a 24-23 victory and begin his legendary career.

Not everything was great with Brett right off the bat, though. The Packers struggled through a 3-6 record halfway through the season before things finally turned around. We won six consecutive games to get back into the playoff race before losing the season finale at Minnesota, 27-7. The Vikings killed us in the trenches that last game. They were the better team and won the division by two games. The fact that we were able to win six in a row was amazing. It was an example of how good a coach Mike Holmgren was, because we weren't a good football team.

Our home record—which at that time included three games a year in Milwaukee—was 6-2. We expected to win at home. In fact, during Holmgren's seven seasons, the Packers had a 49-7 regular-season home record, including a remarkable 25 consecutive wins from the second game of the 1995 season to early in the 1998 season. For a few years the Packers were literally unbeatable at Lambeau Field.

Since eliminating distractions and knowing the landscape was such an important part of going on the road, it wasn't long before we started holding travel meetings on Tuesdays before every away game. We'd go over all the details, from the layout of the hotel to our transportation plans. Our director of administrative affairs, Mark Schiefelbein, would call other teams for their input whenever we were headed to a city we didn't visit often.

Nowadays, before the team arrives, our advance team checks out the hotel, finds out what other events are going on there, and takes note of things as detailed as where the restrooms are located in relation to our meeting rooms. We have a team meeting in a large room, then break it down into offense and defense, and then by position coaches. The offense goes through its list of the first fifteen plays. Usually a team of six off-duty police officers who accompany us on the trips secures the whole area.

We select hotels based on where they are in relation to the airport and the stadium, what's around each hotel, and the typical post-game traffic conditions. We try to pick a hotel that provides us enough luxury to be comfortable. The coach usually makes the final call on where we stay, but the travel team gives him options.

Within your own division, you find a comfort zone with a certain hotel. In Chicago, the Packers have stayed at the Westin on Michigan Avenue for many years. We fly into Midway Airport, and the buses—the same bus company every time—are waiting for us on the tarmac.

One of the places we seemed to go way too often in the '90s was Texas Stadium to play the Dallas Cowboys. We played there seven times between 1993 and '96 and never won a game. It wasn't until we got the Cowboys up to Lambeau Field in 1997 that we finally got a win. Because of the historic rivalry between the two teams, the games always carried extra emotion. The Dallas fans would boo us, but I felt so proud—we were the Green Bay Packers! The energy at those games made the hair on your arms stand up.

Bob Hayes, the Cowboys' great receiver from the 1960s, was their honorary captain for the 1993 game, which Dallas won 36-14. After Coach Holmgren got done talking to the media, he mentioned to me that he wanted to go congratulate Coach Barry Switzer and some of their players. Coach would always look for the other team's skilled players, such as Michael Irvin and Troy Aikman. It was his way of showing respect.

We walked down the hallway toward the Cowboys' locker room with a half dozen security guys. We met Hayes inside, and I could smell the alcohol on his breath. We've all got Packer clothes on, of course, and he says, "What the f--- are you guys doing here?" Maybe he was still upset about the Ice Bowl or something. Being who I am, I challenged him, and there were some bad words said between us. Alcohol will do that to people, but I lost some respect for Bob Hayes that day. I got caught up in the moment, and the media would've had an ugly picture if anyone had seen it. I didn't want Coach to have to deal with that kind of situation, and I think Hayes never even knew he was there. Cowboys owner Jerry Jones happened to be right there, though, and he apologized for Hayes's behavior. It was just a brief episode, but one I'll never forget.

We had a major disturbance prior to our game in Minnesota on December 1, 1997. Kickoff was late that day, so I had time to get up early and go for a run. When I got back to the hotel, someone said to me, "Jerry, did you hear about the story that Frankie (Winters) and Brett had someone in their room last night? A radio guy said he knocked on their door and a woman came to the door."

I went up to talk with Brett and Frank right away. I had a good relationship with both of those guys, and they assured me no such incident had ever happened and that they'd never had anyone in their room. The story got way out of hand, however, and the next thing I know it was on the national news. I told Coach Mike that it hadn't happened, but the main problem now was it had become a huge distraction. This was around the time of the Vicodin issue with Brett, too. I know someone must've made some money off this stunt, because it affected the entire Favre family. It was such a concern that Irv Favre and Brett's agent, Bus Cook, immediately flew up to Minneapolis on a chartered flight.

We were staying at the Marriott downtown, a hotel that's very difficult from a security standpoint because of how spread out it is. The main lobby isn't even on the ground floor. I think Coach knew the incident never happened, but I was a nervous wreck.

When we got to the Metrodome that night there were a lot of signs up around the stadium, many of them referencing Brett's admitted misuse of pain medication. It's always a hostile environment when we play there, but we ended up kicking the Vikings' butts, 27-11.

An Expectation of Excellence

The excellence that Ron Wolf and Coach Mike brought to the Packers made me want to work that much harder to bring my position and my security team up to that level. We tried very hard to keep the players in line, and Coach was very good at reminding them that they were representing the Green Bay Packers off the field as well as on. He told them many times during his time here that they were going to have to deal with him if they got in trouble. I picked up on that piece, since it was my particular area. If players made mistakes off the field, I was usually involved, at least at the start.

Often, Coach would have me sit in with him and a player if we were dealing with an off-the-field incident. We'd let the player tell his side of the story, and after he left the room, Coach would ask if I thought he was telling the truth. Mike respected my opinion and learned he could throw anything at me. Sometimes I had to deal with some very interesting and dangerous people.

I never met a coach that didn't want to know about everything. That's their business, just like the security business is for me. I've always felt that if a player gets himself into a bind, I want him to be honest with me so I can look at the severity of the situation and determine whether we need to involve a lawyer. In a sticky situation, I can usually tell which way things are going, but I can only know for sure if players tell me the whole story. Players have to be smart because in today's world things are a lot worse, not better. They get themselves into areas where they shouldn't be, and there are too many ways to get in trouble.

Sometimes, even the security director and team executives will find themselves in places they should avoid. Ron Wolf is a very interesting guy, regardless of whether you're talking history with him or traveling to a game. Ron likes to go first class, and he loves to peel hundred-dollar bills off his money clip. On our Super Bowl run in 1996, we were in St. Louis just before Thanksgiving to play the Rams, and Ron flew in separately after scouting a college game. He rented a gold Cadillac, and I was assigned to drive him from the airport back to the team's hotel. Unfortunately, I took a wrong turn on the way downtown, and before I knew it, we were heading across a bridge into East St. Louis.

Now, East St. Louis has a reputation for being a very tough town, and I didn't like the idea of two older white guys riding around that neighborhood in a gold Cadillac. I was sweating, in fact wringing wet, driving through there. I ran every red light trying to find my way back to that bridge. Ron always thought I had everything under control, but if he was getting a chuckle out of the situation, I didn't know it. I certainly didn't want to stop and ask for directions. I just kept turning, hoping the next street would lead us back to the west side of the river. If a cop had stopped us, I would've happily paid the ticket and asked him to lead us out of there. We eventually found our way back to the hotel without anything bad happening.

Changing of the Guard

The Packers' current general manager, Ted Thompson, was a comfortable hire for me when he came back to town in January 2005. He originally joined the organization at the same time I did, when Ron put together his front-office team in 1992. Ted worked under Ron through the 1999 season, and then went to Seattle to serve as Coach Holmgren's vice president of football operations. Ted is as obsessed with football as anyone. I don't think there's a head coach or general manager who isn't like that. Football people aren't home half the time, and they eat most of their meals at the stadium or St. Norbert College during training camp.

Thursday was Coach Holmgren's night to be with his family, and all his girls had to be there. No matter what was happening with the team, he and Kathy made a point of having dinner together. It might not always be a home dinner, but if their daughters were home, Mike and Kathy would make sure to have as many of them at the table as possible. The amazing part of the football business is that coaches have to actually make a point of having a home life during the season.

Ted's a single guy, so he can put all his energy into his job. When Ted was here in the 1990s, he and I and Mark Schiefelbein would go running and play basketball together. Ted takes care of himself, and I like his idea of working out to vent. I knew Ted was going to go places since he was always highly respected in football circles. He's a quiet guy, so being out front is a challenge for him. As the GM he has to make decisions that he never had to make before, and he's a public figure now rather than working under someone else.

As Bob was preparing to take the GM duties away from Mike Sherman in 2005, he sat down and talked with me about the situation. He made the move with the approval of the executive committee and was confident our program was going to get better. Time has shown that to have been a good move. Their priority is to do what's best for the Green Bay Packers, and sometimes those are hard decisions to make.

Bob's mandatory retirement age of seventy was approaching in the spring of 2007 when he and the executive committee had another tough decision to make. John Jones (J.J.) had come from the league office to join the Packers organization in 1999 as senior vice president of administration, and Bob began preparing him to be his eventual successor.

Within the first couple years of John's time here, a group of administrative employees approached me about attending a meeting where they planned to discuss John's ability to lead. Having been involved in management and union positions with the police department, I didn't like the idea at all. I told them they shouldn't be meeting about someone in the organization, that it's not the way to do things.

I thought that if someone had a complaint, correct protocol would be to talk with Bob.

They eventually dropped the idea of having that meeting, but some of the unhappiness with John eventually got back to Bob. The two worked on an improvement plan, and John tried very hard to change. The board of directors elected him team president on May 31, 2006, officially making him the heir apparent to Bob as president and CEO.

Suddenly, however, things began to change. John developed major heart problems soon afterward and was unable to perform his job duties for a while. In his absence, Bob brought corporate counsel Jason Wied into all aspects of running the organization. Jason had joined the Packers in 2000 at age twenty-eight and was already representing the team at league meetings. As a nice perk, he and Missy got to attend the owners' meetings and travel to some fabulous places.

After John returned to work, Jason and director of finance Vicki Vannieuwenhoven were promoted to vice president positions. I was very proud of Jason. He was doing well and really liked his job.

As Bob's retirement date approached, I started to hear rumblings that all was not well with the succession plan. There were concerns about John's health, and some people in the organization still didn't appreciate his approach to doing things. It meant everything in the world for John to be the president of the Green Bay Packers, but it was becoming evident to Bob that John's management style and personality weren't a good fit for the people working at Lambeau.

Meanwhile, the clock was ticking on Bob's tenure, and the board meeting to make the leadership transition was coming up in July. Bob and the executive committee decided at the last minute that John's issues were too serious and pulled the plug on his promotion, and Bob agreed to stay another year as a search committee was formed to identify the next CEO.

I thought they'd give Jason a chance at the top job. He had so much responsibility already that I think John would've tried to groom him as his eventual replacement. As the search process progressed, Jason started receiving support from some key members of the board.

Finally, one day he said, "Well, Jer, I applied."

Whatever process the executive committee had put in place for this search, Jason was now officially a part of it. A lot of people who knew me knew that Jason was my son-in-law. I was very honored by all this, and before long I knew it would be a letdown for our families if he didn't get the job.

If published stories were correct, the search committee narrowed the field of applicants down to a handful for second interviews, including Jason, Andrew Brandt, and board member Tom Olejniczak. No one knew that Mark Murphy's name was even part of the discussion.

Jason's a lawyer and very good at controlling his emotions, but Missy shared with us that the process was hard on him. "Jerry," he said, "it's going to hurt if I don't get this job, because I think I have a chance."

There were people within the organization who supported Jason, but others strongly supported former CFO Mike Reinfeldt. There's no doubt Mike would've made a good CEO for the Packers, but he was under contract as executive vice president and general manager for the Tennessee Titans. Mike's also very close with Ted Thompson, and his daughter is Ted's godchild. I was hurt that those people felt that way. I felt that if they questioned Jason's ability, they were challenging Jerry Parins, too.

Jason is so respected within the organization that he represented Ted Thompson in his contract negotiations with the Packers and Bob Harlan, and then represented the team in negotiations with Coach Mike McCarthy on his new deal. That tells me a lot about Jason's integrity and his ability to work with people.

Eventually, the team announced that Northwestern University

athletic director and former Washington Redskins safety Mark Murphy would be the Packers' next CEO. The news hit our families hard; it was even difficult for Jason to go to work for a while. I think his age was a major factor in his not getting the job. If the organization had been one hundred percent behind him, like Bob Harlan was, it would've put more pressure on the executive committee to pick him.

I was very upset, but Sandy was a rock. She's stronger than I am, and I think her difficult childhood made her better able to deal with adversity. Jason's parents were visibly upset, and it was hard on Missy, too, though she had some concerns about what effect the job would have had on their family. They have three young kids, and Missy kept telling me that family was more important than any job. That was impressive to me.

Who knows where Jason will be in ten years? I hope he's still a part of this organization. He's made some inroads in the league office as well as in this community. Even though Ted favored Mike Reinfeldt, he came up to me at practice one day and said, "Jason's very important to me. I need him." That made me feel much better, and I think Jason felt better after hearing that from Ted, too.

Bob Harlan must be proud that his legacy with the Packers is one of success. We had only one losing season from 1992 through 2007, which is amazing. Bob let people do their jobs and he hung his hat on that. I'm so happy for his success, and I'm sure Ted Thompson and Mark Murphy will ensure that that success continues. As a member of the security team and a fan, it's a good feeling to know the Packers are in capable hands.

Chapter 7
Life with Coach Holmgren

I RESPECT MIKE HOLMGREN so much so that I seldom address him by his first name. Usually it's either Coach Holmgren or just Coach. Even though he hasn't been with the Packers since 1998, to me he's still Coach and a true friend. In the football room at my house—which we use for our grandchildren when they stay overnight—I've got a signed picture from all the coaches I've worked for. Mike's photo is one I'm very proud to have.

I worked closely with him for seven years, doing a job I wasn't quite sure about because I was new to the position. Our friendship eventually grew very close, but it wasn't always easy working for Mike. He's a very intimidating man because of his size and demeanor. He's very detail oriented, so you have to be thoroughly prepared when you're going to talk to him. He was a teacher, so he's very articulate, and he uses his hands a lot when he talks. I was intimidated by him, but not to the point of feeling uncomfortable going in and talking with him.

Mike would be the first to say it isn't just the head coach who should get the credit for a team's success, it's the whole program. When you look at all the great coaches who were on the staff, it's no wonder we were good during those years. I can hardly believe we had so much coaching talent at one time. The 1992 staff included five future head coaches: Jon Gruden, Dick Jauron, Steve Mariucci, Andy Reid, and Ray Rhodes. Gruden was the "get-back coach," meaning that one of his responsibilities on game day was to yell at guys to get back from the edge of the sideline. Sometimes he'd yell at me, too.

Like the captain of a ship, Coach Mike would be the last person off the airplane on road trips. He'd sit in first class and I'd wait for him as he left the plane. He would always thank me, whether we had won or lost. He was very good at signing autographs at the airport, but I knew that sometimes he just didn't want to deal with people.

Over time, Mike began to trust me with details of his personal life, and that meant a lot to me. The Holmgrens maintained a home near San Francisco that they'd use as a getaway from the intensity of being a head coach in the NFL. Mike would leave me the keys to their Green Bay home, and I'd check on it while they were away just to make sure everything was okay.

Mike's mother was living in a local nursing home when one of his daughters got married. They planned a small outdoor ceremony, and Mike asked me to take care of getting his mom there. I felt specially honored. Green Bay police officers Tom Hinz and Gary Smith helped me make sure she was comfortable and get her around that day.

When you get older, you don't get yelled at as much as the younger guys. In fact, in the seven years Mike was here he almost never yelled at me. I did get myself in a bit of hot water one day during training camp when I had my motorcycle down at the practice field. Brett Favre jumped on the back and asked me to give him a ride up to the stadium following the morning practice. Coach wasn't happy to see that, and I knew it right away. I was sitting in my office a little later, and all of a sudden the whole door frame was filled with the imposing figure of Mike Holmgren.

"Jerry," he said firmly, "I don't ever want to see that quarterback on the back of your motorcycle again."

Coach also talked to Brett about it, so that was the only time Brett ever rode on the back of my motorcycle. After seeing the accidents that happened to the Browns' Kellen Winslow II and the Steelers'

Ben Roethlisberger, I can see why Mike felt that way.

The only incident I was involved in where Mike really got angry came at the very end of his time in Green Bay, right after we lost Super Bowl XXXII to the Broncos. We were heavily favored to win our second straight championship, but they played a great game and pulled off the upset.

The Denver players were feeling cocky and hollered into our locker room after the game. I was offended at their lack of respect. The way the Broncos handled themselves after that game was the complete opposite of how Coach Holmgren and the Packers conducted themselves after the previous Super Bowl, where we were the ones who came out on top. I'm happy that we went over to the New England Patriots' locker room after that game and showed them some respect.

Some of the players and coaches had to go out and talk to the media following the loss. The post-game press conference is really a circus at an event like the Super Bowl. Everyone felt terrible as we got ready to go back to our hotel and join the party that was going on there. I stayed with Coach while he completed his interview responsibilities before getting into a waiting limousine with him and his agent, Bob LaMonte.

Ralph Ockenfiles, the Packers' assistant marketing guy, was in charge of transportation at the Super Bowl and was supposed to have another limo there to pick up Coach's wife and daughters. It's awesome to get to a Super Bowl, but it's awful to lose one. It's very hard to stay around the stadium after losing, and I'm sure they wanted to get out of there. Apparently that limo never arrived, and it left Coach's family temporarily stranded.

I didn't hear anything about it — and neither did Coach — until later. Kathy must've said something to him and he wanted to get it cleared up. Everybody in the organization felt very down the following week, kind of licking our wounds. Mark Schiefelbein, who was also very close to Coach, had been talking to him and knew he was hot about something. "Jerry," Mark said to me, "Coach wants to talk to you and me and Ralph. He's really livid."

We went into his office and Coach was really hard on us. I knew it was more than just this incident, but I also knew how much his family meant to him. I took it that he was upset and didn't want to hear any excuses. I felt really bad for Ralph, who was catching it left and right. I was catching some, too.

Coach was probably still upset that we had lost that game. Not that Denver didn't play well, but I think we had too many distractions. We certainly should have won that game, which would've given us two Super Bowls in succession. Vince Lombardi had won Super Bowls I and II, and it would've been nice if we'd won XXXI and XXXII. Coach lost his composure with us. Did he handle the situation badly? No, I don't think so.

Mike had decided to leave the Packers by the end of the 1998 season. The crushing playoff defeat to the 49ers on Terrell Owens's last-minute touchdown catch was the end of the Holmgren era in Green Bay. Coach didn't say anything immediately, but I had a feeling that was the last time he'd be coaching the Packers. He signed every autograph at the airport when we got back to Green Bay that night.

Within the next few days, Coach pulled me aside and said, "Jerry, I want to buy you a motorcycle. Go over to McCoy's Harley-Davidson and pick out whatever you'd like."

His generosity just overwhelmed me. I had tears in my eyes.

"Coach, you don't have to do that," I said. "You've taken very good care of me."

But Mike wouldn't take no for an answer, so I had the great pleasure of picking the ride I wanted. Coach took care of everything—the bike, taxes, everything. I picked out a pretty expensive "Hog," too, a 1999 Harley Heritage Soft Tail.

Our friendship had grown over the years because of all the time we'd spent working together. When Mike left Green Bay to take the job with the Seattle Seahawks, he asked if I'd be interested in going with him. Rumors were flying around the building that he was going to ask various people to go with him, so I was honored that he asked me. For a short time, I thought about going out there just for the football season, but it was a ridiculous thought. My whole family was in Green Bay and I was sixty years old. Eventually, I said no.

Whenever the Packers play the Seahawks, Coach and I still try to spend some time together. We even spent a few minutes talking about our grandkids on the way off the field following warm-ups prior to the Packers' snowy playoff victory in January 2008. I enjoy our visits every time, and I'm proud to call Mike my friend.

Chapter 8
Cancer–Battling
The Ultimate Foe

I LEARNED I HAD COLORECTAL CANCER on Monday, February 10, 2003. That's a date anyone on a cancer journey will never forget. I was sixty-four years old, and of course I was devastated by the news. I'd gone for a colonoscopy after noticing some blood in my stool. Dr. John Gray, the Packers' associate team physician, got me in the next day to meet with a surgeon, Dr. Scott Ruggles. Even though the appointment was only a day away, I still had twenty-seven hours of believing my whole world was coming to an end.

I had read some things about Coach Lombardi and his brief battle with the same type of cancer. The story I got from the players was that Lombardi was also bleeding, but he was a very proud man, and wasn't about to let any doctor examine that part of his body. Coach Lombardi might have had a chance to survive had he gone to the doctor earlier. It's an uncomfortable few hours preparing for a colonoscopy, but that's the only way to check for the possibility of colon cancer. It's nothing now to go and get a checkup. We all have our personal dignity to deal with, I guess, but if you care about your health, you've got to give your body over to medical people.

My family went with me on that first trip to Dr. Ruggles's office. I felt like a noodle as nurses Beth Schuurman and Ann Dollaway asked me a slew of questions about my medical history. These two ladies would become special caretakers through my cancer journey.

Afterward, we met with Dr. Ruggles and he made my whole family feel more comfortable. He's a very compassionate person. He went over the colonoscopy report with us. Then the nurses took me to another room where the doctor examined me. The first thing he said was, "This growth is mobile, and that's good." He explained that the tumor wasn't affixed to the rectal area, meaning it wasn't a foundation. It appeared to be an early growth, not too deep, and could be removed easily. I hung my hat on that.

When we left the doctor's office, I was already feeling a lot better emotionally. Those were the first positive words I'd heard about my condition. While this was good news, I still had no comprehension of how difficult the journey would be. And even if the treatments were successful, I knew there was no guarantee of long-term health.

The Packers were fantastic to me from the very beginning. Bob Harlan told me to just take care of myself and that my job would always be there for me. I wasn't able to work much during that 2003 season, but I stopped in for a little while whenever I could.

Dr. Jules Blank became my oncologist and handled my chemotherapy, while Dr. Pamela Vanderwall was in charge of the radiation treatment. I received chemotherapy every Monday for the first eight weeks. I went back to work after the first treatment, still feeling pretty good. I felt a little different, but I didn't think it had gone too badly. I didn't realize that chemo is a process in which you get worse as you go along. Mondays started to come up very fast, and the effects quickly became very noticeable. I felt tired, nauseated, and weak.

The nurses at St. Vincent Hospital prepared me for how my system would break down from chemotherapy's impact. Now that I look back on it, everyone I dealt with did his or her job very well. They were all thoroughly professional. I don't think they allow themselves to get too close to their patients, which is understandable. They treated me with warmth, but it wasn't like talking with a friend.

Several people in the Packers organization made a point to visit and keep my spirits up. One was Rob Davis, our long snapper for punts and field goals. He came to the house when I got sick and was feeling down in the dumps. Rob was on crutches because he'd had surgery right after the 2002 season. He sat with me and tried to pick me up.

Rob married a woman from Green Bay and wants to stay in this area after his playing career is over. They built a home, and are establishing ties here. Rob is a fascinating and very articulate guy from a rough background. He has a brother in the prison system, and another family member was killed on the streets of Washington, D.C. Rob's very patriotic, and donated $25,000 toward a war memorial that was erected in downtown Green Bay. He's learning a lot about history and asked me to tell him about veterans. Because of my father being a war veteran, I have the utmost respect for servicemen and women. My bathroom would be Stars and Stripes if Sandy would allow it.

I'm active in an informal group of Packers employees led by Sherry Schuldes, our manager of family programs. The group mostly visits children with terminal diseases at St. Vincent. We call ourselves The Heart of 1265 (a reference to the address of Lambeau Field, 1265 Lombardi Ave.), and we even had logo T-shirts designed. Our group doesn't include any coaches or players, just non-famous people.

A young man named Nick Gosse inspired the formation of that group. Nick had CF (cystic fibrosis), a genetic disease that attacks the lungs and leaves its victims extremely weak. It's fatal. The first time I saw Nick, in 1995, I thought he was a young girl as he sat on the back of a pickup truck. He was at practice every day, and had to sit up all the time because of difficulty breathing. He'd call me often, and I was able to arrange some special things for him, such as lunch with Brett, Mark Chmura, and me in the gym.

Nick died at the age of twenty-one, and for a long time I kept the card from his wake on my bulletin board at the office. Just because.

Fighting Through Treatment

Following eight weeks of chemotherapy, the doctors rested my body for three weeks before starting six weeks of radiation treatments, Monday through Friday. The first week they just measured me. I dropped my pants and lay on my stomach while they marked up the targets.

Radiation tired me out, but there was no real pain associated with it. I was a sick puppy for a while and had discomfort from diarrhea. My weight dropped from 177 pounds, when I was running and lifting weights prior to the diagnosis, to about 151. The plan was to shrink that tumor and destroy it before surgery, which hopefully would remove any remaining cancerous cells. As if the radiation wasn't difficult enough, I also needed to have chemo injections during the first and sixth weeks.

Those six weeks really pounded my body, and by the middle of May I was in no shape to work the Packers' minicamps. Doug Collins took care of running the security team during my absence, and everything went smoothly.

I had about three weeks from the end of chemo treatments to try to get my body ready for the Bellin Run, a 10K (6.2-mile) race that's a major event in Green Bay on the second Saturday of every June. About 8,000 people participate each year, from walkers through international Olympic stars, and I was determined to complete that race. Turner Construction, led by Bob Bursack and Brenda Rollin, ordered some T-shirts for the people who were supporting me. Pepper Burruss was part of the group that wore those shirts and ran with me the whole race. Fear of that upcoming surgery was hanging over me, and I didn't even know if I could finish the race, but with all their support I just had to do it. Whenever I slowed down, they'd slow down; when I stopped, they'd stop. I ran the race about ten minutes slower than my best time, but I made it. I finished that race on adrenaline alone.

My next major hurdle was surgery on July 6, 2003. I had a lot of anxiety going in because I'd been told there was always a risk of something going wrong. I remember the drive to the hospital, thinking of all the things that could happen. It's human nature to think of the worst, I guess, but you've got to have faith. The surgery lasted four and half hours, and I couldn't believe how good I came out feeling.

They had to open me up again four days later because I got an infection. I couldn't stand to even look at the incision. Our neighbor, Mary Boivin, who was a critical care nurse at St. Vincent, came over every day for two weeks after I returned home. She helped Sandy change the dressing, swab the site with antibacterial solution, and re-bandage me. It was an ugly thing to have to do, and Mary was great. The hospital gave me a supply of bandages and disinfectant, and I had my own dressing kit in our bedroom.

I knew I was in for another round of chemo after surgery, but didn't know to what extent. All I knew was that I wasn't looking forward to it. I wasn't working much during that time, but Doug was a great help. Whenever I was unable to get to work, which was pretty often, he'd come over to the house to brief me and keep me in the loop. My goal was to make it to training camp and attend our first preseason game because it was going to be the Hall of Fame game in Canton, Ohio. I never made one road game that year, however, because I didn't want to be a distraction, and physically I just wasn't up to it. I don't know how in the heck I thought I was going to make that first game.

There was one high-stress incident in which I was able to provide some assistance. Ray Sherman II, the fourteen-year-old son of our receivers coach, Ray Sherman, died after accidentally shooting himself in the head with one of his father's guns in the family garage. Jim Arts, who is now Green Bay's police chief, was called to the scene because of the sensitivity of the case and because Ray was a VIP in the community. Ray was understandably distraught and wasn't being cooperative with the police, so Jim called me to get my help as a mediator.

Jim picked me up at my house because I wasn't yet able to drive much. We went to the PD and I went into a room where the gathering included Ray and his wife, Yvette, Donald Driver and his wife, Betina, Pastor Joe from Bayside Fellowship, and some of the Shermans' neighbors. I took Ray aside and we talked a little bit about the incident. He told me he'd heard a bang, and gave me some other details of how he'd found his son. No parent ever wants to see one of his children die before him.

After a while, Ray calmed down enough that I felt I could bring up the subject of talking to the detectives. I told him they'd want him to make a statement, and he said he was ready. Young Ray's death was initially ruled a suicide, but was later changed to undetermined, and was finally listed as accidental.

Afterward, I sent a thank-you note to Al Van Haut at the PD because I considered myself an outsider in a sensitive investigation, brought in because of my closeness with the Shermans. I don't know if I would've allowed that had the situation been reversed. If the detectives had told me there were too many unanswered questions and this wasn't my place, I would've understood, but the department received me well and I was glad I could be of help.

Rough Travels

I was just coming off surgery and preparing to start a grueling round of chemotherapy treatments when the 2003 football season began in the newly renovated Lambeau Field. I was really beat up physically and emotionally, but was able to be at the stadium for the Packers' 31-6 victory over the Lions in week 2. During a team meeting the next day d, Mike Sherman told the team they needed to address one important issue. He then gave me a game ball and the whole team stood up and applauded. I was so overwhelmed with emotion that I couldn't talk. I just stood there and cried.

"Jerry, you don't have to say anything," Coach Sherman said.

I started my thirty-two weeks of chemotherapy treatments later that September, and it pretty much wiped me out for the whole 2003 season. That was really hard on me. The doctors rested me for two weeks after each six-week stretch, giving me twenty-four treatments during that span. I was a pretty battered guy, and some of that time is just a blank in my memory. Brett was always looking out for me, and we talked regularly. When the team was preparing for the play-off game at Philadelphia in January, Brett told me I could fly on the private jet with Deanna, but I was just too weak. It hurt me to stay home and not be part of it. I almost cried when the Eagles converted that fourth-and-26 play on their final scoring drive and went on to win the game.

Defensive coordinator Ed Donatell took the rap for that play and ended up getting fired over it. I felt badly for him, especially since he was one of the coaches who showed a lot of caring for me that season. Ed had his picture taken with me in the locker room after the Packers beat Seattle in overtime the previous week on Al Harris' interception return.

My cancer journey was one where maybe my being a detail person didn't help, because you don't have to know everything to battle cancer. You just keep on learning, trying to understand the treatment formula and why they need to treat you so extensively. I started questioning the need for it because I was getting sick again.

Dr. Blank said, "Jerry, I can't guarantee that there's not a cell of cancer left in there." He wanted to rid my body of all the cancer so I could go on with my life.

By the time the 2004 football season came around, I was feeling stronger and was able to exercise more often. I still needed to take it easy; the radiation had left the tissue in that area of my body raw, and it seemed like the slightest stress would cause my colon to spasm. I had to be near a bathroom at all times. Needless to say, going to the bathroom was not a pleasant experience. The fact that our home is only a short drive from the stadium allowed me to run home for a while whenever I needed to, and it was comforting to have someone like Doug on board to run the show when I was having a bad day. My biggest fear was having problems on the airplane.

When you're fighting cancer, it's great to have something positive to focus on, so being able to come to the stadium was very important for me. I love being on the sidelines during games, and in 2004 I started traveling with the team again for some road games. My responsibilities were minimal, but the Packers were very good to me. If I was there, fine, if not, that was fine, too. I could've left the job and retired right then, but I felt welcome and there were no demands on me whatsoever—only generous support.

I was just trying to get through every day, every week, and keep focused on my health. I didn't know what to anticipate, but I could tell I was getting stronger. Surviving a cancer journey becomes a mental game, and the support system around you is at least as important as the medical treatment you're receiving. Along with Sandy, my girls and their families provided tremendous support throughout—Shelly and Craig Makholm, Toni Melchior, and Missy and Jason Wied.

The first two weeks of June were a minicamp the coaches called the passing camp. Football didn't really get started until the very end of July, so I had a nice break for several weeks before I had to think seriously about working again. It was so much fun to have Brett on the team and be around him that I didn't really view football as a challenge, but as training camp began, I started to prepare myself mentally for the physical toll the season would take on my body.

During the spring of 2005 I was reminded again of how fragile my health was. Some blood had begun to show up in my stool again, and Dr. Ruggles needed to perform a procedure on my bowel. It turned out that a staple used to put the two parts of my colon back together after my first surgery had become exposed, with no tissue covering the sharp ends. I watched the whole procedure on a TV screen next to me while it was taking place. They didn't use even a local anesthetic, but it was just mildly uncomfortable.

I saw where the bleed was, watched Dr. Ruggles cauterize it, and that was it. After he removed it, the doctor showed me how small the staple was, but when you're lying on your side and looking at a video image of what isn't the prettiest part of your body... There really wasn't much to it, but it scared the hell out of me.

Sandy could already see that I was having fewer spasm clusters shortly after the procedure. Even that little improvement helped. My type of cancer affects the daily function of life; it's not like skin cancer, which you might not think about as much during the course of the day. I'm reminded of my cancer all the time, and that's hard.

One of the toughest parts was going in every three months to see the oncologist, Dr. Blank. I was monitored very closely, and for a long time nobody told me I was cancer-free. For every twenty stories you hear about people beating cancer, you hear ten more about how it came back with a vengeance. Jeanne Otto, a friend of mine from the police department, had breast cancer surgery and was doing really well for about five years. Then it came back hard and she died soon afterward. Stories like Jeanne's tend to linger at the back of your mind.

Two years after my diagnosis, at about the same time as the procedure to remove the protruding staple, Mary Boivin got her own bad news. She came over to tell us she'd just been diagnosed with breast cancer and would need to have both breasts removed. Sandy and I had to give her a hug. Mary had seen a lot in her career, and now she had her biggest battle to fight. The strength of some people is just amazing, and Mary's a special lady.

Sometimes it seems like cancer just keeps coming at me from every direction. The disease doesn't discriminate by age, either. Amanda Noble, the teenage daughter of former Packers linebacker Brian Noble, had a cancerous growth in the upper portion of her leg. She needed surgery to remove it, followed by much the same very aggressive formula of chemo and radiation treatment that I'd had.

People who go through a cancer journey usually experience a lot of fear, but you can't live in that fear. Keeping busy takes your mind off those negative thoughts. I've learned to live every day to the fullest. You've got to have strong faith — and I do — but it's still easy to fall off and get depressed. I became so magnetized to people, and to looking at the obituaries in the paper. I don't know if I ever did that before.

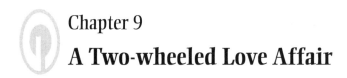

Chapter 9
A Two-wheeled Love Affair

I LOVED MOTORCYCLES when I was growing up. Something about them just always appealed to me. My parents were always against me having one, but I cheated from time to time and rode a Whizzer that my friend Gary VanEnkenvort owned. It was more of a motorized bicycle, really, but I just loved riding that thing. This was long before you needed a special license to drive a motorcycle.

Since I didn't own a motorcycle, the only time I got to ride was when someone would lend me one or if an opportunity arose in the course of my police duties. The most memorable assignment I had as a police officer occurred in October 1970, when President Richard Nixon came to Green Bay for Bart Starr Day. Nixon, who had also been here as vice president in 1957 for the dedication of the new City Stadium (later renamed Lambeau Field), wasn't a tremendously popular president in 1970 because of the country's continued involvement in Vietnam. This was a period of high racial and social tension, especially in the bigger Midwestern cities like Chicago, Milwaukee, and Detroit.

The Green Bay PD was responsible for escorting the presidential car from the airport to the Brown County Arena, located across the street from Lambeau Field. Cy Jacobe was our motorcycle sergeant, and Norel Schaut and I were selected to be two of the officers with him. Our uniforms made us look almost like German soldiers from World War II. We wore Sam Brown belts with our guns on the outside. At that time, the area south of Lambeau Field was all open fields from the airport to the city limits.

We took the lead and led the parade the entire route in a wedge-like three-point formation. Cy was in the center, Norel was on the left, and I was on the right. Thousands of people lined both sides of the street—most of them protesters, unfortunately. I didn't respect them because I believed it was wrong to protest against our country. The president's vehicle was maybe the third or fourth one back, and at least one county vehicle carried Secret Service agents.

Our job was to ride slowly, which is a challenge on a motorcycle. If people along the side had given us a shove or a kick, they probably could've knocked us over. As we rode on, it became obvious that some were there just to harass the president. There were a lot of stereotypical antiestablishment people there. Protesters would jump on the street after us to get their signs up for Nixon to see. The Secret Service never wanted the detail to stop, because that would put the president at risk. I didn't have to be physical with any of the protesters, but we did buzz them with our tires. If they got out too far, we ran over their toes. It was a tense situation.

There were county officers and Secret Service guys hanging off the outside of Suburbans behind me. As I glanced in my mirrors, I laughed at seeing them literally throw protesters to the side of the road if they didn't move out of the way. I was really proud to be at the front of that detail. It was quite an honor.

Coaching the Coach

A year after I left the uniform division in 1977, I went out and bought a cycle. After five years I sold it because being a detective didn't leave me much time to ride. I kept all my riding jackets, but I didn't think I'd ever ride again. I never gave it another thought—until Coach Holmgren came to me in the spring of 1993. He'd heard I was a motorcycle policeman. He said, "Jerry, my dream is to ride one of those cycles. I'm a family man, and my family won't like this (they didn't), but would you teach me how to ride?"

In my career I had taught very few people how to ride a motorcycle. I wasn't a certified teacher, and at the time I didn't even have my own personal cycle, so right away my mind was racing. What do I do for motorcycles? My neighbor had a Harley-Davidson Fatboy. I had taught his brother-in-law how to ride, so I asked if I could use his cycle to teach Coach Holmgren, and he agreed.

I was trying to think of a good place to take Coach where we wouldn't draw attention. The Packers had gone 9-7 his first year here, and football fever was spreading like wildfire in town. I figured if we went out early enough on a Sunday morning, we'd be okay. We started by going through the basics at the Ashwaubenon High School parking lot, not far from Lambeau. I showed him how to start the bike, brake, clutch, and shift. I reminded him that there's no reverse on a motorcycle, and that when you have the clutch in, that stops everything. That first day, I had him just sit on the bike. We never even rode it. I had as much fear as he probably did — I mean, this was Coach Holmgren!

The following Sunday we did it again. We practiced clutching and going ahead a little in first gear. He learned that if you snubbed it, the bike would stop immediately, and that initially you feel as though you're going to tip over. To be safe, a motorcycle's got to fit your body. You need to be able to put one leg down firmly on the road when you stop. That wasn't a problem with Coach, who's a tall man.

The third time out we started making some turns, still just in first gear. We'd go maybe 5–10 mph, just getting him used to the feel of the bike. I would jog next to him as he went. Coach gradually felt more comfortable, but he had a tendency to use the hand brake instead of the preferred foot brake. That comes with experience; the bike can twist on you if you hit the front brake hard.

Coach was doing well and I could see his confidence grow as he continued riding. At this point, he didn't have a helmet on, just jeans and a T-shirt. The next place we went was Northeast Wisconsin Technical College a few miles away. They have large parking lots where we could practice making turns around the islands in the lot.

Finally, we got him to the point where he could shift from first to second gear and so on. We took the lessons at a gradual pace, and every time we'd get together we'd go back and review. From NWTC, we went out on some of the roads in the nearby industrial park. The streets are named for former Packers in that area, and Hutson Street, one of the major streets, is named for the great Hall of Fame receiver Don Hutson. We'd go down a ways, make a turn, and come back to let Coach get a feel for the street. There were no obstructions or cars there on a Sunday morning.

I was probably being overly cautious, but I didn't want to take any chances. Just riding a bike is huge, and then you learn how Wisconsin weather will affect the way you ride. Also, drivers don't see you as well on a bike. Having your lights on can certainly increase your visibility, and I believe noise can be a positive thing.

I once had an incident on my police cycle in which I was riding down Shawano Avenue on a perfectly clear day, coming toward the downtown area right near an S-turn in the road. An elderly gentleman pulled out right in front of me. He never saw me. I almost laid down the bike trying to miss him. Somehow I did avoid him and didn't go down, but it really shook me up. I was scared and irritated. I swung around, put my lights on, and pulled him over a few blocks away. He had realized what happened at the last second and felt really bad about it. As I approached his car, I was trying to calm myself, but I was shaken because I could've gotten hurt. Obviously he hadn't done it on purpose, and he was scared. I started out strong with him.

"Do you know you could've killed me?" I said in a loud voice.

"I'm so sorry," he said, and he was shaking.

The more I talked, the more relaxed I got, so I didn't give him a ticket or anything. But that one incident taught me that you have to be careful when you're on a motorcycle, no matter what the driving conditions. People may pull in front of you because they just don't see you. Lieutenant George Gegere, one of the older riders in the police department, told me that if you can operate a motorcycle safely, you'll become a better driver overall. You have to drive very defensively on a motorcycle, especially on a police cycle with all its extra heavy equipment. That was the understanding I was trying to instill in Coach Holmgren.

We progressed through our lessons to the point where Coach got his temporary permit. "Jerry, we've got to get a motorcycle for me," he said.

Well, there was only one Harley outlet in Green Bay, and that was McCoy's on Velp Avenue. We went there and met with Ken McCoy, who was very helpful. Coach looked at a number of bikes and finally settled on a black and red cycle with an extended fork. It was a nice bike for him, because it gave him room to stretch out his long legs.

Next we had to get him his motorcycle license, so I set up a special time with the Department of Transportation testing office to get that done. We prepared for the test, but I knew they'd probably pass him. We went out there on a quiet day, and the DOT people followed Coach as he rode. When you renew your regular driver's license, it takes care of the motorcycle validation, too, so getting that taken care of was a major step.

Coach was proud to ride that bike. Even though he didn't do a lot of riding, he got out occasionally and started doing a few events. Once in a while he took his motorcycle to work and down to practice. Coach told me I could use it anytime, so I did every now and then. When he'd take a vacation in San Francisco to visit his immediate family, I'd take care of his home and have access to the cycle. Occasionally, I'd hook up with a bike through Ken McCoy so I could ride with Coach, too.

Before long, we started participating in Muscular Dystrophy Association rides. The first event was a 100-miler that went through Suring, a small town northwest of Green Bay. We all met at my house first, where we joined up with a number of policemen to ride along. We kept people around Coach, because we didn't know how he'd handle all the riders and we didn't want him to embarrass himself. Some bikers want to maintain a rough image, and we wanted to make sure no one felt the need to do anything inappropriate.

The whole town of Suring was there when the riders took over the town. Coach and I rode right in the front, but a lot of bikes had already arrived by the time our main group got to town. Coach was great at dealing with people, regardless of who came up to us. Our plan was to walk around and look at other people's motorcycles. We police officers formed a box around Mike and tried to keep some of the people away. We wanted him to have fun, but when you're the center of attention you can burn out real fast.

At one point he said, "Jerry, where can we get a beer?"

"Are you serious?"

"Yeah!"

So we went into a bar, got something to eat, and had part of a beer. Coach handled people really well as they began coming up to him. He signed a lot of autographs and answered questions. He'd always throw the ball back in their court by asking what kind of bike they had. Football was his game, not motorcycles.

One of the biker girls got in line for an autograph and said, "Coach, would you sign this?" She had on this low-cut top, and she wanted his signature just above her breast. He looked at me with one of those *do you believe this?* looks. He said to her, "How 'bout right here," and put his autograph on her shoulder. We got a laugh out of that one.

Coach enjoyed the policemen who were around us as well, and asked about their jobs. I know they appreciated that. We were able to just talk, and it was a great bonding time for us.

Lt. Mike Cygan, a proud rider with the Green Bay PD, helped a lot that day. Since I wasn't with the department anymore, Mike had recruited the other officers to be with us. His off-duty officers rode around us, creating a good comfort zone for Coach and me. I didn't know what to expect that first year on the job, and I wanted Coach to have fun, knowing that if the first year wasn't fun, there wouldn't be a second year. As it turned out, we did it every year until Coach took the Seattle Seahawks job in 1999.

The MDA ride falls on the first Saturday of June, and the Lombardi Classic golf tournament is held that same weekend in Milwaukee Coach was very supportive of both events. Some players also began to ride in the MDA event, such as offensive linemen Marco Rivera and Ross Verba. MDA made about $13,000 the first year Coach participated, and that number increased each year. We began contributing Packers items for the auctions, and the rides now clear about $75,000.

Coach was a lot more tolerant of players owning Harley cruisers than he was with the guys who owned the speed bikes we call crotch rockets. Two of our running backs, Edgar Bennett and Dexter McNabb, wanted cycles and had sales lined up at the Kawasaki shop in town. Both had ridden a little, but I wouldn't call them expert riders. Coach found out about it and put a stop to the sale. E.B. and Dexter were shocked that they couldn't have bikes. Coach could ride, but he didn't want his players riding unless they were already skilled at it.

Seeing Coach Holmgren having so much fun riding, Ron Wolf asked me to teach him how to ride. I had Ken McCoy get Ron a Honda because it's a much lighter bike. Ron didn't want to go out on the street to learn, so we went inside the Hutson Center to practice on the artificial turf. The first day we went through the same basics I'd gone through with Coach, but Ron wanted to move faster than that. In one day, we got him up on the bike and riding straight ahead.

Ron didn't have as much patience for learning the basics, and I was getting tired running next to him.

He said, "Jerry, I can't get this shifting. Don't they make an automatic?"

That ended that.

Bill Nayes was Coach Holmgren's administrative assistant and a motorcycle rider. He's a Wisconsin kid and like a son to me. He came here in 1993, shortly after I joined the organization full-time. He was Coach's right-hand man, and he went to Seattle when Holmgren took the Seahawks job.

Once Bill got involved in our rides, Coach would take us out on the bikes for a burger or some refreshment to just get away. For the first five minutes, there'd be three people in this little country bar. Fifteen minutes later, the place would be packed. It was kind of fun; everybody was calling their friends to tell them Mike Holmgren was there.

Depending on the time of year and the city, Coach wanted to go for rides on road-game trips. When we played in Tampa, I worked with Ken McCoy to set up something with the Harley dealerships down there. We'd get there on the Friday before a Sunday game, and after the Saturday morning walk-through we'd go for a ride. The local folks directed us so we'd ride in safe places.

The league mandated that we arrive in Dallas on Friday for the 1996 NFC Championship game. That gave us time for some riding, and Coach took full advantage. On the team buses, the players were waiting for us to go to practice at Texas Stadium. We came around from the side on cycles, had an escort into the stadium, and rode right in front of the buses. It was a lot of fun.

The following year, Ken trucked six motorcycles down to New Orleans for us to use at our first Super Bowl, and he and his son were guests of the team. We did it the next year in San Diego, too, and it got to be a thing of pride for Ken. We took the bikes out two or three times in New Orleans, usually from the hotel to practices at the Saints' facilities. One day, the buses went out ahead of the four of us who were set up to ride there. A heavy rain began to fall while we were on the way. It really came down, and when the bikes started hydroplaning, we drove under the overhang of a shopping mall to wait out the storm, even though we knew we'd be late for practice.

Coach became more and more comfortable on a bike and even got Kathy to ride with him. When you have a rider on board, though, it's very different. The passenger has to learn to relax and go with the flow. They took a road trip up to Door County, a tourist area an hour northeast of Green Bay. Instead of his regular bike for that weekend, we got Coach a Harley Road King, which is bigger and has a nicer backrest and seat for the passenger. That was a mistake, because every bike has a different weight and feel to it, and riding an unfamiliar one is like playing golf with someone else's clubs. I found out at work the following Monday morning that they'd had an accident. They weren't injured, and Coach had someone take care of the bike, but I think he was embarrassed.

A few years later, Coach called me when he heard I had cancer, and we visited when the Seahawks came to town for a game that October. His team beat the Packers, and was he pleased. I went over to the visiting team's locker room and we chatted for a long time. It was pretty emotional, since I was a very sick puppy.

As the 2004 preseason approached, I started talking to Bill Nayes about arranging a ride for Coach when the Seahawks came to town for a Monday night game. Details started to fall into place, and sure enough, we got it scheduled for the morning of the game. Our party included Coach, Bill, Pat Doherty, a high school friend of mine whom I'd taught how to ride five years earlier, and Dale Jaeger of Vandervest Custom Cycles.

We met at my house because Coach wanted to see Sandy. While enjoying sweet rolls and coffee on our back porch, we talked about my health, since I was still recovering from my cancer treatments. Then we went over to Vandervest's to get the bikes. The guys there had jackets for us to wear, and I had a route planned. We left the store and headed south toward Lombardi Avenue. Coach wanted to see what Lambeau Field looked like after the renovation, and I pointed out where the coaches' offices were.

After leaving Lambeau, we stopped across the street for a few minutes on Packer Drive. We turned around to look at the east side of the stadium, because when teams come to town, they're on a bus and they never really get to see the place from this angle. From there we headed a block east to catch Holmgren Way — the street they named for Coach after the Super Bowl win in 1997 — and headed south toward De Pere on Ashland Avenue. We rode past the Black and Tan restaurant, because that's where Coach took us to dinner right before he left to take the Seattle job.

We wound through De Pere toward St. Norbert College (site of the Packers' training camp), then south along the Fox River on Lost Dauphin Road. Our plan was to ride along the river to Wrightstown and back. Dr. Pat McKenzie, the team physician, had a new home on the river, and Pepper Burruss had it set up for us to have breakfast there anytime after 9:30.

We were near St. Norbert when we saw a familiar white Ford pickup. It was Brett Favre. He realized it was Coach and turned around, and we pulled over by the campus, trying to be inconspicuous. Brett came over and we just let them talk off to the side. They chatted for maybe fifteen minutes, some of it about Brett's loss of his dad, and then Brett was bustin' on us a little bit about the bikes.

After that we continued all the way to Wrightstown, turned around, and rode back. We weren't sure where Dr. McKenzie's house was, but we eventually found it. It was a relaxing, beautiful August day. After breakfast, it was getting late, about 11:00, and Coach wanted to get back by 11:30. It was interesting coming back through De Pere with these five Harleys making noise. People recognized Coach and started waving. Having a comfort zone on a motorcycle is important, and this wasn't a perfect situation, but Coach waved back anyway.

Coach has a good sense of humor. He was told us a story about Paul Allen, his boss in Seattle, and the yacht Paul owns that's 400-some feet long and has a submarine that comes out from the bottom. Coach was very relaxed, and I know he enjoyed the ride. So did I.

Chapter 10
The Ride of My Life

DURING MY RECOVERY from cancer treatments in 2004, Rick Vandervest of Vandervest Custom Cycles, Pat Doherty, and I began planning a motorcycle ride as a fundraiser for needy cancer patients and their families. It's called the Jerry Parins Cruise for Cancer, and takes place on the second Saturday of every June. The Packers organization plays an important role in organizing and staging the event.

I wondered how we could promote the first ride, and the idea of inviting Mike Holmgren back to Green Bay sounded good. Coach and I had done MDA rides when he was here, so I knew this could be a big event. I talked to him every few months during my treatments, and he'd ask how I was doing. I said, "Coach, I want to invite you to this ride. We're doing it for cancer, and it would be an honor to have you ride with me. I'll have the motorcycles here for us."

He seriously thought about accepting the offer, but as it got closer to May, he told me he couldn't because one of his daughters would be graduating from medical school that weekend and he'd have to be in Chicago. In the meantime, he asked what he could do to help with the Cruise for Cancer, and promised to send some stuff for the auction and raffle. I didn't know what to expect, but a box arrived from the Seahawks with some very nice items, including an autographed jersey from their quarterback, former Packer Matt Hasselbeck, and a football signed by Shaun Alexander, their star running back.

I was going through intense cancer treatments during the planning stages for the inaugural ride in 2004 and was really only at half strength. Our planning team meets about every two weeks or so right up until the ride date. We break the team down into departments, and team members are assigned specific responsibilities. This is the warmest group, and we receive tremendous support from the Packers.

More than fifty people volunteer the day of the ride for things like registration and concession sales. Bob Harlan and John Jones of the Packers' front office were on hand to kick things off that morning in the Lambeau Field parking lot. Being able to use Lambeau as a starting and returning point—how many groups get that opportunity? The Packers are extremely generous to me and to this ride. The two weeks leading up to the event are hectic. Nobody questions the time our team members take away from their regular jobs, and not one of these people asks for anything in return.

We leave Lambeau Field at 11:00 a.m., ride through Ashwaubenon, and skirt the city of Green Bay on our way north. We work with the various police departments along the route to determine the best roads to take, steering clear of major highways. We return to Lambeau later in the afternoon for live music, food, and drinks, all to support a silent auction and live auction. Everything wraps up late in the afternoon.

Mother Nature plays a huge role in the day's success. Leading up to our first ride, it rained every day for a week, and it was still cold and cloudy that morning. That was great for the morning's Bellin Run participants, but not good for our ride, as many people decide that day whether they're going to participate. The weather changed for the better that afternoon, and by four o'clock everyone was overdressed and hot. As long as it's not raining, though, that's okay.

I had some health issues the day of the second ride in 2005. Sometimes I don't handle stress very well, and it shows up in how my body reacts. Everyone tells me to just have fun and not worry about anything.

Then they all laugh. For me, it's easier said than done.

The weather held out just long enough for a successful event that year. At the end of the afternoon, as things were coming to a close, a tremendous storm sent us rushing under the stadium concourse. The tornado warning sirens started going off and rain came down sideways. Somebody ran out and got a pail of beer from the concession stand—I think that was the first time I relaxed all day.

The ride has become a big part of the day for some of the small towns and villages of northern Wisconsin along our route, as about 800 bikes roar through. While Harleys make up about 90 percent of the bikes involved, all riders are welcome. A growing number of women participate each year. Owning a Harley is an identity thing for some people, but there's really no stereotype. Bike owners' careers might not mesh with the Harley image at all. The parade of bikes is a huge noisemaker as it moves along, and it becomes sort of a fashion show. You almost have to be involved in motorcycling to really appreciate it.

We do something special for a few cancer families or individuals each year by taking them along on the ride in four-wheeled vehicles. This is a small but very important part of the ride. The second year we had a seven-year-old boy who'd been dealing with leukemia almost since birth. Looking at him, you knew he'd been through a war. We also had a thirty-five-year-old man and his two little children who were referred to us by St. Vincent.

The night before the ride, we do a presentation for the cancer families. We give them a jersey with their name on the back; the jersey number signifies their age. The Packers' president says a few words, and Vandervest Harley-Davidson gives each person a camera and a "do-rag," one of those small scarves that bikers wear on their heads. It's a special kind of get-together. What we do for the cancer patients and their families that day can mean as much or more than any monetary assistance.

Through the Internet and cancer circles, word about the ride reaches far beyond Northeastern Wisconsin. The Packers have even helped with a website: www.cruiseforcancer.org. Who knows how big this fundraiser can become? Will it continue to be an annual event? I hope so. When you're a cancer patient, you can't help but feel that way. Riders can pre-register on the Web site, and it serves as an information source for people around the country.

One year I received a very touching note from a lady in New Jersey named Annette Wells, who found me on the ride's website. Annette had lost her younger brother, Anthony, to cancer. She sent $200 and asked me to carry a picture of her brother in my pocket on the ride. Anthony was a motorcycle guy who had died young.

Some people just know how to write things that touch your heart. I've met some warriors in this battle against cancer. One who was in a really tough fight was Kathy Miller of De Pere. She sent me this note following our second ride. It's what makes all the effort worthwhile:

Dear Jerry,

Thank you, thank you, thank you for inviting us to be a part of your Cruise for Cancer! We had a wonderful time, and it was awesome to see all the bikes and bikers there to support the cause. You had everything planned just perfectly, including the van for Rick and me. We enjoyed meeting and visiting with your wife and daughter and Jim.

I believe that every day is a gift, and I thank God for what a gift it was the day we met and the day of the ride! Jerry, you never cease to amaze me... all that you are going through, yet you have the strength and energy to organize an event like this. We both fight different cancers, but know that your enthusiasm and sense of hope will be with me as I continue this battle! I like to use visuals to help me through the tough days, and the image of the Lambeau parking lot that day will be one that I will use. Know that I will be wearing my Packers jersey with pride.

With love and thanks,

Kathy and Rick Miller

That kind of thank-you is invaluable, and it gives me a much-needed boost when I'm feeling a little down. Sadly, we lost Kathy to cancer in the summer of 2007.

The emotional ride of producing this event is kind of like a wedding: Afterward, it's easy to look back and think *so what?* and laugh about all the issues that came up, because there are so many details to attend to. From the second year on, I was in much better condition, physically and emotionally, and better able to handle the stress, but then I was more involved, too.

The heart of the ride's purpose is raising money for a variety of nonprofit organizations. We handle the finances as a sub-account of the Green Bay Packers Foundation, which is fitting because of all the assistance we receive and the marketing attachment we have with the organization. Our association with the Packers get us a lot of media attention, and it's very effective. The media is extremely helpful in getting the word out about the ride.

The foundation accepts applications for grants from a number of organizations and decides at the end of the year where to disburse the money. After the first ride, we were able to donate $27,500 to eight different organizations, which still left us $10,000 in seed money for the second year. Money went to the Breast Cancer Family Foundation; the American Cancer Society; Ribbon of Hope (a breast cancer organization); Families of Children with Cancer; Unity Hospice; A Woman's Place at St. Mary's Hospital Medical Center; the Leukemia and Lymphoma Society; and a fund we established at St. Vincent Hospital called the Compassionate Care Fund.

I worked on creating the fund with Connie Worzella at St. Vincent, whom I had met a month into my own cancer journey. Connie's one of my best friends now. She helps families of cancer patients who are financially strapped, and I've even heard stories of her spending her own money to buy them groceries on occasion. We gave her $6,000 to spend at her discretion so she could help more people. Joe Neidenbach, the former hospital administrator at St. Vincent, sent me a super letter about what that gift meant to their hospital.

I was disappointed with the turnout our second year, but as I shared that with someone, I was reminded that even if we made only $1,000, it's a lot more than nothing. As it turned out, we grossed about $50,000 that year, which was pretty good considering that we'd cleared a little over $40,000 the first year. Coach Sherman gave us $10,000 in 2005 from fines players had paid during the past year. Every year he distributed money to a number of charities from that fund.

I was just awed by this donation, because it covered the majority of our expenses for things like T-shirts and food and drinks. Coach said, "Don't thank me, thank Mike McKenzie." He was referring to the roughly $160,000 in fines that the former Packers cornerback paid in 2004 while he was holding out. Coach added, "In a way, there are a lot of things I do for the players, and maybe this is a way they can do something for me." Whatever his motivation, I was tremendously appreciative of getting those funds for the ride.

The variety of items that come in for this ride, and all the logistics and planning that go into pulling it off, are just amazing. Two of our major partners are Vandervest Harley-Davidson and the Wildfire Chapter of the HOGs (Harley Owners Group). The Wildfire Chapter takes care of the halfway pit-stop party in Peshtigo, about sixty miles north of Green Bay. They set up the food, beverages, and music, and even auction off a few items there. Some of the key people in that group are Tony and M.J. Kapla, Dave and Bernice Campshure, and Rod Malfroid.

We get some truly unique things to auction off during the post-ride party back at the Lambeau Field parking lot, including NASCAR items, hotel stays, and a variety of autographed items. We've received things from the Packers, the Detroit Lions, and from their then coach, Steve Mariucci. "Mooch" is a former Packers assistant and a native of Iron Mountain, Michigan, which is only about two hours north of Green Bay. We've also received auction items from the Seattle Seahawks and Mike Holmgren, the University of Wisconsin, and many others.

One of our prized items one year was a football autographed by four current or future Hall of Fame quarterbacks from the Packers and the Dallas Cowboys: Bart Starr, Brett Favre, Roger Staubach, and Troy Aikman. We didn't know how to adequately market so special an item, so we figured out another way to get a worthy price for it later on and applied the money toward the ride fund.

We had jerseys autographed by Brett and Deanna Favre for the 2005 ride. The funny part was we got more for Deanna's jersey than for Brett's — $1,350 to $1,000. She signed hers "Deanna Favre 4½."

For the last month before the 2005 ride, Rick Vandervest worked on building a mini-chopper for kids that we could raffle off. He had it painted green and gold by a gentleman in Upper Michigan, and it had my picture on it. The bike went about 20 mph, and the rider would be only about a foot off the ground. It was designed to be used on parking lots or cul-de-sacs where there's very little vehicle traffic.

We took that bike up to Peshtigo in a limousine along with some of our cancer patient guests, figuring we could sell some raffle tickets at that midway party. My grandson, Brock, was able to collect several tickets from bikers there. On the way back to Green Bay, he said, "Grandpa, I've got sixteen tickets for the chopper!"

When we got down to the end of the post-ride raffle, and the time came to draw for the mini-chopper, I was busy signing T-shirts and hats and had forgotten about Brock's collection of raffle tickets. I picked out the winning ticket and began to read off the numbers over the loudspeaker. The ticket had a little tear in it, and I almost put it back because I couldn't tell right away if one of the numbers was a 6 or an 8. Then I saw Brock come running out of the main tent with a big smile on his face. He'd probably bought about 10 percent of the tickets, and this was one of them. Now that mini-chopper is in the Parins family, and that's how the 2005 ride wrapped up. It was a great way to end the day.

The 2007 ride was my last one as security director for the Packers, and it turned out to be one of the best yet. We had over 1000 registrations at $10 each, and our line of about 800 cycles held up traffic for fifteen minutes as we went through our route. We had some weather before and after, but it turned out to be a fantastic day.

With my health better than it had been the first few years, I was more involved. I didn't sleep much the night before, so I got up early to get to the stadium and help out. I guess I was back to my old type-A personality again. I was worried that the morning's rain would make the roads slippery, and recalled that the MDA ride had had an accident caused by wet roads. I'm thankful we had a safe ride, and the fastest we went was 47 mph on our way to Peshtigo. It's a nice, comfortable ride, and our police escort made it possible to go the whole hour and twenty minutes up there nonstop. Our biggest expense each year is for police services, but it's worth it. If it's at all possible to avoid it, I won't take the highway. It's just not safe, and there's something about it I don't like. We take a nice route on county roads where we can follow the bay.

We had three special cancer families with us for the ride. The first was Ricky Sandoval, my colleague from the Detroit Lions. He's in his forties and battling tumors. He had worked with Mike Holmgren at the 49ers before getting caught up in a "housecleaning" there. Ricky knew Matt Millen, Detroit's president, and Coach Mariucci, and was able to hook us up with the Lions. The second was Todd Dessell, a forty-four-year-old who's fighting prostate cancer. Todd works in our facilities department at Lambeau Field. He and his family were going through a really tough time with his complications from surgery. The third family was that of one of my true friends, Stan Keckhaver. Stan and I started at the police department together and had even tended bar together in our younger days. His daughter, Cindy Keckhaver-Anderson, had breast cancer, and was also going through a difficult separation.

Each of these three got a Packers jersey autographed by Brett Favre. This was the first time we had that for our cancer families, and I couldn't thank Brett enough. You can't put a price on what that was worth to those families. Several players participated as well. Pepper Burruss drove A. J. Hawk in the pace car, which was donated by Casey Cuene and his dealership. Aaron Kampman, Cullen Jenkins, Jason Spitz, Coach McCarthy, and Ted Thompson also made appearances, and Bob Harlan was there to meet riders and sign copies of his book.

The support I receive from people like Mr. Harlan is priceless. I'm costing the company money with all the time and resources that go into this ride, yet there's no pressure on us to make money for the organization. A team of about twenty-five people from across the Packers' operation, and some from outside, give freely of their time to help with this event, attending planning meetings and soliciting prizes for the raffle. Carla Schrank and Nicole Ledvina are two of the key people who've been with me since day one, and Gary Rotherham of The Elite Group has been a great help in securing items such as T-shirts and hats. These generous individuals are willing to meet after the end of their regular workday, taking time away from their families for this cause.

How do you thank them? I give them all hugs, but that just doesn't seem enough. In 2007, I bought them all fleece jackets out of my own pocket, and it felt good.

The 2007 event grossed over $100,000! A central contribution to that number came from someone in the area of Eau Claire, Wisconsin, who donated a motorcycle to be raffled off. We sold 2,800 tickets at $10 each, with some folks spending hundreds of dollars on tickets. The guy who ended up winning it had bought two tickets at a bar and didn't even know how to ride. Another person contributed a sizable amount of money, but the individual $10 and $15 donations are just as important.

I remember saying once that I wouldn't care if we only made a hundred dollars on these rides, because it would be a hundred more than we started with. But the more money we raise, the more we can give to the organizations I believe in. We don't have a major sponsor yet, but we keep adding good people with connections around town.

We announce our donations to various organizations every May as we're gearing up the publicity for the next ride. Prior to the 2007 ride, we gave away more than $65,000 to seven organizations, including a distraction machine for the pediatrics unit at St. Vincent. We bought some Cruise for Cancer pink hats for the hospital to give away to patients starting their breast cancer treatment, and Brett and Deanna autographed them because they believe strongly in the cause. I can't tell you how much those hats meant to the people who received them — one woman started crying when I gave her a hat.

As the ride keeps growing, we'll be able to give away even more money in the future. I hope we're able to keep the ride going for many years to come, whether I'm able to be as directly involved or not.

Chapter 11
The Kid from Mississippi

BRETT FAVRE CAME TO THE PACKERS early in 1992 — the same year I started being the team's full-time security director. Ron Wolf traded a first-round draft pick to the Atlanta Falcons for a guy that few people in Wisconsin had ever heard of; hardly anyone could even pronounce his last name correctly. Brett rode the bench his rookie season in Atlanta, and Coach Jerry Glanville was happy to get rid of the wild kid known as "Nightlife" because of his partying ways.

Brett didn't impress me when I first saw him, and he certainly didn't look like a future Hall of Fame quarterback. He was throwing everything high and hard, two or three feet over the receivers' heads. About ten days into training camp, I met a man outside the Oneida Street practice field who introduced himself as Irv Favre, Brett's father.

"That's my son out there; he's one of your quarterbacks," Irv said. "Is there any way to get on the field?"

He was alone, so I said, "Sure." I figured I'd hide him among all the other people on the sidelines, and address the issue if Coach Holmgren noticed.

The next day, Irv came back with his wife Bonita. We talked some more and Irv mentioned that he was a football coach and this was his first time up in Wisconsin. He asked if there was any chance for both of them to get inside the fence. Again I said yes, but bells were ringing in my head right away. Coach didn't want anyone on the practice field who didn't belong there.

I mentioned this to the Favres, and Bonita said she understood, so I took only Irv inside the fence. But then I thought *how can I leave this player's mother out there*? So I went back out and brought Bonita in as well. It was a one-time thing, and I don't know if Coach noticed because nothing was ever said.

That first year as the department head, I was walking on pins and needles with everything I did. I was thrilled to be part of the Packers, and didn't want to screw up. I had been working out there assisting the staff for many years, but now the whole thing was on my shoulders. I broke a lot of rules that first year, and was learning as I went along.

My relationship with the Favres soon developed into something special. Before long, Sandy and I began getting invited to Brett and Deanna's house for parties after home games. Their home was just west of the stadium in the Park Place neighborhood. They lived right around the corner from Steve Mariucci, who was our quarterbacks coach.

Irv and I would go out of our way to get together every time he came to town. He even started coming to Mass at the team's hotel the on mornings of Sunday home games. I saw much more of Irv than of Bonita, but I got to know them both very well along with other members of the Favre family. They're all such fine people. We began to make some exceptions in our security routines for Brett and his family as his popularity grew. If his parents had a vehicle at an away game, we'd make them part of our motorcade to and from the stadium.

Brett was our guy after replacing Don Majkowski as quarterback in week 3. That 1992 season, the team won six games in a row to finish 9-7 and barely miss the playoffs. However, the Packers had struggled with their young quarterback for the first half of that season, standing 3-6 heading into a November 15 game against the Philadelphia

Eagles at Milwaukee County Stadium. The team took buses to the game and stayed together at the Pfister Hotel, but Coach Holmgren allowed the players to drive back from Milwaukee in their own vehicles rather than ride the team bus if they wanted to. Brett's grandmother and mother were here, and they drove down to Milwaukee. Irv wasn't in Green Bay, but he did attend the game.

Reggie White was playing for the Eagles then, and he laid a hit on Brett that almost separated Brett's shoulder. The Packers ended up winning the game 27-24 to begin their six-game win streak. After the game, Brett came to me and said, "Jerry, my shoulder hurts so bad I can't drive."

The training staff gave Brett some painkillers, and I drove the car back to Green Bay with Brett in the passenger seat, reeling in pain. By the time we got back, almost two hours later, he was ready for another pill. I drove the family to Brett's house and Sandy came to pick me up from there.

Brett's admission in 1996 that he was addicted to Vicodin, a prescription pain medication, came as a complete surprise. I didn't have a clue that that was going on, but Coach Holmgren got me involved once we found out how serious Brett's problem was. I tried to find out how he got so many pills, and there were stories he was getting them from other players. We weren't privy to all the information regarding his case because the NFL was watching Brett through its substance abuse program.

Dealing with various difficulties brought Brett and me closer through the years. On occasion, he'd come to our house for dinner with my family before he and Deanna got married in 1996. As Brett's status continued to grow, I began helping out with a variety of issues some of them related to his tendency to party with his buddies, tight end Mark "Chewy" Chmura and center Frank Winters. Those three did their share of drinking and partying over the years, and I was involved in put out a couple of fires.

In 1997 we played against the Buffalo Bills in an exhibition game in Toronto, and the team spent a few days there. That left plenty of time for the guys to go out on the town. There were all sorts of stories flying around about their escapades. I had hired some extra people to help watch the floors of the hotel that week, because I was concerned about all the extra time we were spending there. Toronto is a huge metropolis with plenty of potential distractions.

A couple nights before the game, we did bed check. I knew something was up. Brett and Frankie were in bed, but I could see they were half dressed. We finished up with bed check about midnight—which was later than normal—and I felt suspicious. I went back to their room with the master key, and sure enough, the room was empty. I noticed they'd stuck a washcloth in the emergency exit at the end of the hall to prop the door open so they could get back in later.

By now I was a nervous wreck, so I grabbed Tom Hinz and Gary Smith and we went looking for them, searching the area bar to bar. I knew Brett and Frankie were gone, but I didn't even think to check on Chewy. Of course he was with them, since the three did everything together. We never did find them, so at about 2:00 a.m. I pulled the rag out of that emergency door so they couldn't get back in that way. It turns out they'd been picked up outside the hotel and were out drinking with Jim Kelly, the Bills' future Hall of Fame quarterback, and a few other guys. When they decided it was finally time to get back, they first went to the wrong hotel. They finally found the right place, but couldn't get back in the way they'd planned, and had to come in through the lobby. My staff was on alert to tell me when they got back, because there was no way I could sleep until I knew those guys were safely in their rooms. I was very much like a parent in situations like that. One of our strength coaches stayed up with me that night.

Coach Holmgren found out the next day when I told him during breakfast. I felt bad because I figured the players would get fined, but sometimes the right thing to do is just tell the coach and get it over with. I was just happy that it didn't become a media issue; it could've been embarrassing to a lot of people if something had happened that night.

Early in Brett's career it was common to see him out with friends or teammates—they didn't call him "Nightlife" for nothing—but he became more reserved later on. There were a lot of times when Coach and I would listen together as Brett told his story.

"Jerry, do you believe him?" Coach would ask.

He wanted to know if there was more to the story than what he was hearing. We went through hell with Brett at times. His struggle with Vicodin was very scary—addiction to any drug is serious business—and I'm sure it was one of the darker spots in Brett's life. Going through that made him a much stronger and better person, because he learned from adversity.

Despite all the challenges Brett created through the years, you just can't dislike him. I'm very fond of him. He's the most down-to-earth superstar I've ever met. I've called him a warrior for years because of all the hits he's taken. He and I are both missing parts of our colons (Brett from a traffic accident while he was in college), so I understood why he had such problems with gas during meetings. He and I would kid each other about that.

When I was diagnosed with colon cancer in February 2003, Brett made sure to call me a couple times from his home in Mississippi. He was very worried when he saw me at training camp a few months later, too. For Christmas 2005, he surprised me by giving me a beautiful Rolex watch with the inscription "Jerry, you're the real warrior."

A lot of people in Brett's life are important to him, including his grandmother, whom he calls "MeMaw." Brett's a great storyteller, and over the years MeMaw was part of some of those stories. Brett would get all of us crying with laughter, because he has such comical presentation. Sometimes, when I wasn't there, he'd talk about how hyper I am, too.

Many other family members are important to Brett, but his wife, Deanna, is by far the most treasured person in his life along with their daughters Brittany and Breleigh. Sandy and I often talk about what a warm person Deanna is, and one of the most beautiful women we've ever met.

Deanna is shy by nature, but she found herself much more in the public eye after being diagnosed with breast cancer in 2004. I spoke with her after the diagnosis, and wrote her a letter offering counsel from my own cancer journey. I tried to help her prepare for what she could expect. Brett's been through a lot of tough things, but this one really hit him. Deanna was a pillar for the family, and now she was the one who needed support.

Deanna makes more public appearances than she ever did before, especially since her book came out in 2007, and is now just as recognized as her famous husband. She gets a lot of attention now, but she doesn't seek it out. Deanna is very active with the Brett Favre Fourward Foundation, which raises funds for disadvantaged and disabled children in Mississippi and Wisconsin, and her own Deanna Favre Hope Foundation, which raises money to provide assistance to women who are under-served or underinsured in their battles against breast cancer. Deanna's got the poise and elegance to be a great representative for both foundations, and I think she's starting to enjoy it, too.

Sandy and I were able to spend some time with Brett and Deanna during Super Bowl XXXII in San Diego following the 1997 season. Two nights before the game, *Sports Illustrated* writer Peter King took Brett and Deanna, some members of Deanna's family, and us out to dinner. Our group went in through the back door, and nobody even knew Brett was in the restaurant. Brett and Peter have always had respect for one another, and the evening was very special.

The 2004 season was especially stressful for Brett while Deanna was going through her cancer treatments. After her second chemotherapy session in early December, her beautiful dark hair began to fall out. She had the rest of it taken off rather than watch it get thinner and thinner, so Brett got his cut really short, too. By now, his hair was getting pretty gray. Deanna stopped going to games, and I could tell that Brett was always concerned about her.

Earlier, when I got sick, Brett would call to see how I was doing. Now, after Deanna's cancer battle, it became easier for him to talk to me about the "C" word. He must have received advice from countless people on how to deal with a spouse who's fighting cancer. I know how I was during that time, and it wasn't always good. I could be short with Sandy, and it was hard to be upbeat when I felt so sick. Your spouse may not have your pain or sickness, but their heart is with you as they go through the journey alongside you. The fear and the ups and downs are just as intense, if not more so, for your spouse as they are for you.

Deanna's illness was one of many family crises that hit the Favre family over the years. Brett's had so much adversity in his life that it seems like he gets tougher every time something bad happens. I think he might get bored if everything went smoothly. Maybe coping with the bad times helps push him to focus on something positive like football. Just because he has talent and money doesn't mean his life is easy.

One of the most challenging events Brett had to deal with was his father's sudden death in 2003. Irv died of a heart attack on December 21, a day before the Monday Night Football game at Oakland. The team was already in Oakland when Irv died back in Mississippi. I didn't make the trip because of my illness, and Doug Collins called to tell me the bad news. Irv was driving at the time he was stricken and went off the road into a ditch at about 5:30 in the evening. He was pronounced dead forty-five minutes later. The incident occurred near the spot where Brett had his accident in college. Brett honored his dad the next night by playing one of the best games of his career in front of a national TV audience.

The bad news came in waves for the Favre family after that. Ten months after Irv's death, Deanna's younger brother, Casey Tynes, was killed in an ATV accident on the Favres' property in Mississippi. That was followed a week later by Deanna's diagnosis of breast cancer. The family suffered through Hurricane Katrina in August 2005, which destroyed Bonita's home in Kiln and damaged Brett and Deanna's house in Hattiesburg. Thankfully, no family members were injured by that terrible storm, but Brett's grandmother suffered a severe stroke a few months later.

The next shocker occurred during training camp 2007, when Ricky Byrd, Deanna's stepfather and Brett's confidant, died of a heart attack at the age of fifty-six. Brett was very close with Rocky—as close, he says, as he was with his dad. In fact, he could tell Rocky things he didn't feel comfortable telling Irv.

It was critical for the Packers that Brett clear his mind and play at the highest level. Brett had a lot on his plate, and it's amazing that he was able to concentrate on playing football. Brett loves the game, and he's the kind of guy who doesn't blame anybody else for his poor play or take all the credit for the good things that happen. If receivers ran the wrong routes, he'd occasionally get on them, but it was all in the spirit of playing to win.

When Reggie White was here, the Packers were his and Brett's team together. In fact, the reason Reggie even came to Green Bay was because of the respect he had for Brett as a player and a leader. There were two sides to Brett in the early part of his career—those were the days when he was young and foolish in his personal life, yet he was a team leader because of the way he played the game. He was a gunslinger on the field, and even talks that way. He's not a polished, pretty guy, but he doesn't want to be. You don't have to be eloquent to be a leader.

Thank God Brett was at his best physically during the period when he was partying too much and abusing Vicodin. He's a different person now, and has been since the late 1990s. Many people don't realize how smart Brett is; he knew our offense, could play effectively without practicing during times when he was nursing an injury, and could sit down and do a game plan. As he got older, he got even better at the study part of football.

His aggressive style generated some criticism at times because he threw the ball into coverage too often, but even late in his career, he retained his great arm and sense of balance. One time I was standing on the sideline during practice when one of Brett's throws headed toward an equipment guy. I managed to knock it down, but that ball came in so fast that I felt like it was going to take my hand off at the wrist. I'm telling you, it hurt. Brett throws a tight knot, and it's like a bullet coming at you. The equipment guy thanked me because he never saw it coming. It would've just drilled him.

Brett usually rode on the number-one bus in our group when we were on the road, and everybody on the other teams—including the coaches—would drop their kids off beforehand just so they could get a glimpse of him. One year, during pre-game warm-ups in Philadelphia, Brett was out on the field talking with an assistant coach, and three offensive linemen for the Eagles were nearby doing some stretching. All of them wanted to talk to Brett.

One of the said to me, "You know, I could be playing with the Packers. I love hunting and fishing."

It was about two hours before kickoff, and those guys stayed out on that field just to spend time with Brett and burn off a little anxiety. He went over and shook their hands and talked with them. It was a special scene, and the kind of thing Brett carried wherever we went. He could play a terrible game, but what he did one week to the next didn't change how people saw him. Brett got a lot of respect because of his consecutive games streak, which was a testament to his toughness.

I'm sure Brett's rock-star status could be frustrating for others on the team, because there are a lot of egos walking around an NFL organization. On November 29, 2004, Doug and I were getting Coach Sherman to the middle of the field to shake hands following the Packers' 45-17 win at home over the St. Louis Rams. He greeted a few of the Rams players and their coaches, and then as we headed toward the tunnel we noticed a massive media crowd off to the right with the fans over there cheering. Brett was getting a lot of attention, and I felt bad for the coach. He stopped and shook some more hands to let Brett have his time, then continued on his way toward the tunnel and got the cheers he deserved from the fans.

I don't care if Brett was playing for the biggest coaching star in the world, he'd still be a bigger attraction. When I first met Joe Montana, he received the same treatment. Joe had his own private guard because people would mob him. Brett handled things well, and he knew how to say no.

Most players don't realize how much of an impact they can have on young lives. One year we were in Detroit for a game and some young Pop Warner League kids were on the field during halftime to play a little game. When they came off the field, they stood in line to watch the teams come back on the field. Their eyes were huge as they saw the players go past them.

"Who won? Who won?" Brett asked them.

All the kids started talking to Brett at once with all the excitement you can imagine. It was just a special two or three minutes that Brett spent with them, and it was a great reflection on our organization and the NFL as a whole. It was also a great example of Brett's maturation as a player and as a man.

The 2007 season turned out to be a season of records for Brett, as he passed Dan Marino to own virtually every important passing record in the NFL. He probably didn't expect to reach some of them, and he knows it's only a matter of time until they get broken. The great part was Brett had so much fun with how well the team was doing that the records became secondary to winning games. Do I believe the records were still important to Brett? Yes. He's worked incredibly hard to maintain his level of play. He truly had a passion for the game and enjoyed being one of the best, which is why he played as long as he did. You've got to be lucky to play as many games as Brett did, because one hit can end your season. Brett spoke for a long time at press conferences, and the media really loved him. He doesn't seek attention, but he doesn't shy away from it, either.

I think the most dressed up I ever saw Brett was when Steve Mariucci's mother passed away in 2007. She and I went through chemotherapy together at St. Vincent in 2004. Ted Thompson, Brett, and I took a private jet up to Iron Mountain, Michigan, for the funeral, and Brett had some dress slacks on. He'll always be just a guy from Mississippi, never one of those pretty boys you see in the NFL. You very seldom see Brett clean-shaven or wearing anything fancier than a T-shirt. Brett is what he is, and people love him for it.

I was lucky to be able to watch Brett firsthand throughout his career. The only games I missed were when I was sick with cancer in 2003. Otherwise, I was his security man on the field, on the bus, and on the airplane. I'm probably the luckiest security man in the world, coming into the job with Mike Holmgren, Ron Wolf, and Brett Favre. I don't know what this organization will be like now that Brett has finally retired. He brought so much to this organization—it's going to be different to walk by that locker and see a different name there.

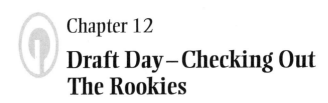

Chapter 12

Draft Day – Checking Out The Rookies

LIKE MOST FOOTBALL FANS, I really look forward to the annual NFL draft in April. It's a new beginning for every team, and provides a ray of optimism that the next great Packer will have just joined the organization. What most people don't realize is how much work goes into preparing for the draft, not only by the scouts and other player development personnel, but also by our security team.

Since my cancer journey began in 2003, Doug Collins has been a big help in making this time less stressful. His computer skills are much better than mine, and we use all our resources to complete background checks on potential draft picks. We look into each player's personality, find out how much baggage he may have, and even define what that baggage is. We hope there's nothing there, of course. Looking at a police blotter oftentimes doesn't tell us the whole story; we have to collect as much information as possible and break it down from there. When we come across something that's a red flag, we do some more digging to really understand the young man.

Tyrone Williams is a good example. Before the 1996 draft, Ron Wolf came to me with a list of thirty to forty possible draft choices for background checks. Tyrone was on that list. He was an excellent cornerback for the University of Nebraska, but had allegedly fired a gun at an occupied car. I needed to find out if this was an isolated incident or if he truly was a bad guy.

Tom Hinz was a detective for the Green Bay Police Department at the time (he's now the county executive), and I contacted him as a point person. He helped me reach several people in Lincoln, Nebraska, in my efforts to discover what kind of person Tyrone was. I even talked to a cleaning lady in Tyrone's dorm to find out all I could. She gave me a whole different perspective on him, which showed that you can't rely only on what the front-line people tell you as the final word. When my mom had cleaned buildings, I could remember her telling stories about people she'd met. This woman said Tyrone had always been respectful and didn't cause any problems. What it came down to was Tyrone was basically a decent kid. The prosecutor was helpful in giving me some information on the case, and told us it was possible Tyrone could get off without going to jail if he'd enter a plea.

I wrote up a report for Ron and he selected Tyrone in the third round. He probably could've been drafted higher, but his baggage likely dropped him down. I'm sure Ron drafted him because he wanted a good player, a good cover guy, but he also wanted to be sure he didn't have a bad seed on his hands. Once Tyrone signed his contract and became a member of the Packers, the court ruled he had to hire his own attorney rather than use a public defender. The PD formerly assigned to the case was very good and helped us hire an attorney. I went back and forth to Lincoln with Tyrone, usually flying from Green Bay to Minneapolis to Lincoln. It gave me the opportunity to spend some time getting to know Tyrone.

The case revolved around Tyrone's having made a series of bad decisions that culminated in his shooting at another car. He shouldn't have had a gun in the first place, much less opened fire with it. Tyrone's girlfriend was in a car with a former Nebraska player who was already in the NFL. Tyrone knew they were out together, found them riding around, and pulled up next to them at a STOP sign. As they pulled away, Tyrone fired a shot that hit the other car's trunk. At least he had the good sense not to fire at the occupants with the intent to harm them. If he'd hit the gas tank, the car might've exploded, killing two people. As it was, no one was hurt. The prosecution had no evidence that Tyrone was shooting at the people in the car; without proof of the intent to cause bodily harm, they had to back off a little.

Tyrone finally pled to a lesser charge and served some jail time after his rookie season with the Packers. Once that was completed, he still had two and a half years of probation. I dealt with his probation officer several times because Tyrone didn't always fulfill his probation requirements. One time we even had to involve Coach Holmgren.

I said, "Tyrone, we've accomplished so much, and you're a starter on an NFL team. Please, get these things behind you and stay good. Your probation officer has the authority to jail you for up to seventy-two hours."

We went through some trying times with Tyrone. If he hadn't had the support of the Packers, I'm not sure what would've happened. He ended up playing here for seven seasons and made a good living. He came from a very hard life growing up in Homestead, Florida. I hope he did something good with the money he earned.

We all make mistakes, and those mistakes can really stay with young people in this game. Running back Najeh Davenport will probably never live down the story of how he defecated in the closet of a girl's room at nearby Barry University while he was a student at the University of Miami. Anyone hearing that story would've thought *what the hell kind of guy is this?* As it turns out, Najeh is one of the warmest players I've ever met. Other than that story, our background check showed no problems, so Mike Sherman picked him in the fourth round of the 2002 draft.

Najeh was facing a felony charge of second-degree burglary and a misdemeanor count of criminal mischief, and, as the legal process was going on, Coach Sherman told me we needed to deal with this situation. During my first meeting with Najeh in Green Bay, I was trying to break through the police image that I was thinking he might have about me. He was new here, and didn't really know or trust me yet. I was trying to be objective and set up a defense, because from the Packers' standpoint, we wanted him to get the issue behind him and play football.

During our interview, he suddenly said, "I don't like the way you're talking to me."

I took that personally, since I was trying to give him respect. "What you tell me stays between us and an attorney," I said. "I'm on your side."

Eventually, Najeh accepted a plea bargain in which all charges were dropped in exchange for his completing a hundred hours of community service. Najeh and I soon came to be the best of friends. When I got sick the next year, he was very concerned when he arrived for minicamp. He came up to me and gave me a bottle of the special drink that he uses to cure everything. I thought t was so considerate that when I was down and out, he offered me something that he thought would help. After that, we gave each other a big hug whenever we met. Najeh plays for the Pittsburgh Steelers now, and I miss him.

We derive our list of potential draft picks from a variety of sources. John Dorsey, the Packers' director of college scouting, oversees the pre-draft background-check process, and the league provides us a list of players who show up at the NFL Draft Combine, and an information sheet on each player so we can have a starting point. The scouts put together their own reports, including anything negative they've learned, and we check the Internet for any public information that's available. If a player has been reported for an incident, it'll be out there.

I don't know whether Ron Wolf ever declined to select a player because of negative off-the-field information, but that wasn't always the case with this organization. The Packers were known for having some bad characters during Coach Forrest Gregg's tenure in the mid-1980s, which contributed to the team's poor public image. That changed under Lindy Infante and Tom Braatz's watch, when the team seemed as concerned about each player's character as it was about his ability to play the game.

Every club takes chances on players, whether in the draft or the free agency market, because you're always looking to improve your football team. I'm very confident in our program's ability to bring out the best in people—maybe it's partly because of our small community. It seems like we can take players into our organization and very seldom encounter a major problem.

You have to remember that a lot of these players are basically kids when they get here. We have to teach them how to be responsible in their off-field lives as well as on it. Professional football affords players just a small window of time in which they have an opportunity to make a lot of money and be set up financially for life. Even at the minimum pay rate, these guys earn more in a short time than a lot of people make in a lifetime. We try to prepare them to make good decisions, but sometimes they get directed the wrong way by agents and other financial people, or even friends or family.

Like all NFL clubs, the Packers have programs that gets players and front-office personnel in touch with the community. There's a lot asked of players once they get here, and it's not just the stars of the team. Even the minimum-wage players are asked to do a lot. The loners are out of here before long if they refuse to fit in—some players just aren't good for a team, and it doesn't take long to weed them out.

After the 2005 draft, we were contacted by a sports company wanting us to bring our number-one draft pick, quarterback Aaron Rogers, and his college teammate, tight end Garrett Cross, to a guest appearance at an elementary school in Two Rivers, about forty-five minutes southeast of Green Bay. Doug Collins and I arranged to drive them to the school, and our group had a nice day. I'm sure the players got paid, but it was fun for me just to get to spend some time with them. You get to learn about people in situations like that, and both of these guys are quality people. How players treat staff reveals a lot about their character, so the trainers, doctors, and equipment staff are all very important, because they get to know the players intimately.

I've been fortunate since I came on full-time, in that the mood in our locker room has always been positive, and a good locker room will carry over to the football field. Obviously, part of that is having strong leaders like Brett Favre, Reggie White, LeRoy Butler, some of the offensive line guys, and others. Key skill players can be leaders just by virtue of who they are. Reggie, for example, was phenomenal; he was a fun guy who brought a lot of faith into the locker room, and a lot of laughter, too. He was definitely a leader, especially for the African American players.

It was Mike Sherman's idea to do something special for all the draft choices, and that's continued under Mike McCarthy. The Packers bring each and every drafted player — not just the ones picked in the higher rounds — to town along with their immediate families, usually their parents and maybe even a grandparent. We fly them in for the minicamp that immediately follows the draft and put them up in a hotel. While they're in town we take them on a bus tour of the city to show them the various things Green Bay and Brown County have to offer.

Matt Klein, the football administration coordinator, heads up the team that brings the players' families to Green Bay. Sherry Schuldes is the manager of family programs, and does a lot of work with the families when they come to town. Linda Nuthals helps with the travel logistics involved in getting everyone to Green Bay and back home again. Matt, Sherry, and Linda are with the families the whole time they're here, and really give them hands-on care.

The group has a nice dinner together, and we show off our facilities to them. They get to meet a variety of people in the organization, including those behind the scenes: the trainers, equipment people, public relations, security, and marketing. We tell them about how we try to protect our players. The coaches make a point of projecting the Packers as a real family-type organization where everyone is cared about.

Sure, doing all this is costly, and the payoff is unknown, but we believe it has a strong positive effect. It puts our organization in a caring light, it's a great first exposure to the Packers, and it gives the players and their families a clear look at what they're getting into. The visit really highlights the tradition of the team and the integrity of the organization — twelve-time world champions and more than eighty years in the NFL. It's a legacy we're proud to share, and we hope they're proud to be a part of it.

Minicamps help the rookies begin making the transition out of the relative safety of their college programs and into the professional atmosphere of the NFL. A higher level of intensity greets them when they return to town for preseason training camp.

Chapter 13
Starting Over Again

PRESEASON TRAINING CAMP is one of the most grueling parts of the year for both players and staff. The Packers have used St. Norbert College in De Pere as their training camp base since the late 1950s, making it the longest training camp relationship in the NFL. Located just a few miles south of Green Bay, St. Norbert offers convenient housing, dining, and meeting facilities, and is a short drive from all the great practice and workout facilities at Lambeau Field.

Having camp in town is great for our fans, too. It gives them an opportunity to see the team day in and day out. People even plan their vacations around training camp. Lambeau Field tour guides tell me that visitors from all fifty states and at least thirty countries come through during camp.

Fans stake out a spot in the bleachers or on the sidewalk just outside the cyclone fences surrounding both outdoor practice fields. There's a field on both sides of the Don Hutson Center, the Packers' enclosed practice building that sits across South Oneida Street from Lambeau. Fans who watch training camp practices are called railbirds. This refers back to the time when there was nothing more than a rail fence around the lone Oneida Street practice field.

Returning to St. Norbert every summer is like going home, because we're so familiar with the surroundings. Our security team has a ground-floor office in Victor McCormick Hall (VMC), which is where the players stay. This includes married guys, other veterans who live in the area during the off-season, and the rookies and other new Packers getting their first look at Wisconsin. The head coach and top coordinators stay in the campus townhouses, and coaches occasionally have guests whom we lodge there as well.

Each suite in VMC includes two main rooms separated by a bathroom and dressing area. When school is in session, four students occupy each suite, but even two players per suite is a tight fit during training camp. Rookies are assigned rooms on the third floor, seasoned veterans on the ground floor, and younger veterans on the second. A room on the ground floor is kind of a status symbol. The basement recreation room has video games, and guys gather down there for Bible study as well.

VMC is located near the south end of campus, across the street from the Schuldes Sports Center and the training rooms. The Sensenbrenner Memorial Union, just north of VMC, holds the dining facilities. The longest walk the players have is for meetings in the Minahan Science Hall, just a few more buildings to the north.

Many people outside of the upper Midwest assume it's always cool in Wisconsin, but that's not true — it's not uncommon for temperatures to get above 90 degrees in July and August, with high humidity often adding to the misery. The training staff works hard to make sure the players stay hydrated during the practice sessions, especially the bigger guys who can lose up to twenty pounds of water on a hot day.

The cafeteria staff at St. Norbert does a great job feeding the team. Until Coach McCarthy's tenure, the staff prepared four meals a day, starting with breakfast at 6:30 a.m. and ending with a late-night "snack" that wraps up at 11:00 p.m. Coach McCarthy began his first camp by having the players eat most of their meals at Lambeau Field, but eventually gave in to their requests to have dinner back on campus. Dinner alone can include beef, seafood, chicken, and pork selections, a baked potato bar, a soup and pasta bar, a salad bar, and a dessert table. With all the calories the players burn during the course of the day, they arrive with healthy appetites, but healthy eating isn't always high on their priority lists. Most of these guys are still kids, and they eat like it.

Players are up early most days to eat breakfast and get to Lambeau Field by 6:30 or 7:00 a.m. Under Coach Sherman, the players returned for lunch and meetings in the afternoon, but Coach McCarthy had the team spend most of the day at Lambeau and conduct their meetings there. Bed check is usually at 11 p.m. By then, players are either exhausted from the day and ready to go to sleep, or they act like the youngsters they are and want to go have some fun. There are all sorts of stories involving players trying to sneak out for some late-night partying. We're dealing with a lot of young men, and they make us work hard to keep a football-focused operation.

From a security standpoint, we handle training camp differently today than in the past, using off-duty police officers rather than a private security company. The officers enable us to protect the players more effectively and monitor them more closely. Two officers work from early evening until morning. Their duties include helping with bed check. One or two assistant coaches are also assigned to do bed checks every night.

Keeping an eye on the players and their would-be visitors is more difficult on weekends. As the players get more comfortable with the St. Norbert area, they'll walk over to the downtown pubs and get to know people; plus, there are all sorts of activities going on around campus, including cheerleading camps with lots of pretty young girls around.

Coach Holmgren started the trend of coaches taking a very hard line on fraternizing with the St. Norbert staff and requiring players to maintain the fullest respect for all the housekeepers and the people who feed us. The campus hosts weddings on the weekends, and conferences throughout the summer. Our job is to keep the public away from the players, and we're tested. Autograph seekers can become a problem, so we monitor the parking lots and don't allow guests into the dorm rooms. We do authorize permission for visits on occasion, such as when parents come to town.

VMC is "locked down" at 11 p.m. You can walk out, but then you can't get back in. I'm sure guys have beaten the system without our knowing it, but coaches make rules that entail fines for those who break them. There are occasional exceptions; we'll work with a player if he lets us know ahead of time that he has an issue. For example, one player's wife was flying up to Green Bay and not getting in until 11:30, so we allowed the player to go pick her up and take her to the hotel before returning to campus.

Is training camp hard on the married guys? I think so. Other than a player's mother once in a while, we don't allow any women in the rooms, and certainly no drinking. VMC is a tight place, and the open courtyard in the center of the building lets us hear a lot of what's going on from our office. De Pere is a small community, so we'll usually get wind of any problems occurring at neighborhood bars.

Marijuana is an issue in the NFL, and random testing is an ongoing process. I know better than to say the players don't use it, but we attack it strongly, beginning with the head coach, and since I've been here the whole security system has worked to eliminate it. Ricky Williams had a highly publicized affection for marijuana when he was with the Miami Dolphins, and the habit eventually led to his suspension from the league. Ricky just scratched the surface as far as the drug's popularity with NFL players.

I'm amazed that some athletes can function as well as they can when drugs or alcohol are involved. This includes people like Lawrence Taylor, the New York Giants' spectacular linebacker, who was allegedly high on cocaine during part of his career. Drugs take a heavy toll on the body, and I can't help wondering how good an athlete could be if he didn't use any.

Illegal drugs are among the top issues we face as a security team.

Fortunately, we no longer have to be quite as involved, as the league has now set up a system to address drug problems; a whole infrastructure deals with testing, and people with drug or alcohol issues are treated under league policy.

Ken Van Lanen and Louie Runge, who administer drug tests in Wisconsin, are retired police officers who were my riding partners years ago and worked the Broadway beat with me. Both are employed by the NFL — not the individual teams — and work through a testing system mandated by the league. They follow a protocol that includes four-hour notices for random tests. Their main objective is to maintain confidentiality. Tests are done in a private room where the testers have an unobstructed view; they make sure the player actually urinates into a vial, which is then sealed, labeled, and sent out of state for processing. The results are reported to each team and the league office.

We're heard stories about players finding ways to beat the system, from drinking lots of water to dilute their urine when they've done something that would be a problem, to carrying someone else's urine in a bag for the test. That's where the supervision and credibility of the individuals doing the testing are crucial.

Pepper Burruss, the team's liaison, makes sure our players get the message regarding test appointments. We have to give the testers access to Lambeau Field or St. Norbert at any time. They meet the players at the appointed time, and every date and time is documented.

Around 1990, several teams held their training camps at college campuses around Wisconsin, and the retired officers handled testing there as well. The Kansas City Chiefs had their camp at UW-River Falls; the Chicago Bears at UW-Platteville; the New Orleans Saints at UW-La Crosse, and the Jacksonville Jaguars at UW-Stevens Point. Since it was common for these teams to scrimmage with each other during the course of training camp, it was referred to as the Cheese League. The name was a play on baseball's spring training Cactus

League and Grapefruit League in Arizona and Florida respectively.

The crew not only handles all in-state testing during the season, but also tests any player with off-season requirements. This includes every player from any team in the league who spends his off-season in Wisconsin.

We don't get many reports of pot smoking in the dorm. We have our suspicions at times, but it's not something that's in our face on a regular basis. If guys are smoking weed, they're doing it someplace else. I think the random tests we conduct pretty often during the preseason are a strong deterrent. The players have to get up at 4:00 a.m. for a urine test, so they'd be taking a big chance with their career. Any player with drug-abuse issues — including alcohol — goes right into the league's substance-abuse program.

Marco Rivera, a great guard here from 1996–2004 and one of my all-time favorite players, got a DUI citation and was tested at least three times a week after that. He didn't know when the tests would be, so he literally had to quit drinking. The system is quite intense, and the players are closely monitored.

If you want to play in this game, you simply have to stay away from drugs and alcohol. I often think about a sign I saw in a hospital elevator when I was going through cancer treatments: EVERY LIFE EXPERIENCE IS AN OPPORTUNITY. WHAT WILL YOU DO WITH THIS ONE?

Part of our job is to protect the players' valuables and cars. They bring a lot of jewelry and music with them, because camp is their home for a month or so. We protect their property as well as possible, and have gotten much better at it since hiring the off-duty police officers. On one of the first days of camp each year, the coach would have me say a few words to the team about our security staff and its role in protecting them. I'd introduce my top assistants and give the players a brief history of my career, making sure to hit four key points: identity theft, weapons, domestic violence, and safe driving.

Regarding identity theft, I tried to make them aware of the good and bad associations they have with people around them, and let them know that even people they're tight with can create problems. Offensive lineman Rich Moran (1985–93) was on injured reserve at the end of his last season and had gone back to California. The team put players' paychecks in their lockers, and Rich's check for the last game was in there. Rich called me a few days later to say he never received it, so our accountant did a trace and found out that someone had cashed it.

A lot of players use the same bank, and a teammate had taken the check from Rich's locker and forged his signature. The funny part was Rich is a white guy and the offending player wasn't. Unfortunately, the young lady at the bank didn't know and took the check. We were able to get restitution paid through the player's agent, so the offense never went through a court.

Concerning weapons, there's no gray area — they're flat-out banned by the NFL, and Wisconsin has tough guns laws. Domestic violence is a touchy subject that seems to come up every year. I let the guys know that if a policeman is sent to his residence, the officer must take some action by law, regardless of whether any actual violence has occurred.

"This is a family and we can help," I tell them. "You just have to give us a chance."

Just after completing cancer treatments in 2004, coming to camp was difficult for me because I'd lost that close contact with the team. We had a lot of new players on the roster for the minicamps, training camp, and preseason games. When you're with the team all year, you get to know every player's face. You learn a lot about the guys during the course of the season, and they get to know you, especially on the road. You're on airplanes together, eat meals together, and sit in meetings together, and you become someone they can trust. Being at home is less intense than being on the road; more kidding and laughing goes on, and we're more like a big family. There's a lot more to this job than just the work part. While I was sick I even missed getting the players into their rooms on road trips.

I go in with the coaches for hotel bed checks, and that's when I start getting to know the new guys. I tend to pick out a few favorites early on, and quietly pull for them to make the team. For some young players, training camp is like starting their first job — but there's not a lot of money coming their way unless they actually make the team.

I expect our officers and security staff to be polite to all the players, and we ask the players to be respectful to our officers. I tell them, "Even if you don't agree with what's happening in a particular situation, you can always deal with it the next day. If things escalate, you'll never win. Police officers have the power to take your freedom away — they even have the right to take a life if it's justified." Players have asked me if I've ever had to shoot anyone. Thankfully, I haven't.

Driving issues may not be as big a deal as some other problems that arise, but they seem to take the most time. We've got our share of people on this team who drive expensive vehicles and do some irresponsible things. I try to be proactive, but there's only so much I can do. You'd think some of them would be more responsible, but I guess we spoil them sometimes.

I tell the players there are five police jurisdictions in the six miles between the St. Norbert campus and Lambeau Field, and all of them is more than willing to write speeding tickets. Of the five (City of Green Bay, City of De Pere, Village of Ashwaubenon, Wisconsin State Patrol, and Brown County Sheriff's Department), De Pere officers are the most likely to cite speeders. If you don't have the cash to pay the fine on the spot, they'll occasionally take you to headquarters rather than let you just pay it later. De Pere is a college town, and the officers treat out-of-towners differently than they do the locals.

In my years as a police officer, I saw so much death and so many injured people that I take driving very seriously. We lost Wayne

Simmons and Lewis Billups to traffic accidents after they finished their careers here, and Derrick Thomas of the Kansas City Chiefs was killed in a traffic accident. The Green Bay area isn't as small as people think; in fact, some players and coaches are surprised that it's as big as it is. They think it's the size of Mayberry or something, but the population of our metropolitan area is about 240,000.

After the team wraps up for the day at Lambeau, the players and staff can create a traffic jam while returning to campus, and traffic enforcement here is tight Tickets serve a purpose beyond bringing in money from fines: they're a wake-up call to get your mind on what you're doing instead of talking on your cell phone. Some guys get so many tickets that they lose their licenses, and then think they can just drive anyway without anyone noticing.

"Guys, policemen aren't going to forget you just because you're driving a Rolls Royce," I would say.

Veteran players usually gave me some grief about my concern for their driving issues, because they knew it drove me crazy. Officers don't care how big a star you are when they pull you over.

"Five times," Brett said during my talk one summer, raising five fingers to the laughter of his teammates. Brett got some tickets in his first few years here, but he became a lot more responsible later in his career.

I'm not the players' father, but my job was to help them in dealing with the system. Yes, sometimes I think officers are just waiting for these guys to write them up, but players have to be more careful, too. If I'd been smarter, I'd have had the Packers pay me a retainer fee for all the help I've given the players.

Every year at training camp, Coach Holmgren would say, "Jerry is not the guy to help you get out of tickets." But it never worked; they'd still come to me. I'm sure some of the officers cut players a break now and then, but I still saw so many tickets that if they were getting any favors... my God, that's a lot of tickets!

Players are more concerned about the points that come with speeding tickets than the fines. I can get the points reduced sometimes, but if a gut gets three speeding tickets in two years and then gets one for doing 30 mph over the legal limit, my powers of negotiation are limited.

In the second year of Reggie White's time here, he came into my office and told me he'd received a speeding ticket the night before. He and Sara were out to a movie, and he was hurrying to get back to campus by eleven o'clock after dropping her off at home.

"I was fine until I got to De Pere," Reggie said. "They got me going forty in a twenty-five, and it was two minutes to eleven."

I told Reggie I'd see what I could do.

I'm no attorney, and Coach Holmgren always told me, "Jerry, don't fix tickets." Reggie was embarrassed about it, and my personal opinion was that, given the circumstances, the officer probably didn't need to write it. I wasn't able to make the ticket go away, so I ended up getting a check from Reggie to pay the fine and that was that.

Following the loss to Denver in Super Bowl XXXII, the players and coaches received "NFC Champions" diamond rings as consolation gifts. Jermaine Smith was a backup defensive lineman on that team, and qualified for a ring even though he was injured and didn't play at the end of the season. The next spring, Jermaine was in Green Bay during minicamp season, and had an accident that almost killed him.

He jumped on one of those low-slung motorcycles — a crotch rocket — and took off for a ride down I-43. He lost control around a curve and wiped out. He was injured and was lucky to be alive. I saw him about a week later in the locker room and we talked about the accident.

"You know the worst thing about it, Jerry?" he said to me. "I lost my ring. It came off in the accident."

I thought the chances of ever finding that ring were pretty slim, but Bill Nayes, Jermaine, and I jumped in a car to search for it at the accident scene. We called the Brown County Sheriff's Department because we were going to be stopped along the side of the interstate, and they came out to provide some safety. It was June and all the plants were in top foliage. We spent more than half an hour there, pulling grass aside and looking for that ring. It was like looking for an angleworm in a field. We never found anything, and we didn't expect to.

I told Jermaine he should check with his insurance company to see if his policy might cover replacing it, and started back up the grade to return to the car. I glanced down to watch my footing, and there, sitting on the stem of a milkweed flower, was the ring! If it had fallen all the way to the ground, we probably never would've found it. By taking the ride out to search, I was trying to pacify Jermaine more than anything, but that had to be one of the luckiest days of his life — other than surviving the accident. I think I was more excited about finding the ring than he was.

Sometimes it's the little success stories that really made my job enjoyable.

Chapter 14
Security Team Ready? Hut!

NOTHING COMPARES TO THE EXCITEMENT of a football game. We always have a team meeting the night before, and the coach addresses the team. Each coach handles that time a little differently, and listening to those talks is one of the highlights for me. That speech is even more important than the one the coaches give right before the team goes out on the field, because the night before is when players start focusing on the game.

A lot of our games are at noon, which is ideal — you wake up and go play football. The challenge is to prepare for night games, especially on the East Coast where the starting time is even later. The players have all day to sit around, so how they fill their day is important. If I were a player, I certainly wouldn't sit in my room all day long. Some guys like to go shopping, and a lot play video games.

Fans drive here from all over Wisconsin and Upper Michigan. For home games they begin arriving in the Lambeau Field parking lots and start tailgating four hours before kickoff. Lots of fans from the visiting teams also make the trip, because Lambeau is such a special place and our fans make them feel welcome. Business in the city virtually comes to a halt during the three hours the game is being played. In fact, ESPN did a funny ad in 2005 that showed police officers patrolling empty streets in Green Bay. For people who aren't football fans, it's a good time to go shopping.

For a noon kickoff, our security team is already off and running at

5:30 a.m. The team includes about a hundred police officers, sixty-five private security personnel, and twenty to twenty-five of our own security people. That sounds like a lot, but keep in mind we've got more than 70,000 people in the stands alone, not counting players and other team personnel. Many members of the security detail are on the job until eight o'clock at night.

A home game is quite an event, and it's our job to make sure things go smoothly. Our goal is to provide a quality entertainment experience for all our guests, and that takes cooperation and seamless execution by a variety of teams in both the Packers organization and outside agencies. Considering how many people come to games, the number of problems we have is very low.

Predictably, alcohol is a contributing factor in much of the unruly behavior we see. Most people drink responsibly, but there's a certain percentage that abuse alcohol. We can see the difference in fan behavior between games that start at noon and those that start at 3:15 p.m., and it steps up to an entirely other level for night games. Police officers who work the games have portable Breathalyzer units to speed the processing of potential arrests. The legal limit for driving in Wisconsin is a BAC (blood alcohol content) of .08, but we've had some fans well over .20.

Even with all those people and all that drinking, we average only five arrests and twenty-five ejections per game. Those numbers can escalate when a division rival is in town or if the game starts later in the day. Statistics show that we have more problems at night, and obviously most are related to excessive drinking. People start right after work or take the afternoon off prior to night games.

The Packers and many other teams have designated driver programs that are cosponsored by soft drink companies. While these programs help keep impaired drivers off the road, they can sometimes have a less desirable effect: people who know they won't be driving have a tendency to hit it a bit harder in terms of alcohol consumption.

The Packers try very hard to provide a family-friendly environment at games. We send letters to season ticket holders to let them know that they're responsible for the appropriate use of their tickets, whether or not they're actually the ones attending the game. It doesn't happen often, but people have had their season tickets revoked because of poor behavior.

As at any stadium, fan behavior at Lambeau can get ridiculous at times, ranging from swearing and spilling beer to passing out or even vomiting on people. We make people pay for dry-cleaning bills in such cases, and I'm proud of that, because not many organizations would follow up an incident so thoroughly. Because season tickets are so hard to come by, everybody respects that ticket. That respect provides the leverage we need to take action and gets fans to pay attention to who's using their tickets. The Packers have an internal group that handles complaints, and if we consistently have problems in the same part of the stands, we observe that area ourselves. Behavior has to be pretty bad before we'll pull someone's tickets, but it does happen.

Just as the coaches have meetings during the week to prepare for the upcoming game, so does the security force. We have weekly meetings with the police and fire departments, the county sheriff's department, the State Patrol, the FBI, airport security, and county highway and city street departments. Any new or continuing complaints by fans are put on a hot-list sheet for more intense focus. The people who work security at games don't get to watch much of the action; they take their jobs very seriously. We have a great group of people who all care about our fans enjoying a safe event.

Jim Arts was on our security team for a long time before becoming Green Bay's police chief in 2006. Fire Department leaders such as Chief Jeff Stauber, John Rodgers, and Cal Lintz head up the medical aspect of our operation, which is huge. That team may handle a hundred service calls during the course of a game for issues related to either heat or cold, depending on the time of year. The weather is a big factor in how busy we are.

Departments within our organization share all kinds of information with the various law enforcement agencies. One department affects the others, so communication is vital. We have to make decisions on the fly during the course of the day. I feel comfortable having such a great working relationship with all of Brown County's emergency people.

Football quickly became big business during the 1980s and '90s, and the NFL put in guidelines limiting the number of people a team could have working on the sidelines to twenty-seven for home games and twenty-five on the road. Those numbers include coaches, trainers, equipment guys, et al., and an organization can be fined if it exceeds those limits. Most coaches are in agreement, because they want the sidelines to be well organized.

Security personnel wear yellow to stand out from the rest of the staff. In January 1997, when we were preparing to leave for Super Bowl XXXI, we had some sharp-looking black jackets made for Tom Hinz, Gary Smith, and me that say SECURITY on the back in gold letters. I was really disappointed when we got to New Orleans and the NFL told us we couldn't wear them because they felt it created a negative image. In the post-9/11 era, it's entirely the opposite — security is very evident on every sideline in the league.

The Lambeau Field renovation and expansion coincided with an increased focus on security throughout the league after 9/11. The Packers hosted the first Monday Night Football game following the attacks. No games were played the following weekend, so it was two weeks after our opening-day win over the Lions when the Washington Redskins came to town. It was a very emotional time for everyone in the country, especially for the people in New York City and Washington, D.C.

The sudden increase in all aspects of security was tremendously challenging for our organization. There were a lot of meetings that week, and that Monday was a very long, intense day—you could see it on the faces of all the policemen. We were still living 9/11, and images from Ground Zero in New York were everywhere. People would watch the news for hours, as CNN ran onsite coverage of the recovery efforts all day long. Our whole staff was packed into my office on September 11 because I had the only TV on the administrative floor of Lambeau Field. I don't even think Bob Harlan had one.

It was a chilly night for the September 24 game, but it was a very special night, too. Chris Gizzi, one of our linebackers and a graduate of the Air Force Academy, led the Packers onto the field by sprinting out with an American flag in his hand. The energy from the crowd was fantastic. Members of the police and fire departments then stretched a giant flag in the shape of the United States over the field. Players from both teams also helped hold it, and I got to hold part of it as well. Country music star Martina McBride did a great job with the anthem, and military jets did a flyover at the conclusion.

Playing that game might have been harder on the Redskins than it was on the Packers because of the emotional drain of the attack on the Pentagon in their hometown. The Packers dominated the game, winning 37-0.

Later that season, the Packers went to New York to play the Giants in the last regular-season game. The game was scheduled for a mid-afternoon start, so we had a little time the day before to take in some sights. Pepper Burruss is friends with Steve Donohue, the head trainer for the New York Yankees. Steve arranged with someone in the NYC Fire Department to escort a few of us down to the hole, as they called it, where they were still cleaning up debris from the World Trade Center. Steve also took Pepper, assistant trainer Bryan "Flea" Engel, Bob Harlan, and me to visit Yankee Stadium. Lambeau Field has tradition, but Yankee Stadium is really something special. We walked out of the dugout and across the field to the outfield monuments. I imagine we felt just like someone walking onto Lambeau Field for the first time. I was awed.

I credit our fans for adjusting to the additional time it now takes to get into the stadium. Precautions such as pat-downs and bag checks by uniformed police officers before fans enter have been SOP ever since that terrible day. Every team makes its own decision on that issue, and the Packers are one of only about ten teams in the NFL that continue that policy. Pat-downs are a costly security expense, and anytime you slow down the flow of people it can cause problems.

Our fans have accepted it well; people actually wanted it for the increased safety. Additional security precautions since 9/11 include fortifying the four corners of the stadium by blocking the roads. This ensures that no one can drive a truck full of explosives onto the premises.

The Oneida Nation Gate, located on the east side of the stadium, is our highest-attendance gate and the spot where the longest delays can occur. That's where fans coming from the entertainment district and the main parking lot typically enter. We lost 2,000 parking spaces with the stadium renovation, and the buses that bring people to the games now have found off-site parking in the entertainment district. It's a festive area, and a lot of people try to get into the stadium within a half hour or so of kickoff.

With so many people in the parking lot and walking to the stadium, there's always the potential for someone to try taking advantage of the situation. We use a bicycle patrol of Ashwaubenon and Green Bay police officers to maintain a presence in the parking lots, and the security presence both around and inside the stadium during games is very good.

You can have all your procedures set and an agenda to follow on game day, but there are many variables that you've got to be ready to handle. There are always last-second changes, usually from the TV networks. Add 72,000 people and some bad weather to the mix and there's plenty of concern to go around.

Calling off a game because of a bad storm, or pausing the action to send everyone for cover, is the league's call. Lambeau Field is much better able to accommodate a weather issue now than it was before the renovation. There's more room on the concourses behind the stadium bowl than there was in the old stadium. Our real concern, in fact, isn't even the storm; it's how to get the message out to the people without causing panic. That's always the main thought in the minds of those who have to make the decision.

Water, wind, and cold won't do much harm, but lightning and heat can. We hope fans will dress appropriately on cold days, but we've got to be ready to treat people for exposure. That also goes for abnormally warm games in August and September. It's not unusual to have a hundred calls for instances of heat exhaustion, so we need to have plenty of water available.

Security efforts don't stop when the game ends. In fact, some of the most challenging issues happen after the game, when all those people try to leave at virtually the same time, and many of them have had something to drink. The stadium gates are monitored right until the end of the game because we don't want anyone coming back in. We can't open the gates after the third quarter like we used to. Getting the stadium cleared out is crucial so we can do a sweep of the building from the top down about an hour after the game. We even check all the bathrooms to make sure the only people inside the stadium are those who are supposed to be there.

This business has changed substantially with the elevated security concerns brought on by 9/11 and the 365-day operation of Lambeau Field. We've had Saturday-night events in the atrium that don't end until midnight or 1:00 a.m., and our maintenance crews have to work through the night to have everything cleaned up and ready to go for game day. That doesn't leave much turnaround time when we have a noon game.

Two separate full-time services are employed to take care of maintenance at Lambeau Field. One group sees to the administrative part of the building, while another maintains the public areas such as the atrium and areas where the organization rents out space. We do background checks on everyone during the hiring process. Workers at the various concession businesses in the atrium aren't Packers employees, but they work under our roof, and the team has no say over whom those businesses hire or fire. We made sure to hire some bilingual people for our security team, because some of the folks who work here don't understand English very well.

The ability of the Lambeau Atrium to function year-round is critical to the Packers' ability to generate income, but it creates additional security challenges that didn't exist with the old stadium. Since the renovation, we've gone to a full-time security center that's manned 24/7. We have alarm systems and cameras mounted in select areas both in and around the stadium so we can watch every spot where the public has access. Multiple security challenges occur when the atrium hosts a major event such as a vendor fair. It's important that we maintain separate areas for people paying to attend that event, while ensuring that people here for other events or to visit the Packers Pro Shop don't jump into that adjacent area. We try to make sure that people renting space at Lambeau Field can have a private, protected, and fun event.

Taking Care of the Visitors

Each NFL team has someone assigned internally to act as the liaison with the visiting team to make sure the locker room is set up their preferred way. Getting the training room set up right is very important because most stadiums aren't set up anything like what teams are used to at home. Security teams have to manage that room space as best they can. We have to keep the training area private, separating it from the rest of the locker room because there are media people all over the place after the game. The training room acts as a hiding area, really. When we're on the road, Brett's always in there until we take him out to the bus.

The Chicago Bears' equipment guys usually come up with a motor home on Saturday before a Sunday game and get their training room all set up. Then they have their own tailgate party in the fenced-off visitor's area that night. With the renovated Lambeau Field, we now have a secured lot about 150 feet square for visiting teams, where they can get off the buses and walk right into the locker room.

Back in the '80s, when the San Francisco 49ers were the class of the NFL and winning championships, I was able to assist their security team when they came to Green Bay. The team would come to town two days ahead of the game and work out in the green barn, which is what we called our indoor practice facility prior to the dedication of the Don Hutson Center in 1994. The Niners had players such as Joe Montana and Jerry Rice, and I was just awestruck. Here I was, just a policeman helping out the Packers, and I was able to sit and watch the superstars practice. The next day I'd work the game as a Packers employee, helping Bob Noel with the team's equipment.

The Packers do a good job of taking care of visiting teams, and even after 9/11 the league didn't add anything to that part of our game-day process. Our NFL rep, Mike Armitage, and his alternate, Bob Langan, make sure we take care of the game officials. We usually know who's working the games about a week ahead, and we arrange to get them to the stadium from their hotel and back again in complete safety. We'll even get them a police escort if needed, especially if there's any controversy during the game.

Most visiting teams stay at the Radisson Paper Valley Hotel in Appleton, about a half hour from the stadium. If they don't travel with their own staff, as we do, teams hire security through the hotel.

The Cleveland Browns stayed in Appleton prior to the 1965 NFL

Championship Game and almost didn't make it to Lambeau on time. It started snowing heavily at about four in the morning, and by late morning there were several inches of snow on the ground. The Browns didn't have an escort to the stadium, and by the time they got to Green Bay it was only an hour before kickoff. It was Jim Brown's final game as the Browns' star running back, and I'm sure the travel problem was a big distraction for them—the Packers won easily, 23-12.

The league now mandates that teams be in town at least twenty-four hours before kickoff and make arrangements to get to the stadium. If the same situation occurred today, the Browns would probably have a police escort with a plow clearing the way for their buses. Teams typically bring four buses to games—two for the players, one for non-playing personnel, and a fourth for guests and fans.

While he was head coach from 1988–91, Lindy Infante had let the Packers stay at home the night before games. That practice came to an immediate end when Ron Wolf took over as GM in 1992 and hired Mike Holmgren. Ron thought allowing the players to stay at home created a country-club atmosphere. The first year under Ron and Mike's leadership, we stayed at the Embassy Suites in down-town Green Bay. It's a nice hotel and was easy for our security team to secure, but it was difficult in terms of meeting rooms.

Since then, the Packers have stayed at the Radisson across from the airport, which is only about five minutes from Lambeau. The Radisson is a very difficult place for us to deal with for team meetings. There are a lot of hangers-on at the hotel, and a lot of our fans stay there, too. The main issue is there's only one way to get to the meeting rooms, and that's to walk past the Oneida Casino on the main floor. The casino is obviously off limits for players, but maybe we don't make that point often enough. I happened to walk over there once and saw a player in the casino. He wasn't aware that he was doing anything wrong, and not wanting to embarrass him, I whispered in his ear, "You need to get your butt out of here right away." Half the people there probably didn't even know who he was.

There were stories about Ray Rhodes spending a lot of time in the casino when he was head coach in 1999. In this community it's hard to do things without people finding out about them. We've won a lot of games while staying at the Radisson, though, so there's probably no sense in looking for a different hotel. In fact, after losing the season opener in 1995 to the Rams, the Packers didn't lose another game at Lambeau Field until week 5 of the 1998 season when we lost to the Vikings. We had a twelve-game win streak at Lambeau in 2001 and 2002. Overall, home has been a great place to be since Mike Holmgren took over in 1992.

While a lot of team owners come to town separately from the players, our executive committee is part of our travel package. Some owners come in on private jets, and we get them an escort to the stadium. Chicago Bears owner Virginia McCaskey uses a wheelchair. We provide a golf cart to transport her around Lambeau Field and get her up to the visiting owners' box. That's an example of the little things we do to make people feel welcome. We get very few complaints. I'm not saying things never go wrong, but we do our best to handle every situation, and we offer our sincere apologies when necessary.

All sorts of dignitaries, public officials, and famous people come to Lambeau Field for games, and sometimes the owners of visiting team are famous in their own right. We had an incident involving an altercation that 49ers owner Eddie DeBartolo Jr. had with some of our fans. It was embarrassing for everyone involved. The Niners were on a downward slide after many years of dominance, but they were still a good football team. The 49ers themselves have a great security staff, but Mr. DeBartolo had his own man.

A couple fans started heckling DeBartolo from behind the safety of the cyclone fence that separates the visitors' area from the public. Mr. DeBartolo made the mistake of coming out from behind that fence to confront the fans, and he and his bodyguard instigated a physical incident. If I'd been there, I wouldn't have allowed them outside the fenced visitors' area. No matter what's said, public figures have to be above any type of fan behavior and just move on, even though it can be challenging. Let fans make fools of themselves if they must, but don't react to their behavior.

Both sides in that altercation ended up being charged. Eddie DeBartolo and his man paid fines. It was a big story because of who was involved, and was an embarrassment for both organizations.

My daughter, Toni, who works as a hostess in the visiting owners' box, was there for Dallas quarterback Troy Aikman's last game here in 1997. The Packers beat the Cowboys soundly, and the fans outside the box were taking out years of frustration by harassing Jerry Jones, the team's high-profile owner. They pounded on the outside of the box and chanted, "Jer-ry, Jer-ry." Toni said it was really annoying, even for her.

Often, visiting teams will bring their own VIPs to the game and even onto the field. We've had musicians, celebrities like Donald Trump, and even Kato Kaelin, O.J. Simpson's buddy, come to Lambeau. We didn't care much about Kato, but it sure created a buzz around here. Whenever anyone like that comes to Lambeau, we want to know which box they're in and if they're going to be leaving immediately after the game. We want to avoid issues with fans if at all possible.

Brett Favre has had some of his celebrity friends here, too. NASCAR star Matt Kenseth, who's a Wisconsin native, has been here. He's a great guy, and is my favorite NASCAR driver now. We even got to see his shop when we went down to Carolina for a game.

Of course, the worst nightmare for everyone would be a terrorist event or even a natural disaster in which fans or players were hurt. Security teams around the league do everything they can to prevent problems, but there's no way we can prevent everything. We have to jump through hoops to get approval for aerial photo shoots, even for our own purposes.

In 1997 we were in Indianapolis when I got a call at the hotel from the NFL rep. It was the morning of the game and he told me they'd received a bomb threat at the stadium. The league planned to keep it quiet, and I wondered if I should tell Coach Holmgren or not. I asked how they were evaluating this threat and was told they had swept the stadium and found nothing. I wasn't concerned about it, but I ended up telling Coach later on, just so there wouldn't be any surprises in case anything happened. I didn't tell any of the players, but I did tell our trainers and doctors.

In hindsight, such a threat would now be a very big deal in the wake of 9/11. The risk of an attack is much higher on our list of concerns than in was in the past, and we've got procedures in place to deal with any such issue.

Unwelcome Visitors

An incident that occurred on September 13, 1998 would've received a lot more attention had it happened after September 11, 2001. The Tampa Bay Buccaneers were in town for the second game of the regular season, when a mysterious man named Raoul Farhat turned that beautiful day into a potential nightmare.

Farhat, a man of Middle Eastern heritage, apparently was a Bucs fan who'd created some type of forged credential that he used to gain access to Lambeau Field and get into Tampa's secure area. He arrived in town two days before the game (coincidentally, on September 11) and checked into the Hampton Inn near Appleton, claiming to be the Buccaneers' team doctor. No one else in the Tampa Bay organization was staying at the Hampton, but the desk clerk apparently didn't find this suspicious. In fact, she even faxed some documents for him to a Realtor in Florida.

Farhat arrived at Lambeau Field before the Bucs, probably because he figured he'd be discovered if he waited till their arrival. He handled himself professionally, using his phony ID to gain early access into the visitors' locker room, a place he had no business being. He wore army fatigues when he came onto the property, but changed into a pair of shorts he'd lifted from the Tampa coaches' office. They were easy for him to grab, since the locker room had been set up the night before the game, and it was normal for shorts to be sitting out. He walked around with that Buccaneers hat on for some time and was brassy about it. He'd drawn attention to himself earlier that morning when he went out on the field and ran around on the Tampa sidelines.

A Tampa Bay security employee later saw Farhat come out of a hall closet in the locker room area and notified Steve Jobelius, who handles the visitors' locker room for us. When the two men realized Farhat didn't actually work for either team, they called for police support.

Farhat was wearing a white NFL Game Day shirt taken from the closet, and a black Tampa Bay ball cap, which we later learned he'd taken from Bucs linebacker Hardy Nickerson's locker. He also carried a black doctor's bag, inside of which was a plastic bag containing marijuana, another plastic bag containing pills, and a few ID cards with different names. One of the cards was from Saginaw, Michigan Cooperative Hospitals, in the name of Raoul Farhat, M.D.

Farhat was arrested and taken downtown for questioning and processing. During pat-down, the jailers found a disposable camera in the crotch of his pants. The photos on the film were nothing more than shots of an empty Lambeau Field taken while he was on the field that morning, a band, and two photos of Farhat himself. It was as though he was a tourist recording his visit. We don't know if he just wanted to prove he was there to the young son he claimed to have back home in Florida, or if he was casing the property for some other purpose.

Farhat was smooth throughout the entire police questioning process. Whenever the officers asked a question whose answer could be verified, Farhat refused to answer. He kept changing his story and talking about other problems he claimed to have. He continued to assert that he worked part-time for the Buccaneers and had been a medical tech during training camp. He also stated that he'd left an army duffel bag and some other items in the locker room and wanted them back.

Ted Eisenreich, our director of facility operations, showed the items in question to police officers, who confiscated one green army bag, one black duffel bag, one black suitcase, and a pair of black army boots. Back at the station, they inventoried the items inside the bags. What they found was amazing: wads of cash and multiple credit cards. When they tried to open a brown briefcase that was inside the black suitcase, only one side would open. They peered in and saw a large wad of hundred-dollar bills. They consulted with the district attorney's office and were told they were within their rights to open the briefcase. Inside, they found a lot of cash and a cashier's check for $52,000. The amount of money and checks in all of the bags totaled $112,004.89, plus two Canadian dollars.

Then things got even more bizarre. The officers found a rubber ink stamp with the name Gerald Payne on it, and some paperwork from Greater Ministries, Inc. A Hillsboro County, Florida detective told the Green Bay officer that the FBI and IRS had files on this Mr. Payne and his connection with Greater Ministries. It turns out he was involved in a con game that amounted to millions of dollars swindled from people in the Tampa area.

Farhat was released on bond, but was re-arrested the next day in Appleton after a dispute over his room bill at the Hampton. In a September 21 police interview, he claimed he'd come to Wisconsin to meet Lee Mezrah, a financial guy who was a friend of the Buccaneers' owners. He said he'd met Mezrah at a Bucs father-son function, and that Mezrah was going to assist him in financing a house he was buying in Florida.

When asked how he was able to get into the stadium, Farhat said he showed the lot attendant an EMT badge, and next to it was the Tampa Bay pass he had put together. The attendant let him in and allowed him to park inside the stadium lot. He then went to an area of the stadium where non-police guards were stationed, and since he was wearing a hospital shirt and carrying his doctor's bag, they let him in.

To add more stress to the situation, just prior to this incident, the FBI had put the NFL, the Packers, and all law enforcement on alert for possible terrorist activity at public events. Coupled with what was unfolding here, it was now apparent that this could be a much bigger issue than simple trespassing, and officers notified the FBI.

A terrorist threat was the first thing that came to mind for Ted Eisenreich and me. Everything you could imagine was going through our minds. Even before 9/11, the word "terrorist" was big, and the attacks magnified it a hundred times. In fact, when Brett got hurt in a game at Tampa after 9/11, stadium security kept one of our coaches from going onto the field by because he wasn't wearing his credentials.

What was Farhat's motive? The money he had with him threw up another red flag. I don't know what that money was for, but we had to wonder why the guy would have that kind of cash on him. Was he involved in drugs? Was he buying something here to be transported?

The FBI took over the investigation and provided very little feedback to us or the Green Bay PD. The communication between the various organizations is much better now, thanks to improvements put in place in accordance with the Homeland Security Act, and the FBI is now much easier to work with than it was then.

We later found out that Farhat had connections to some militia organization and had spent time in Michigan for college and medical jobs. This brought to mind the 1995 Oklahoma City bombing; coconspirator Terry Nichols was from Michigan.

I often think how lucky we were that the incident turned into nothing more than an embarrassment. Nobody got hurt, and being embarrassed isn't a bad thing if you can learn from it. In the end, we weren't able to pin much of anything on Farhat. He was convicted of burglary and fined $1,000 plus court costs by Judge Naze. It was a very strange scenario that never really came to a satisfying conclusion.

After that game, in addition to private security, we started stationing a uniformed officer outside the visitors' locker room as a deterrent. We ask for the same officer for each home game so he can get to know the people in that area. Having that uniform there really makes our security that much stronger.

When someone gains improper access to Lambeau Field, it's a big deal. Farhat wasn't the first person to do it and he won't be the last. Sometimes it's more a matter of pride for us than an actual threat. That was the case in 1997, when a radio personality from Dallas snuck into the stadium the week before the Cowboys played here. The Packers had won the Super Bowl the previous season, ending a string in which the Cowboys had won three of the last four championships. It was a big rivalry period, and we were on our way to a second straight NFC title.

It had gotten dark, and I was just about to take a shower before heading home. A maintenance guy came into my office and said, "Jerry, did you know there's somebody sitting on the fifty-yard line? He's doing a live radio show back to Dallas, and he's saying he's on the field."

A Packer fan living in the Dallas area had called our switchboard to tell us he was listening to this show. I couldn't believe it. My mind racing, I got dressed fast. I felt violated, like someone had broken into my house. I figured I couldn't go out there, but I had to get this guy. I called the Green Bay Police and told them I needed some officers.

One of our cleaning people and an equipment man went out on the field to confront the guy. They asked him if he'd like to come in. After all, sitting outside in the middle of a dark stadium in Green Bay in mid-November isn't a very comfortable place to be. The incident was a big hit back in Dallas, obviously, but not here.

"Do you know you're going to be arrested?" I said to him.

He tried to egg me into doing something wrong, but I wouldn't bite. He took off running and I wouldn't touch him. The cops caught him running underneath the stadium and charged him with trespassing. Dallas got a laugh, but we got the last laugh. The radio guy got a ticket and then we kicked the Cowboys' butts, 45-17.

Fan-antics

Is there any mistreatment of visiting fans at Lambeau Field? I hope not. I know the Carolina Panthers fans got great treatment when they came up here for the NFC Championship Game following the 1996 season, as did the New York Giants fans for the 2008 championship game.

We had one unfortunate incident in which two African American women attending a game felt they were the victims of racial harassment. We were very concerned. The story got a lot of press for a few weeks. Mayor Paul Jadin and the Green Bay Police Department even investigated. I submitted the season ticket list so investigators could interview anyone who'd been sitting nearby. Overall, our fans have enough respect to treat people well.

That isn't always the case when we go on the road. The Bears played their home games in Champagne, Illinois during the 2002 renovation of Soldier Field. A woman and her son went to the game dressed in Packers clothes and were treated horribly. Unfortunately, they got near some University of Illinois students who didn't show the maturity and restraint that adults might have.

Our standard procedures take on a slightly different tone for road games. It's a big challenge, and I've learned how important it is to have a sense of stability when going into a hostile environment. The league is very much involved with and concerned about the security of visiting teams.

A member of our advance team meets with representatives of the host team about two days prior to the game to go through the stadium layout and any logistical issues. They cover details such as the location of the will-call window for family and friends to pick up tickets; where the executive committee will be seated; and where the coaches and players can meet their families after the game. Following halftime, some of the team's equipment will already be loaded onto the buses and ready to head to the airport.

The home-team fans can be both a challenge and a source of entertainment—sometimes it's hard to decide. The secret to game security is keeping your players from responding to the fans. It's tougher to do this in some places than in others.

We played the Redskins in Washington during the 2004 season, and some young Packer fans were sitting behind our bench next to a group of Redskins fans. One guy in the Redskins group was very vocal throughout the game, calling out to the players on the bench and giving our fans a hard time. The guy looked and sounded like Jackie Gleason's character in the movie *Smokey and the Bandit.*

I spoke with the Redskins' security people and found out the guy is there for every home game. They said, "You should see what this guy's like when the Eagles or Cowboys are in town. He's livid and he's steady."

Thankfully, he was drinking water during our game, which was the key to keeping the whole thing under control. By halftime he'd worn himself down, but he perked up when the momentum changed and the Redskins rallied. I could hardly believe our fans would stay there and take it from him.

After making an interception, Al Harris even went over to the guy and shook his hand. We won the game, and I gave a young lady in the Packers group a game ball afterward. The guy admitted she deserved it for putting up with him. For her to stay there through the whole game was impressive, because he could be intimidating. He was having fun, but he made his points, too. He got into it with William Henderson, our fullback, telling Henderson that he'd paid his hard-earned money and could say whatever he wanted. I was proud of the way our players handled that guy; for the most part they either ignored him or played along.

We got a taste of Philly fans' level of class a few weeks later, where we suffered an embarrassing 47-17 loss. Probably nine out of ten people gave us the finger as our buses pulled into the stadium. They really know how to welcome a team. Unlike their fans, the Eagles are a class organization. Coach Sherman is from the Northeast and had some family in town for the game, but we didn't have enough credentials for everyone. Fortunately, I had a great relationship with the Eagles' security guy, Anthony "Butch" Buchanico. Butch was a former Philly police officer and kind of a redneck in the NFL security world. He brought me over to show me the Eagles' locker room, and he got us credentials for the rest of Coach Sherman's family.

Visiting Philly is a pleasure, especially because of Coach Andy Reid and his wife Tammy. Andy's a good friend, and was the quarterbacks coach for the Packers in 1997–98. Brett stopped over to hug Tammy, who then yelled at me, "Jerry Parins, get over here and give me a hug! You're the second-best security guy there is." I feel badly for all the difficulties they're having with their two sons' highly publicized drug issues.

For all the challenges we face with fans on the road, that's not to say our fans at Lambeau don't occasionally step over the line as well.

When Randy Moss was playing for the Vikings, he'd come to Lambeau every year, and his abilities would make life miserable for us. He was getting into it with some of our fans behind the Vikings' bench one time, and we were concerned that further trouble might occur after the game. We protected Randy, got him off the field, and later protected him all the way to the Vikings' bus. I wouldn't want it done any other way. Randy gave no respect to Green Bay, but the officers respected him and got him on the bus safely. One of the NFL guys told us that if a similar situation had happened in most other cities, the host team would've left Moss to deal with it on his own.

Fan behavior can be an issue at home games, too. Sometimes the players give away their tickets to ticket brokers; fans from visiting teams buy them and end up sitting right behind our bench. You certainly can hear them at times. When the game's in your house, that's something you shouldn't have to deal with. The area behind the bench should be your holy land, a comfort zone filled with people giving strong support. My job was to make sure our players didn't get involved with the fans. If the game's going the wrong way, it can get to be a problem.

The emotions of a game can even affect the better judgment of the security director and the head coach. When the Packers played at Tampa on November 24, 2002, an ugly incident occurred that I didn't prevent — in fact, I even encouraged it in a way. The Buccaneers were long-time members of the NFC Central Division through 2001, so the players and coaches knew each other very well from playing twice each year. This was another hard-fought contest. Brett was trying to make something happen midway through the third quarter when he threw a pass into coverage. It was intercepted, and during the return, Bucs defensive tackle Warren Sapp laid a blind-side hit on Packers tackle Chad Clifton that left our guy motionless on the field. Sapp was doing a celebration dance while Clifton lay severely injured. The Packers' bench was really upset, from the players and support staff right up through Mike Sherman.

The Bucs ended up winning, 21-7. Afterward, as the network's Pam Oliver was interviewing Sapp, I led Coach Sherman right past him on his way off the field. Coach was headed in the wrong direction, but I didn't correct him and he didn't need to tell me who he was looking for, either.

Sapp thought Coach was coming over to shake hands, but instead it got into an F-word exchange between the two of them on national TV. Coach walked off, Sapp screaming at him all the way. Sapp's eyes got so big—he saw Sherman as provoking him. Sapp is one crazy football player, and it would've been no problem for him to take a piece out of Sherman. In fact, while playing for the Oakland Raiders in 2007 he got so out of control in a game that he had to be forcibly removed from the field after receiving three unsportsmanlike conduct penalties.

Sapp was never penalized for his hit on Clifton, so I'm sure Sherman wanted to make certain Sapp knew his type of play wasn't appreciated. Clifton was taken off the field on a stretcher, and didn't have complete feeling in his limbs for a while. The bones of his pelvis were so badly sprained from the hit that he had to spend the next week in Tampa and Green Bay hospitals, and couldn't walk on his own for another six weeks. Thankfully, he recovered during a hard off-season of rehabilitation, and reclaimed his starting left tackle position the following year.

After winning the 2004 season opener, the Packers lost the next four and looked bad doing it, especially on defense. This was the season immediately following the famous playoff loss to Philadelphia, when the Eagles converted a 4th-and-26 play late in the fourth quarter and went on to win. The last of those four losses was a 48-27 setback to Tennessee on a Monday night. Our home fans at that game were the worst I'd ever dealt with. Because people were losing patience with the team and Mike Sherman, things got uglier with every point the Titans scored.

The players did well to endure the abuse that night. They were hurt, especially after being booed off the field at halftime. The guys were getting embarrassed on both sides of the ball, physically pushed around by the Titans. The players didn't seem to get angry at the fans' reaction—I guess they felt they deserved it. Marco Rivera, truly one of the toughest players I've been around in all my years, was over by the sideline heater and the fans there were yelling, "You overpaid sonofa-----."

Marco said he didn't know what to do. I spent the fourth quarter behind our bench to make sure we didn't have any trouble, something I'd never had to do before. I got annoyed with the police, too, because they were letting fans walk down to the railing and deliver their verbal abuse rather than turning them around. I got involved and told some fans to turn around, and I said something to my police friends the next day.

It was embarrassing that night, especially when fans began to leave early in the second half. They were just disgusted, and the unruliness was at least two or three times worse than at most games. For our own fans to sit there and boo us was terrible. The police made three times the normal number of arrests and ejections, and my office handled triple the usual number of complaints after the game. It was a bad night for both the Green Bay Packers and our fans.

The true heart of the players came out after that, though, as they went on to win nine of their next eleven games—including six in a row immediately following the loss to the Titans—to finish 10-6 and make the playoffs.

I'll never be able to sit in the stands for a game. It's not in my personality to accept the opinions of the fans. It's like hearing someone talking about your family: it's okay for me to criticize, but I don't want to hear you do it. No matter how the game's going, some people can't see that their behavior causes problems—and alcohol fuels that fire.

Mike McKenzie's training camp holdout and continuing unhappiness with his contract was having an effect in the locker room and on Coach Sherman's ability to focus on the bigger picture. Unfortunately, McKenzie became a target of hate mail because of his dreadlocks, and some of the letters turned vicious and racist. Mike was a very good player and a key part of our defense, but his personality had changed by the time he rejoined the team early that season. He was no longer dedicated and loyal to the operation and to fellow players, and Sherman had to get him out of here while trying to get some value for him. Coach eventually traded him to New Orleans.

The Bench in a Fishbowl

During the course of the game things can get heated in a team's bench area. Football is a very emotional game, and the players and coaches feel a lot of passion for what they do. Sometimes our security team has to protect the players from themselves.

During the 2004 season, the defense was struggling as the Packers were trying to earn a wild-card spot in the playoffs. Some of the defensive guys started pointing fingers, and it felt like a volcano getting ready to blow. It finally happened when defensive lineman R-Kal Truluck and his position coach, Jethro Franklin, got into a heated exchange in front of the whole defensive unit during a 28-25 home loss to the Jacksonville Jaguars in week 15. It was close to getting out of hand. There were a lot of accusations, finger-pointing, and name calling. It got to the point where I grabbed Hannibal Navies, one of the veteran linebackers, and told him to get Truluck away from Franklin. They were standing toe to toe and I didn't want the situation to escalate. That was Truluck's only season as a Packer.

In that game, Jacksonville defensive back Donovan Darius put a wicked clothesline hit on Packers receiver Robert Ferguson, sending him to the hospital with a neck injury. When we went to Minneapolis the next week, a Vikings fan showed no class, displaying a sign that read DONOVAN DARIUS FOR MVP. It was part of an emotional Christmas Eve there; we had to get through a number of challenges in addition to beating a good Vikings team.

The visitors' locker room is quite a distance from the field inside the Metrodome. There's a shortcut through one of the baseball dugouts; however, the stadium had chained the door for security reasons, and that forced us to take a lot more time, both before the game and during halftime, going back and forth to the field. Larry Beightol, our offensive line coach, had a bum knee and had trouble walking that far. We were able to get him a cart and take him through the Vikings' area of the building, but that didn't save much time. Then there was trouble with the lights: the Metrodome staff didn't have the game lights on during our warm-ups, so we complained to the referees but didn't get anywhere with that, either.

Later, we finally won a battle later after seeing that DARIUS FOR MVP sign. Some of our players were really upset about it — you can't ignore everything — so I went to the NFL rep to complain that it was in poor taste. He agreed, and we grabbed a policeman for support. The NFL rep was being diplomatic, but I just ripped that sign right down.

Coach Sherman told the team before the game that if they could keep things close, we'd win. He said the Vikings would choke at the end, and it was amazing how right he was. The Packers pulled to within four points at halftime after a late field goal by Ryan Longwell, but the Vikings kept scoring quickly with one-play drives and an interception return. Defensive backs Mark Roman and Ahmad Carroll got into it with each other at one point.

After the offense and defense broke from their halftime huddles in the locker room, tight end Bubba Franks called the team together and said to the defense, "Hey, we need you guys. Let's all hang together and get this one."

I thought Bubba handled it very well, and I think the guys on defense said to themselves, "Let's play better this half."

Sure enough, Longwell hit another field goal at the end to win the game 34-31 and give the Packers the division title. Having been in the middle of my cancer journey at the time, I missed out on being in the locker room the previous year after Brett's great game at Oakland right after his dad died, so I really enjoyed being there for this one. It made Christmas in Wisconsin a lot better that year.

One of my main jobs during games is to keep distractions out of the locker room and get everybody in and out at halftime as efficiently as possible. By the time everyone gets off the field, uses the bathroom, and, late in the season, just tries to get warm, several minutes of halftime have already gone by. When the coach speaks, everybody shuts up. Then the offense goes to one end of the locker room and the defense to the other with their respective position coaches and coordinators. If the coaching staff changes the game plan, they get that in as quickly as possible; the discussion becomes all about Xs and Os and what the opponent is doing or expected to do. Sometimes the veterans will inject their own tips as well. For instance, Brett Favre might tell the defensive backs to play tighter on the receivers during cold games, because they most likely won't be going long. The equipment staff provides oranges and bananas for the guys to snack on, there's another round of bathroom breaks, and that's about it. Halftime goes by really fast, and then it's back to the field.

You never know who might be watching when sideline incidents happen. You'd think everyone would be watching the play on the field, but a whole network of people keep tabs on what's going on in the bench area. Doug Collins and I usually work there, and one of our duties is to help the Packers avoid penalties. The day after a particularly intense game, it's not uncommon for one of the coaches to thank us for preventing them from drawing a flag. The tempo and emotions of the game get everybody in the bench area involved, especially with regard to his own position.

I can observe how people react to various situations and sense how tense things are getting both on the bench and the field. Sometimes the officials will turn and glare at someone in the bench area who might be getting too abusive. I've even had a ref yell at me, "Get him out of my face!" We try to help out without being a distraction for the team.

Tempers and egos can get out of control at any time, players' and coaches' alike. Virgil Knight, tight ends coach under Lindy Infante, and somewhat of a hothead, got into a fight with a fan after a game and was arrested. Defensive backs Ahmad Carroll and Joey Thomas, the Packers first- and third-round draft picks in 2004, had a much-publicized weekday fight in a Lambeau hallway. They were battling for playing time, and for a while Thomas was getting more than Carroll was. Only a few players saw the fight, and I didn't realize anything had happened until the next day when I noticed that a photo had been knocked off the wall. I knew something was wrong, got the details, and Coach Sherman got involved later that day.

You don't see the game very well from the sidelines, but you get to see how your team produces the game and what goes into it. Sandy has been taping televised games for me ever since I went full-time with the Packers, and it's nice to hear the announcers' perspectives when I watch them later on.

Wins and losses can have a major effect on the mood around Lambeau during the week, and that extends beyond the football operations. Some people take losing a lot harder than others. I thought it was just me that didn't watch ESPN's *SportsCenter* after losses, but the more I talked to people, I found I wasn't alone. There's a lot of pride in this building. I wish some of our players would take losing as hard as some of the staff and coaches do. We put in our time, too, and are paid only a fraction of what the players make. The coaches can do everything in their power to help the team win, but it's the players who have to play the game.

Our Off-season

Once the business of football is done, it gets very quiet around Lambeau Field, and we can recharge our batteries. When you get where you're not dealing on a Sunday-to-Sunday basis or working on the game, a lot of your daily anxiety fades away—but you miss the excitement, too. When the season is over, all the different departments in the organization, from football to security, critique it to see where we can make improvements next year. Our security team looks at cost breakdowns—what we pay for services to the city, where our manpower expenses are coming from—and details such as whether there are any patterns regarding ejections or other fan issues.

Movement in the football area keeps us active all year, and there are major events that have nothing to do with games. Packer Fan Fest is a big event that happens in mid-March, followed by the draft parties in April as football fever starts up all over again.

We have to prepare our security budget by April 1 for the coming season. Prior to 1991, that didn't amount to much. Now, with all the electronic security we have around the property, and personnel to handle a 365-day operation, the budget is at least twenty-five times higher in salaries alone. Following the stadium renovation, we went from providing security services primarily on game days to a 24/7 setup.

We spend thousands of dollars for services associated with every game. The organization has a variety of contracts in place, including one with the police department for overtime. Our costs for emergency services are probably in the top five in the NFL, and we're always looking to see which jobs we can get done with internal teams.

We take a lot of pride in our fan behavior overall, but it takes an army of private security, team security, and police officers to insure that there's good reason for pride.

Chapter 15
Special Treatment For Special People

POLITICIANS OR HIGH-RANKING government officials coming to Green Bay presents a whole different level of security issues. If you're a sports fan — as most of these people are — and don't get a chance to see Lambeau Field when you're here, you feel you're missing something. The Packers make an effort to avoid letting candidates use Lambeau Field for their own publicity purposes, so public appearances at the stadium are rare. The organization just doesn't want to be put in that position.

I had the opportunity to meet George W. Bush and his wife Laura when he was running for office the first time. As a former owner of the Texas Rangers baseball team, he's a big sports fan. He visited the Don Hutson Center in September 2000 and showed up at practice while Laura remained in one of the cars. He still hasn't visited Lambeau, but I know he would've loved to.

The level of security for a presidential visit took a major step up following 9/11. Security had already been tightened twenty years earlier after President Reagan was shot on March 30, 1981 and President Anwar Sadat of Egypt was shot and killed on October 6 that same year. At that time, security forces feared that an assassination attempt would come from a person with a gun. After 9/11, the job of protecting the president became even more difficult; we had to take into consideration everything from car bombs to suicide bombers.

The Resch Center, Green Bay's major arena, was chosen as the venue for a rally when President Bush came to town during the 2004 campaign. The Resch sits across a side street from the Hutson Center. Since the Lambeau Field parking lot is used as the primary lot for Resch events, I knew we'd be right in the middle of the security efforts for the rally set for the evening of Wednesday, September 14.

Planning began as soon as the press release confirming the visit came out in early July. The president's itinerary had him riding in a bus up Highway 41 from Milwaukee to a stop in Fond du Lac, and then on up to Green Bay. I knew from past experience that I'd be contacted by the Secret Service's Milwaukee office to help the agents with the Green Bay part of the day. In 1988, while working for the Secret Service as a police liaison, I had spent three weeks at their training facility in Washington, D.C. I was highly impressed working with them, and honored during the last five years of my police career to be their local contact for setting up Green Bay visits.

The advance crew came in on Friday, five days before the event. Doug Collins and I gave a two-hour tour of Lambeau for that group, which included thirty-five members of the Secret Service, Air Force, and Army personnel. Some were directly assigned to the president, and the next week I saw them on stage with him at the rally. They were from all over the country and really enjoyed the tour, which lasted twice as long as the public ones led by our tour guides. We talked about the tradition that this organization thrives on, and since a lot of these guys were from big cities with NFL teams, they were really into it.

Word must have filtered back that the tour was very enjoyable, because the following Monday we got a call asking if we could do some tours for the uniformed division and the capitol division. These were the guys who handled the scanning equipment that would check people for weapons when they entered the Resch. We ended up giving two tours for seventy-five people on the day of the event.

They were all based in Washington, D.C., and none had ever been to Green Bay. Most of them were Redskins fans, so it was a fun telling them about the history of the teams. Vince Lombardi was with the Redskins when we lost him to cancer in 1970.

On the ninety-minute drive from Fond du Lac to Green Bay, the president's motorcade pulled into an ice-cream store in the Fox Valley, where he went in and surprised the people. You don't give criminals a chance to set up when you have a surprise visit like that, but you don't give your security people a chance to do any advance work, either. Normally, the Secret Service does background checks and researches the employees in every venue where the president goes. It puts a lot of pressure on local law enforcement to help out with such a huge task. The Secret Service's job became much more detailed with President Kennedy's assassination, then the Reagan shooting, and the more recent terrorist factor. A lot more planning takes place, and they even do overhead checks of the route to make sure nothing has moved or looks suspicious.

The big difference with moving a president around today is air power. Two Apache helicopters flew cover all the way up from Milwaukee, so if anything went wrong they could get him out of there immediately. Air Force jets are also on standby or even in the air. I was told they were only four minutes away, coming from Madison. Once in Green Bay, the motorcade went to the Radisson first, where the president probably showered and ate dinner before the evening's event.

Doug and I were offered the opportunity to meet the president in a VIP room at the rally. We were all fired up for two days ahead of time, but the meeting never materialized. It would have been nice to shake his hand and be acknowledged by him, but that's how things go in this business. We had fabulous seats at the rally, just above and behind the president, only two rows behind his daughter, Barbara, comedian Dennis Miller, and entertainer Wayne Newton. A number of players wanted to attend, so we made a few calls a couple hours ahead of time and were able to get Marco Rivera and Aaron Kampman in with us.

If we didn't want to attend the rally, another option was to tour Air Force One out at the airport, but Doug was really eager to meet the president, and I love watching the processions and how the police do their jobs. I spent half the time at the rally observing the Secret Service agents. Their every movement said something, and I could tell when the president was about to come out on stage.

At one point the president left the stage and went out into the crowd, and the way the agents handled themselves and protected him was impressive. Everybody in the arena had been checked, and no chances were taken. There are eight agents around him at all times, including one right on his belt to pull him out of a crowd if necessary. The president has to listen to his protectors, and I'm sure they don't share everything with him as they react to situations.

If I had it to do over again, having already met the president back in 2000, I would've grabbed at the chance to tour Air Force One.

Vice President Dick Cheney was in Green Bay for an official visit at the same time that Bart Starr, a good friend of his, happened to be here. Cheney wanted to see Lambeau Field, and since we had done something special for Ted Kennedy not long before, a special tour was approved. Bart asked if he could stop by and visit, and I accompanied him as he met with Cheney's wife and daughters. As we sat there talking, the vice president walked up, and Bart introduced me by saying, "Jerry is one of the outstanding people in the Green Bay Packers organization." I didn't deserve that, but it meant so much to me. The Cheneys went on to enjoy their tour, and the whole experience was quite a thrill for me.

Tommy Thompson, former governor of Wisconsin, came to Lambeau while serving as the Secretary of Health and Human Services for President George W. Bush. Even when a cabinet-level type of visitor is in a private suite with his own security team, we have to be in communication with them to avoid any embarrassing situations. Their security people are likely to be armed, and we don't want to have any recognition mishaps — especially if they're in plainclothes.

In 1996, during his second campaign, President Bill Clinton visited Green Bay on Labor Day. It was very interesting how laid back everything was when he came to see Lambeau Field. We had some of our people out on the field with him, and many Packers employees sat in the bleachers to watch. There were pictures being taken all over the place. Even though it wasn't a public appearance, things would certainly have been much more tense had it occurred in today's post-9/11 era.

We did have a minor issue prior to Clinton's visit. Pepper Burruss has a gun collection at his home and keeps a bullet collection in his office. It's just a hobby of Pepper's, but one of the Secret Service people did a double take when he saw it, and we had to explain what it was. We walk by that collection every day and think nothing of it. The agent was just doing his job, and was concerned that the scent of gunpowder would set off their dogs.

We had the opportunity to visit President Clinton in the White House in 1997 following the Packers' victory in Super Bowl XXXI. A noticeable change from 1988, when I was there for Secret Service training, was that the atmosphere around the White House felt more relaxed, and there seemed to be many more female staff members — attractive female staff members — than I'd seen in previous administrations. The president greeted us very warmly and spoke to us in the Rose Garden. He met with us in a private area of the White House, too. He was on crutches at the time, so he couldn't move around too well. I always thought it would be a great honor to be a Secret Service agent and go running with the president, like some of the guys did with Clinton.

Additionally, the whole operations area of the White House had been revamped and its technology upgraded since I was there during the Reagan presidency. I thought things were handled more professionally back then.

The Men of Honor

On March 2, 2007 I received a call from retired FBI agent Tom Azier who told me that the Congressional Medal of Honor Society had chosen Green Bay to be the host city for its annual convention. They had their pick of all kinds of places, but they chose Green Bay because of Lambeau Field. What an honor for the Packers to be involved in this event! As of June, I'd begun my transition into semi-retirement as a senior security advisor for the organization, so this event gave me something to focus on now that I wasn't security director anymore.

There are only 110 living recipients of the Congressional Medal of Honor from conflicts dating back as far as World War II. Fifty or so were expected to attend the convention, but that number quickly grew because so many of these men wanted to see Lambeau Field and the Green Bay Packers. They ranged in age from fifty-seven to ninety-seven, and some were in wheelchairs.

The convention was a federal government-protected event, so security was a major issue. The week's worth of activities would be capped off by on-field introductions prior to the Packers' September 9 regular-season opener against the Eagles. Adding to security concerns was the very real chance that First Lady Laura Bush would attend and accept the group's Patriot Award, their highest honor for a civilian. There was even an outside chance that President Bush might be here.

As it turned out, neither could attend. Laura had a surgical procedure to relieve pain from pinched nerves in her neck, while the president was attending a conference in Australia. We found out about

Mrs. Bush's surgery plans only a few days before the event. I was disappointed that she wasn't able to come, but her presence would've changed a lot of the security preparations and the Secret Service would've become more involved. We had our own Patriot Award recipients, though: Brett and Deanna Favre were recognized at the Saturday night banquet for citizenship, while NBC anchor Brian Williams was honored for journalism.

For months leading up to that week, the local planning committee held meetings to deal with issues ranging from donations of game tickets for attendees to how we should handle the pre-game ceremony. Some of our people who were the most involved were Doug Collins, Packers Pro Shop manager Kate Hogan, and the Packers' marketing entertainment coordinator Kandi Goltz. It was a huge logistical undertaking with an incredible number of details to account for, and this team pulled it off without a hitch.

The Men of Honor really enjoyed their visit, especially the string of appearances they made at schools throughout the week. What a treat and an honor it was for me to work with this group of people. And it wasn't just the recipients—their wives were wonderful, too. I had a chance to meet them during an autograph session the first day. Kind of like football coaches' wives, they seem to take a back seat and don't want to be conspicuous at these kinds of events. I made a point of talking with them, which was the best thing I did that week. They told me about their husbands and raved about the treatment they were receiving from the hotel staff at the Radisson and everyone they were meeting in town. In my estimation, security was probably overdone, but there's nothing wrong with that. From going places around the country for years, these people know that they like to have hands-on attention to make them feel more secure.

One of the wives told me about her husband, an eighty-three-year-old World War II veteran from Boise, Idaho. They were big fans of the football team at Boise State, where Packers offensive lineman

Daryn Colledge and fullback Korey Hall went to school. I waited around for this couple outside the Radisson banquet room to make arrangements for them to meet Daryn and Korey. I was wearing a pair of jeans, a nice, white long-sleeved Harley-Davidson shirt with black print, and a Harley hat. A guy came up to me and said, "What is this... biker trash?" Someone told the man who I was, and he shut his mouth and walked away.

I was able to bring my Boise couple up to the players' floor of the hotel a little later that night so they could get autographs from Daryn and Korey. I get a kick out of doing little things like that for people, and they really appreciated it.

As far as our preparations were concerned, Sunday was the big day. Not only was it the regular-season opener, with all the challenges that presents, but we had a window of only eight minutes before the game to get all the veterans on the field and the introductions completed. We were working with the national TV schedule, and some of the veterans weren't mobile.

Jim Arts came over to the stadium that morning in full-dress uniform to help us coordinate the veterans and get them into the stadium on time. We had to split them up because there were so many — sixty-two in all, including four from Wisconsin. The group came in through the rear dock area, which gave them a place to meet before the excitement of going onto the field. When we brought them out, our fans immediately stood and started cheering.

NBC's Brian Williams handled the announcing duties from the field, having each group step forward from the visiting team's sideline in the chronological order of the war in which they fought. The largest group by far was the Vietnam vets, and they received the loudest ovation — that is, until the men from Wisconsin were introduced as honorary captains. I was standing with these men on the Packers' sideline, and I could see the pride on their faces as a huge cheer went up from the crowd. It was quite an honor just to be standing there next to them, since I wear my flag on my lips. A lot of our players shook their hands, and it was a great scene. A squadron of F-15s executed a perfect flyover at the end of the national anthem, and the ceremonies concluded without a hitch. Or so we thought.

After we'd escorted the veterans off the field, an automatic siren and announcement suddenly came over the stadium's public address system. "Attention! Attention! This is an emergency. Please go to the nearest exit and evacuate the stadium."

Fans didn't know what to do. Because it was right before kickoff, we now had a situation in which people were trying to come into the stadium and trying to get out at the same time. Thankfully, most of the fans just stayed put. We didn't know what to do down on the field, either, and I could see concern on the faces of the Medal of Honor people as the announcement kept running. The emergency system overrode the P.A. announcer's microphone and didn't allow Bill Jartz to address the crowd. He had just begun introducing the players when the system kicked in, and that automated voice was all anyone could hear, which made the situation all the more troubling.

Doug said, "Jerry, I think this is the real thing."

We had talked about how the Medal of Honor people could be a terrorist target and that they couldn't even go out of the country at one point after 9/11. We knew it couldn't be a weather-related problem, because it was a perfect September day. Then we thought there might be a fire. We tried to connect with the communications center on the seventh floor of the press box. Finally, we learned there was a minor fire in a concession stand and the volunteers didn't know what to do. I told the Medal of Honor people that everything was okay and considered walking onto the field to try to tell more people there was nothing to worry about. We have a three-minute window to shut off an alarm before the fire department shows up, but no one could get the alarm turned off for several minutes, so the fire department arrived just the way they're supposed to.

We won the game, and everything about the day went great except for that emergency-system glitch. That was a good learning experience for us, and now the fire department goes into the concession stands before games to make sure the volunteers know what to do. Thank God there we no injuries that day, because panic can be the biggest threat in that kind of situation.

I got to see some of the e-mails the Medal of Honor people sent back to the committee after the weekend; they said this was by far the most popular city for their annual convention. When you think of all the beautiful places they've visited around the United States, their compliments reflected really well on the city of Green Bay and the Packers.

Chapter 16
Victims, Players, And Knuckleheads

MY JOB IS TO SUPPORT THE PLAYERS when it comes to off-the-field problems. I get to know the players by going to team meetings whenever I can and spending time in the locker room. They have to know the security staff is here for them, and eventually they come to respect us. When they do dumb things, they know they'll have to answer for it, and I feel very good about that.

The word "responsibility" doesn't resonate with some of these guys. This attitude is part of the athletic system in this country, and for many of them it goes all the way back to early adolescence. Sometimes the players are very embarrassed when issues arise. They think their problems will never surface, but in Green Bay it seems like everything eventually does. I can only hope it's not too serious.

Ever since the problem players gave the Packers a bad name during Forrest Gregg's tenure, the organization has put a lot of emphasis on getting guys with solid character. It's harder and harder to bring in good players who've got completely clean backgrounds, but the biggest thing is getting them to realize the opportunity that playing this game gives them. They have to be smart and steer clear of temptations, because football can mean so much to a player's financial future.

Players make a lot of money, yet it's common for them to have nothing left within a few years of leaving the game. It's the people they associate with that get these guys in trouble. It's not as bad in the NFL as in the NBA, but it surely has gotten worse. NFL commissioner Roger Goodell has come out strong with a tough personal conduct policy. In taking that stand, he's fortunate to have a player like former Tennessee Titans cornerback Adam "Pacman" Jones to be his poster boy. Jones has a long rap sheet, highlighted by a shooting incident involving a member of his entourage outside a Las Vegas strip club. Goodell suspended him for the entire 2007 season. That was an easy call, but the commissioner has to be careful with some of the punishments he hands out prior to a player being convicted of anything. This country is based on people's rights, and I can't believe the players union is going to let this go on. (As of this writing, "Pacman" Jones has been given limited reinstatement, meaning he can join his Dallas Cowboys teammates and participate in team activities including training camp and preseason games. A final decision concerning his playing in the upcoming season is expected by Sept. 1, 2008. "Until that time, Commissioner Goodell wrote, "Jones is expected to continue to abide by the NFL's personal conduct program and avoid further involvement with law enforcement.")

In any business, you just don't want word of certain problems to get out. Sometimes, however, it's very difficult to contain those things because people talk. Ron Wolf would get upset whenever sensitive news leaked outside the organization. Sometimes players are so naïve that they don't realize what they're saying, and before you know it someone in the media has the idea that there's a conflict when there might be none at all.

Whenever a problem comes up that doesn't involve anyone from the outside, it needs to be handled entirely within the organization. Just like when you lose a game, you don't point fingers. It can be a tough job keeping everything inside, because you're always under the media's microscope, and those people do their job well. When they're up in the press box watching the game, they don't miss a thing. They'll pick you apart if they see or hear anything on the sideline that hints of conflict. Relations with the media are very different than they were forty years ago. I'm biased, but it's natural for me to protect my turf, and that's not just a game-day process.

Whenever there's any wrongdoing on the part of a player, we as an organization must be careful because anyone prosecuting the case can call us as witnesses. We don't have the confidentiality protection that attorneys do, and by oath I would have to testify if a player had made any admissions to me. I want the players to respect me because I think I've earned that, but I want them to be comfortable talking with me and not fear me. With my police background, I can give them some direction and even help get them a proper attorney, but I can't defend them.

I've had to deal with a lot of players over my career. I've been fortunate to have never had a situation with an African American player in which my being a white police officer got in the way. In fact, I've had more instances of white players not giving me the proper respect.

With some players, you can just tell that they live on the edge of getting into trouble, and you have to be their guardian angel sometimes. They don't make good choices regarding the people they hang with, and you know it's just a matter of time before something bad happens. If an incident does occur, it's my job to get as much information as possible about what happened. It seems that almost every day someone claims that a player owes them money. Everybody thinks all football players are rich, so they're out for top dollar. My role is to negotiate these things so they go away as quickly and quietly as possible.

Being in jail isn't a totally bad thing for a player, because it provides a cooling-off period and gives me time to find out where we're at. Sometimes the less that's said the better off we are. We want to put some time between the incident and any public statements so we can analyze what's going on. It's tough to deal with a criminal incident such as a sexual assault, because the rights of the victim must be considered as well. When I was a policeman, we had to make decisions on the spot that were later scrutinized by the district attorney's office and other legal people. With the Packers, I have the luxury of going slowly with a situation. My job is to protect the property of the Green Bay Packers, but at times there's only so much I can do.

The most common incidents we deal with involve domestic violence. Usually, I know only one of the principle parties, since I rarely know the spouse like I know the player. Domestic violence episodes don't affect just the player — players come and go — they affect the whole organization. Unfortunately, domestic violence is a very common occurrence in society, and the media magnifies it when an incident happens to involve someone from the Packers organization. That's not to excuse the actions of the player or coach, but sometimes their problems are made to appear more severe just by virtue of the fact they're Packers.

Ahman Green and his wife, Heather, had a stormy relationship that culminated in his well-publicized arrest on a domestic abuse charge in April 2005. The morning after his arrest, I was able to get Ahman into the office to hear his version of the story. That's important because it gives us some direction as to where to start as we try to get ahead of the game. The first thing I did was share my thoughts with Jason Wied. We also brought in Coach Sherman, Bob Harlan, and Ted Thompson, the new general manager.

This incident was hard for me because I only knew the good side of Ahman as a caring person. Truly, I didn't know a finer man on the team. He met with the cancer families on my Cruise for Cancer ride. He worked closely with assistant trainer Bryan "Flea" Engel, and went to Flea's house and played with his kids, one of whom had a heart problem. Ahman's a great football player, but he's also a good sport and a dedicated person. He works out and practices hard, and that's why he was one of the best running backs in the history of the Packers.

The domestic violence incident got a lot of publicity, but thankfully Ahman and Heather reconciled and the case was dismissed before ever going to trial. The couple eventually divorced. After the 2006 season, Ahman left the Packers in free agency and followed Mike Sherman to the Houston Texans.

Gilbert Brown, the Packers' massive nose tackle from 1993–99 and 2001–03, also had an assault issue that we were able to assist with. Gilbert was a favorite of mine who always considered himself a mama's boy. He has such a big heart that he bought his mom a house in Detroit. Gilbert's friends used him, and people stole things from him and generally took unfair advantage of him.

Gilbert weighed about 350 pounds and generally was not a violent person, but when he pushed his girlfriend over a couch, the Ashwaubenon Public Safety Department arrested him for domestic violence. I went to court and told Gilbert we would get him into counseling right away. We got him into an anger management course with Betsy Mitchell, the team's player/staff development specialist.

Gilbert didn't have an attorney, so I accompanied him to his legal proceedings. He ended up pleading guilty, but in retrospect I should have advised him to plead no contest in case a civil complaint was ever filed. Judge Sue Bischel had the case, and she complimented us on Gilbert's having already taken a positive step by going for counseling. The media was there for his court appearance, so I used my relationships with sheriff's department officers to get us out through a secure exit.

In terms of being loved by the fans, Gilbert is one of the top five people I've worked with. Even though he had this domestic issue, his play still brought cheers, especially when he would do his gravedigger move after making a big play.

I made certain to confide in Bob Harlan, Ron Wolf, and the coaches on these types of issues. Mr. Harlan's background was in public relations, so he knew the importance of public perception and how to deal with the media. This organization's image was his number-one priority. Some of that image is tied directly to how well the team performs on the field; it seems like when the wheels come off the wagon, we're flooded with complaints ranging from player behavior to fan problems at games.

Ron Wolf took a PR risk during the team's run to Super Bowl XXXI by picking up the very talented wide receiver Andre Rison, a guy with a lot of baggage. In 1994, Rison's pop-star girlfriend, the late Lisa Lopes of TLC, burned his house down, and he'd been arrested several times for failing to pay child support. Ron felt we could hire virtually any athlete and Coach Holmgren could mold him into a good player who'd live a responsible life off the field. His philosophy was that whatever had happened before was in the past.

Was I concerned? You bet. Ron and Mike sat Andre down and had a lengthy talk with him. They let him know what this community is like, that it's very difficult to keep things from surfacing publicly in Green Bay, and that his being an African American might make it even more difficult.

Fortunately, during the one season he was here, we never had a major problem with Rison, though he kept getting in the news for the wrong reasons once he'd left. He made a big contribution while he was here, even catching the first touchdown pass in the Packers' Super Bowl victory over the New England Patriots.

Jerry Kramer had his share of police issues during his playing days back in the '60s. He had a reputation for being a very physical guy, and many of his domestic issues were related to alcohol. Sometimes we'd send the whole night shift of four patrol cars over to his house to calm him down. Thankfully, he never fought with us during those calls, but as officers, we knew we couldn't go there alone because Jerry was a handful. Plus, it's always difficult to deal with someone of stature in the community. Jerry was a very aggressive man in his younger years. He played the game that way, and maybe it was hard to shut that off.

Photo Gallery

"Little Jerry" as he was nicknamed growing up with dad Jerry and mom Florence outside Shea Avenue home in Green Bay, Wisconsin.

Florence Parins with son Jerry at family home, 118 N. Oneida St. Green Bay, Wisconsin. Camera shy. Eyes closed. He later learns to handle media experiences with skill as the Director of Corporate Security for the Green Bay Packers.

A young Parins in Green Bay Police Department riding gear with first born daughter Shelley – 1966.

Sandy and Jerry Parins married April 15, 1961. A family man in the making who would later work for one of the most family-oriented football franchises in the world – the Packers.

The early years – Former Head Coach Bart Starr with Parins far right and his three daughters – Toni, Missy and Shelley on the Packers practice field. Parins was a Green Bay Police Department detective at that time and worked part-time for the Packers in security.

The inspiration – Parins and players with Kathy Miller, honorary cancer patient for the 2006 Parins cancer ride. Miller, a resident of De Pere Wisconsin, died the following year after a several year cancer battle with breast and liver cancer.

Parins watching over Brett Favre during an away game in San Francisco in the 1990s. Photo © James V. Biever

*Packers Coach at the time Mike Sherman and
Parins during a 2000 playoff game at Lambeau.*

*President George Bush is safe-
guarded by Parins during a
2000 visit to Green Bay. Parins
worked closely with the Secret
Service to pull off a safe experience for the President of the
United States of America.*

Parins with former Green Bay Packer running back Sam Gado who was traded to Houston for Vernand Morency. In his role, Parins got to know the players well because their security was his business.

Parins in the Packers locker room with all three Super Bowl trophies – Super Bowl 1, 31 and 2.

Parins keeping pace with the Packers

Favre with leukemia patient outside at a St. Louis Rams/Green Bay Packers game in 2007. "That little boy and his sister wanted to give a present to Brett so I found him. I told Brett 'there's no way we're gonna lose this game today because of what you just did, what you did for those people." In the second picture with both of those youngsters you can see in Brett's eyes the emotion of what they did for him.

Jerry Parins and former Head Coach Mike Holmgren in 1995 before leaving for a local Muscular Dystrophy Association motorcycle ride/ benefit. Parins would later be the founder of the Jerry Parins' Cruise for Cancer. Jerry taught Coach Mike the intricacies of biking.

Parins, Lambeau and cancer support - a Green Bay Packers alliance. The team helped him find the strength and openness to save himself. He continues to try to give back with the organization rallying behind him in the wings.

A Lambeau tradition – Parins Cruise for Cancer participants gather on the back side of Lambeau Field on what is known as Ridge Road in Green Bay, Wisconsin.

Lambeau Tradition

Super Bowl 31 (1996 Season)celebratory motorcade in Titletown, USA. Parins with Coach Holmgren. Parins – "I hadn't slept for 48 hours when that picture was taken, but what a ride."

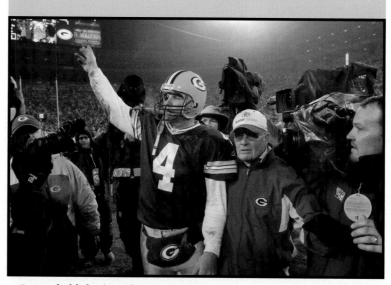

Parins holds back media to give Favre space after a game.
Photo © James V. Biever

Mark Chmura's arrest in 2000 for the alleged sexual assault of a high school girl at a house party was a sensational media event. Chewy, as we called him, was a real upbeat type of guy; he was always positive, very well-spoken, and he cared about everyone. He was there for the trainers, the equipment crew, and the security people. We were a very important part of team chemistry to him, and he always treated us well.

The dumb thing Chewy did was to not go home when he should have. A lot of people who get in trouble can trace it back to having too much to drink, and that was the situation here. What a mess this case was!

I went to Chewy's initial court appearance along with Kurt Fielding, one of our assistant trainers, just to show support. Chewy was such a good friend, and this really hit us hard. I had been to his house in Hartland, near Milwaukee, and I knew his family. I don't know if Mr. Harlan was upset with us for going—as the Packers quickly cut all official ties with Chewy—but this was one of those things you do when a player is a friend. I know that some people in the organization didn't like it that we went down there.

The Chmura case was really hard on Coach Sherman. He had just taken over as head coach, and a few years earlier had coached Mark as tight ends coach under Mike Holmgren. Sherman got to know Chewy fairly well on a whole other level because they spent so much time together. He didn't really know what to do about Mark during this period.

The initial media impact led many people to convict Mark before the trial, but that's why we have a judicial system. If the case had happened in our community, it would've been much easier for me to get involved because I know the local system and how it operates. The farther you go from Green Bay, the harder it is to make contacts and find out the real story. This was a high-profile case, and pictures of Chewy in his orange jumpsuit turned up all over the Internet.

In some cases, players don't have the resources to adequately defend themselves. That wasn't the case with Chewy. To make matters even more spectacular, he hired Gerald Boyle, who had defended serial killer Jeffrey Dahmer, as his defense attorney. The biggest thing for me was trying to get as much information as possible to analyze the case at our level—even just to answer all the Ws: who, what, and where. You've got to be careful asking questions of police agencies, because you don't want to be seen as the bad guy.

Mark was a clean-cut guy who went to Boston College and had a wife and kids, yet many people weren't surprised by the incident. He had a reputation in Green Bay along with Frank Winters and Brett Favre, his "Three Amigos" buddies.

After a highly publicized trial, a jury eventually found Mark innocent of the charges, but the combination of the bad publicity and his poor health kept Chewy from ever playing football again. In the court of public opinion he was certainly found guilty of poor judgment. A couple years later, when I was in the middle of my cancer battle, Mark checked up on me, and his call meant a lot to me.

It's interesting how the team handled this case compared to prior incidents, such as when future Hall of Fame receiver James Lofton was charged with sexually assaulting a woman in the stairwell at The Top Shelf, a downtown nightclub. I was handling a lot of the sexual assault cases for the Green Bay PD at the time, but I wasn't called in on this one because of conflict of interest—and rightfully so. James was a guy I talked to every day, and I knew his wife and kids. His natural athletic ability was incredible. He was the NCAA long-jump champion in track, and I saw him throw a football as far as Brett Favre could. James would have contests with linebacker Mike Douglass to see who could throw it farther.

There was no way I could work on that case, and that was a rough time for the organization. I had my own feelings, but I respected the police department's ability to do the right thing. Bart Starr, who had drafted Lofton in 1978 and was always very supportive of his players, was in court for at least some of the proceedings. Lofton ended up being exonerated, but like Chmura, the case spelled the end of his career in Green Bay.

I don't know if other organizations take the time to get into things like we do, but it's another part of what makes the Packers special. Nobody has ever told me to ignore a situation. I've always tried to listen, even if I thought it was hopeless or the person wasn't a favorite of mine. I would always look at the circumstances and the facts, and help out any way I could.

We had a young offensive lineman who found himself in serious trouble one night during minicamp season. Someone at the Green Bay PD called to give me a heads-up that this player was the subject of an investigation concerning an incident at a downtown bar. They told me that if I had access to the player, they'd appreciate my getting him in so they could find out what was going on.

Doug Collins got a call from one of the night officers, who also worked on our security team, saying that a woman had filed a complaint. The designated driver for a bachelorette party, she was drinking 7-Up while talking to this player when she noticed a pill in her drink. The players had left the bar by the time police were called, and there were other people in the bar who could've been involved. Did our guy slip something into her drink? We didn't know.

The police didn't have an address for the player, so they called Doug at 2:00 a.m. to try to find one. We knew he lived downtown and we were able to track him down. I was very concerned, because this could be a felony if it turned out he'd slipped her a date-rape drug. Not only was there the potential to ruin this player's career, but also the implications of what could have happened to the young lady were awful. In an unrelated case, a girl had died in a car accident, and authorities were later able to prove that someone drugged her drink. This was a very serious matter, and we jumped on the case.

Coach Sherman found out about it the next morning and just lost it; he pulled the player out of a meeting and made a big scene. It became a huge issue internally, and all the players were aware of it. Thankfully, the case just died for lack of evidence, but it was something everyone in the organization learned from. You can't hide in this city. If you do anything wrong, you're going to get caught and you'll be prosecuted to the max. The district attorney will take the case to the highest level, because he knows the entire community is watching him. He can't do any favors for anyone, and any case that deals with the Packers is a public one.

We knew this player had some baggage when we drafted him, and unfortunately that case wasn't the end of the story. About two weeks later, the police called Doug in the middle of night after receiving a call from the guy's girlfriend. She was worried because he had called her in a depressed state, and they'd gotten into a fight over the phone. She thought maybe he would take his own life.

The police went over to his apartment and found the door unlocked. They found him asleep inside and couldn't wake him. The officers called Doug, who jumped out of bed and drove right over. The common thread in both of these incidents was alcohol.

I arrived at work early the next morning and Doug told me what had happened. He and I went over to the guy's apartment to try to find out more. There were beer bottles and cigarettes all over the place. He was in a stupor, so I told him to get in the shower, get something to eat, and come see me in a couple hours. I had built a relationship with him over the past few weeks, and we sat in my office for a long talk. He was injured, so maybe part of this incident was due to his mixing medications with alcohol.

Whenever I saw him after that episode, I always got a warm handshake, and he became one of my favorites. He knew I was sick with cancer, too, but I don't want to have to get sick in order to have a better relationship with players. Eventually, some guys realize I might know what I'm talking about. I think I got through to him, but I was upset and also concerned that there might be a deeper problem.

The players who run into legal problems aren't just inner-city guys. This young man was from a well-to-do family, but that's not the norm. Some of the legal issues come up because players have a hard time making the adjustment from poverty to money. That can create problems if you don't have a good agent or good financial advisors in your corner. Some of the top athletes drafted in the first few rounds have never had a hundred dollars at one time in their lives, so the huge signing bonuses they get can actually be scary because having that much money is so far outside their comfort zones.

Sometimes we forget that these players are fallible human beings. When we have incidents involving alcohol abuse, the players must make a commitment to change. They need to understand that if they're drinking heavily, they're putting themselves at risk. The biggest concern for both the team and the player is falling into the NFL's substance-abuse program. The league has a stiff policy, and it can be a major deal for players.

Caught in the Switch

Antonio Freeman, the Packers' fine wide receiver from 1995–2001 and 2003, got into a double dose of trouble early in the morning of December 22, 1999, by trying to pull a switch with fellow receiver Charles Jordan. I got a call at home from the Brown County Sheriff's Department about an accident at Eve's Supper Club in suburban Allouez. Most of the local law enforcement agencies have access to me at home for issues that are good, bad, or whatever. Usually it's bad, and this was one of those.

The deputy told me the accident involved two players and two women, and that Jordan was being arrested and jailed for driving while intoxicated. Apparently, he had driven into a light pole and one of the women was seriously hurt. Freeman was okay, and someone was taking him home to De Pere. At that hour of the night, there was nothing else I could do. Jordan had been processed and was going to the county jail, and there wasn't any news about how bad the young woman's injuries were.

I got to work at 6:30 and immediately got Coach Ray Rhodes involved. Shortly after seven o'clock, I got a call from Capt. Dennis Kocken in the Brown County Sheriff's Department; the story had changed. During their investigation, they got information from witnesses in Eve's who saw Freeman driving the car. Let's just say that "Free" may not have had his attention fully on driving when his vehicle jumped the curb and struck the pole. Now we've got obstructing an officer and falsifying information in the picture, as well as traffic violations.

Predictably, the officers wanted to talk to Freeman. It was a Friday morning, and I wanted to stall a bit to see if there was anything I could do to help our player while still cooperating with the sheriffs. We set a 9:00 a.m. appointment for them to meet with Freeman at Lambeau, since I knew he'd be here for the team meeting. The sheriff's department was very concerned because they had to get the story straight.

As soon as I got off the phone with the deputy, I called Freeman at his home and told him to get down to Lambeau and see me right away. He arrived around 7:30, looking pretty rough, like he'd been out all night, and I sat him down to get the details. Free admitted he'd been the one behind the wheel, and that Jordan wanted to do him a favor by taking the rap.

"Free, you have to tell me what happened," I said. "Did you eat there? How much did you drink?"

I was asking him the questions I knew the police would ask.

Jordan came in shortly after his release from jail, so I had them both in my office to gather as much information as possible. They admitted to drinking some wine and champagne. Do I believe they had more to drink than they admitted? Sure.

While they were there, I left the room to call an attorney. I knew this incident was over my head, and had to get some legal expertise to protect the Packers and our players. I called Tom Olejniczak, and he sent out Jason Wied, who worked at his firm at that time.

The police hadn't run any breath or blood tests on Freeman, since they didn't know he'd been the driver. Maybe ten hours had passed since the time of the accident, and we still had a little more time before our appointment with the sheriff's department.

"You've got to get yourself cleaned up good," I told Free. "Go work up a sweat, take a shower, and get something to eat."

Both guys smelled of alcohol, which was a big concern since a positive alcohol test would put them in the NFL's substance-abuse program. I was doing all I could to protect the Packers and one of their key players. The team finished 8-8 in 1999 and missed the playoffs, but at that time we were still in the hunt.

When the deputies arrived, both players were very cooperative and gave the correct story. Freeman was arrested and charged with obstructing and reckless driving, and Jordan was also charged with obstruction. Freeman was able to avoid any alcohol-related charges, and that kept him out off the league's substance-abuse list.

Was getting Freeman in more presentable shape the right thing for me to do? I don't know. I saw my job as looking out for the Packers, and Freeman's ability as a receiver was good for our team. It was huge that I was able to help him through that, and fortunate that it didn't affect the Packers.

We had to bring Free downtown to be processed, but he didn't spend any time in jail. He was very concerned about the young lady because he knew she was badly hurt. He called her father and found out her injuries weren't life threatening, but closing up her cuts required a lot of stitches.

This wasn't the end of the story, however; the woman later filed suit against Freeman and his insurance company. I was deposed, since I'd spoken with Free the morning after the accident. I didn't want to get involved, but when you're in this job, it's hard not to. I had to relate what had happened that morning, and I described Freeman as looking "wasted" when he arrived at my office. I had used the word to describe his appearance after not getting any sleep, but it was a poor choice of words, because the attorneys wondered if it meant he'd still been drunk. I had to define how I was using the word. Two years later, the lawsuit was finally settled out of court.

Guns, Cars, and Bling

Along with expensive vehicles and jewelry, guns seem to be a favorite thing for players to spend their money on. The NFL has very strict rules about weapons. Other than law enforcement, no one is allowed to have a gun on an NFL team's property. It doesn't matter if it's loaded or not, and it doesn't matter if it's a hunting rifle you put in the back of your vehicle so you could head out to the woods after practice. We tell the players that if they get stopped for a traffic violation, they should tell the officer right away if they have any weapons in the vehicle. Officers will be much more receptive if you're straight with them right off.

Aaron Taylor, the great Notre Dame guard drafted in the first round in 1994, got in trouble his rookie season because of a post-game celebration involving firearms. The Packers had beaten the Lions 16-12 in a playoff game on New Year's Eve, holding future Hall of Fame running back Barry Sanders to minus-one yard on thirteen carries. What a great game that was for us!

Aaron was a gun collector, and at his house he had about $3,000 worth of handguns that he used for target practice. He fired some shots to celebrate the New Year at midnight, and safety George

Teague did the same with a gun he had at his duplex. That's just not the way people celebrate in Green Bay—the police were called and both players were arrested. Officers confiscated all of Aaron's guns and were going to destroy them, so we had to convince the DA's office that Aaron would behave himself. Teague had bought his gun from a magazine ad, and it was only worth about $175. Both guys ended up paying fines, but the incidents made the papers and were embarrassing to the organization.

The next season, Coach Holmgren asked what we could do to get this gun issue under control. Depending on where they grew up, some players had more access to guns and saw no problem with having them. We also had a lot of guys who were really into hunting, including Brett Favre and his former backup Doug Pederson. I tried to educate the guys about staying away from guns. I'd tell them, "You don't need one in Green Bay because it'll just get you in trouble." Mossy Cade, the defensive back convicted of sexual assault in 1986, worsened his situation by having a gun visible on his dresser. The victim was intimidated by seeing that gun in the room.

We always addressed the issue at minicamp, but obviously that wasn't having the effect we hoped for. Starting in the 1995 season, any player who had a gun was asked to check it in with my office. We signed in the guns and locked them in a trunk until the end of the season. It seemed to work well. Did every guy who had a gun turn it in? I don't know. But the policy was in effect for a while, and it came at a time when we were getting into winning again. That really was the only year where we had a problem with them.

The Five-Six

We can't order players to stay away from certain establishments, but we sure can strongly suggest it. Sometimes we hear from our police contacts about places to avoid, usually because of possible drug-related activity or other rough stuff. We connect with some of the team leaders and have them spread the word. Often that's enough to avert any bad situations.

Unfortunately, one of those rough night spots during the 2005 and 2006 seasons was owned by one of our own players, middle linebacker Nick Barnett. We couldn't very well tell players not to patronize Nick's place, which was called the Five-Six Ultra Lounge — after Nick's jersey number 56 — so we just held our breath and hoped nothing would happen. It's hard for a player to have that type of business, because he's putting himself into a frying pan. Way back when I was on the police force, we worked every extra job we could. I wasn't allowed to drive a cab or tend bar to protect myself from getting involved with people or situations that would put me at risk.

Nick put a lot of money into the place and hired a friend to manage it for him. He was able to get a liquor license for the building, which was a former movie theater, because he planned to serve food rather than alcohol as the primary component. But that didn't happen.

Initially, I didn't realize how rough a place the Five-Six had become. The lounge attracted a crowd that caused numerous problems after bar close, including public urination, littering, fighting, and noise. Word was that many of the bar's patrons came up from Chicago, Racine, and Milwaukee.

The situation became a real distraction for Nick, and it got major play in the local media. The race issue came up when the lounge's liquor license was pulled, while some other bars with similar histories of problems, but owned by white proprietors, were allowed to keep theirs. Then the mayor got involved and requested that the city council reconsider. Nick got his liquor license back after meeting with the police and neighborhood people and coming to some resolutions regarding the after-bar issues, but that wasn't the end of the situation.

After a couple years of responding to complaints at the Five-Six, some members of the police force weren't big fans of Nick's. One day, he was about to cross the street in the middle of the block with two other men when an officer warned him not to because it would be a jaywalking offense. Nick crossed anyway, so the officer wrote him a ticket. The guys with him weren't cited, but Nick was. That incident exploded onto the local media. It became a water-cooler topic of conversation and it did nothing to minimize the accusations of race playing a role in how the city was dealing with Nick and the Five-Six.

The lounge continued to find its way onto the police blotter on a regular basis. Things came to a head after our final game of the 2006 season, a New Year's Eve win over the Super Bowl-bound Chicago Bears. We got out of downtown Chicago as fast as possible because they were expecting about half a million people for fireworks near the stadium. There was no traffic on the freeways going out to O'Hare, and we got through airport security and onto our chartered plane quickly. We landed in Green Bay at 1:30 in the morning, about an hour earlier than expected, and a number of players headed straight downtown to the Five-Six.

Back in the 1960s, when Sandy and I were in our twenties and the Packers were winning, the players would come into the bars and everyone was awed by them. The bar owners would let them run the bar, and every woman who wasn't tied down was over by them. I'm sure it was the same this New Year's Eve, so there was potential for problems right there.

At that time of night, there were people with a lot of drinks already in them. The players got there around 2:00 a.m. and had been there a little over an hour when all hell broke loose. Nick was trying to get people who were smoking pot to leave, and things got unruly with 150–200 people still in the bar. A woman from Milwaukee accused one of the players of hitting her, and a brawl ensued outside. Nick got blind-sided and knocked out, and several other players joined the fight. Defensive lineman Corey Williams also got blind-sided, taking a bottle to the head and suffering a severely cut face.

I think Nick realized he was a victim of his own business. It wasn't long after this incident that he closed down the Five-Six for good and put the building up for sale the following October.

Long-distance Police Work

Many of the cases we deal with never get much media attention—which is just fine—but they nevertheless take a lot of effort on our end. An example is the jam that wide receiver/kick-return specialist Antonio Chatman found himself in during the 2005 off-season. There was a homicide out in Los Angeles, and we received a call from the police saying they wanted to talk to Chatman about it. His name entered the picture because someone got killed in a liquor store robbery, and in connection with the crime, the police picked up a guy who was related to Chatman.

I knew he wasn't involved, since it happened when he was in Green Bay, but he had since gone back home to LA. Was it possible he was harboring someone, or did he know a family member or friend who might have been involved?

I tried to help the LAPD locate Chatman, so I got on the phone in an effort to reach him or his agent. Finally, I was able to talk to Chatman, and he said, "Jerry, I don't know anything about this, and I don't want to talk to the police." As an African American man in Los Angeles, he didn't want to go down to the police station. There's not a lot of love for the establishment there, and if I were a black man, I don't know that I'd want to go talk to the police, either. It was easy for me to say he should, but I told him he had to. I wanted Antonio to know we were supporting him, but that he needed to do the right thing. After a few phone conversations, he agreed to go in. We finally set up a meeting where he could get the issue resolved, and we never heard another thing about it.

Another out-of-town police call came the Monday morning after Family Night during the 2004 exhibition season. It was from a sergeant at the Memphis PD regarding Cletidus Hunt, a defensive tackle who generally underachieved during his time here.

"We have a homicide here, with two black males murdered in a vehicle."

"Okay...?" I said.

"The vehicle belongs to Cletidus Hunt."

I knew Cletidus was here in Green Bay, so that was a good thing, but the players had that day off and he wasn't due back until practice that night. The police had no ID for the victims yet, just a vehicle serial number that led them to Cletidus. According to their records, he bought the 1990 Chevrolet Caprice Sedan in Jonesboro, Arkansas.

I couldn't reach Cletidus at our St. Norbert training camp, so I got his position coach, Jethro Franklin, involved. Jethro left a message for him, and he finally called at 12:30 that afternoon. He had already heard about the shootings from his sister, who's a police officer in Memphis. I told him to come in right away.

Cletidus said he'd bought the car in May and wanted to fix it up, so he left it at a small business that does body and cosmetic work. It turns out one of the victims was an owner of that business, and they'd been driving Hunt's car. I was on pins and needles for about eight hours trying to deal with this thing. I was glad I could help out law enforcement, and they thanked me because our information helped ID one of the victims.

Money, Money, Money

In 2000, the Packers traded with Denver for defensive end David Bowens, a pass-rush specialist who had played for our defensive coordinator, Ed Donatell, when Ed was an assistant coach there. Bowens had some baggage, and Broncos Coach Mike Shanahan had finally had enough of him.

Bowens was one of the nicest guys I've dealt with, but it took a lot of work by me and patience from the Packers to save him from himself. He was like a child: we didn't know what to do with him because he kept doing the same things wrong all the time.

Bowens would spend money like it was going out of style. He'd go out and buy hundred-dollar champagne and then hire a limo to take him home because he didn't want to drink and drive—and both checks would bounce. Finally, he let us help him manage his finances. You can't write a bunch of paper and get away with it. The law calls it uttering, and it can send you to jail. I'm sure David was unhappy that we had to do some things to get his spending under control.

The players normally get paid per game, but Andrew Brandt and I, along with a financial advisor we got for Bowens, changed things so he was paid a weekly salary for fifty-two weeks. We took money out of his game checks, and I'd work with vendors to get money set aside whenever he got paid for a personal appearance. I put so much time into dealing with him. The financial person even tried to train him in how to deal with his money. Bowens had poor judgment, and everything he bought had to be the best.

I really liked David, and always told him that if we could ever get him to the top, he'd make the big money. You see things like this all the time when teams take on projects, players you have to rub and rub to get them to shine, and then they become free agents and go sign somewhere else. Bowens ended up signing a big contract with Miami and became a starter. I'm so proud of him, and I hope his financial problems are behind him.

Up in Smoke

Aaron Brooks was one of a string of quality backup quarterbacks who went through the organization and later became starters elsewhere in the NFL. Brooks was drafted in the fourth round in 1999, but never got to play outside of the exhibition season because of Brett Favre's durability.

In the summer before his second year, Brooks, along with linebackers Jude Waddy and Kivuusama Mays, was sitting in a car in a westside park when a young officer approached and noticed smoke that had a telltale odor coming out of the vehicle. Rather than hauling them downtown, the officer called me to take care of it, and made sure I knew these players could get in trouble. I ended up telling Coach Sherman about it, and he was not happy.

I'm sure officers very often see behavior like this in public. It was kind that he did what he had to do without getting the players into the court system. Back in the 1970s, if somebody smoked a joint it was a big deal, but it's looked at differently now.

Brooks went on to make a lot of money as an NFL starting quarterback, first with New Orleans and then with the Oakland Raiders. This is the type of incident that could easily have surfaced. I don't know how far it might've gone, but it would've been a violation of the NFL substance-abuse policy if they'd been found guilty of possession.

A Piece of Work

Chuck Cecil, the Packers' hard-hitting safety from 1988–92, landed in jail one night after messing with the wrong people on Broadway. To compound matters, he became belligerent with the police. The night-shift captain called me at home about 6:00 a.m. to let me know Cecil had been arrested. The cops had a tough time with him because he was so unruly, and now he needed $1,500 cash for bail. I try telling the players, "Whatever you do, don't start fighting with the police unless you're fighting for your life. Don't let things escalate into big problems, even if you're right."

I called Mike Reinfeldt, our chief contract negotiator, to see if we could get some bail money and get Cecil out before he appeared in municipal court. That way we could keep him off the jail list that media people pick up on their morning rounds. It's a good thing we were successful, because Cecil was a piece of work. The incident occurred at a restaurant on Broadway, and involved some people who knew a thing or two about fighting. Cecil was bleeding, smelled of alcohol, and was still drunk, so we got him into a shower and had him sit in the sauna at Lambeau for a while.

Chuck's one of my favorite guys, and when we get together we still laugh and talk about that incident. I always respected him as a football player because of the way he played the game. He wasn't more than 180 pounds, but he hit hard and always seemed to have that bridge of his nose bleeding. Chuck now coaches the defensive backs for the Tennessee Titans, where Mike Reinfeldt is general manager. It's a small world.

You've Got to Be Kidding

Some of the things players do will just make you shake your head in amazement. LaShon Johnson and Travis Jervey were running backs on the 1995 team. They got into trouble for having two tiger cubs in their duplex in suburban Bellevue. It was in a rural area, but I had to tell them, "Guys, you can't do this!"

Wayne Simmons, a linebacker who was here from 1993–97, had a lot of baggage when we drafted him out of Clemson in the first round. I wasn't here to evaluate his football ability; my job was to keep his distractions to a minimum. I knew he didn't treat women well, especially Caucasian women. Wayne wasn't a popular guy; he even got into a locker-room fight with Reggie White. I don't know if Reggie ever got into a fight with anyone else. Still, I found a lot of good in Wayne. His nickname for me was "The Warden," and I got a kick out of that.

Early in his career, we had an incident in which two sisters came to the front desk and wanted to talk to somebody about a problem they had with a player. I met with them, and they told me they were in a bar when Wayne grabbed one of them on the butt, squeezing her the way you'd grip a bowling ball. Being a policeman, I knew this was a third- or fourth-degree sexual assault. I wanted to treat these young woman with the respect they deserved and was trying to be a good listener and get the facts from them. One sister was taking care of the other, and the victim didn't want to talk about it. They hadn't gone to the police yet—and didn't want to—so I hoped we could take care of the situation ourselves, knowing it was a serious matter and could be a huge story.

I left the two ladies in my office and went to see Coach Holmgren, explaining that we had a possible sexual assault on our hands that could result in jail time. "Coach, I think if these ladies get an apology, this thing might end right here. I don't know for sure, but we might be able to save this if you'll come in with me."

Coach was really impressive. He came back to my office and told the sisters that he'd deal with Wayne. We got a letter of apology out, and fortunately the issue never went any further. The Packers didn't have an attorney on staff at the time—we now have two.

Wayne went on to be a good player for us, and when he was on his A-game he could play as well as anyone. I remember him for his big hit that caused a fumble early in the 1995 divisional playoff win at San Francisco. Our whole sideline jumped up in the air on that hit, and Craig Newsome picked up the loose ball and took it in for a touchdown.

I later found out that Wayne had someone who acted as a kind of guardian and helped him as he went through college. I respected him, and he would call me once in a while to check on Wayne and tell me about another side of Wayne Simmons. Wayne and I had a good relationship. He could make me laugh, but boy, he could be a tough person. He was the type of guy who could easily have gotten in trouble with the law, especially if he'd been drinking. Sadly, Wayne died in a car accident in 2002 while driving too fast.

Certainly, some people I didn't particularly care for came through the organization, but I found a way to be objective in dealing with them. I'm amazed when I hear about some of the things they do—players and coaches alike. It's not that they're bad people; some of it's just irresponsibility. Sometimes, the higher the profile of the player, the more attention I had to give them. Thankfully, there never was a situation in which I had to help out someone I really didn't like.

In a security role, you've got to be a good listener and ask your questions objectively and in a supportive way. It's vital to be there for the player and to safeguard the Packers organization at the same time. In my position, I try to find out what the problem is and get the person some help. My goal is to protect both the individual and our organization.

Chapter 17
New Faces, New Names, New Problems

THOUSANDS OF PLAYERS have worn the green and gold during the five decades of my association with the Packers. Some stay in Green Bay for a day, and some stay for the rest of their lives. I could sense a trend toward more players staying in the area during the off-season right after Ron Wolf arrived. He put in a nice gym to make sure we had topflight workout facilities available year-round, and more guys started to buy second homes or condos in the Green Bay area.

The money players make today—especially if they've got three or four years' experience—allows them to make those types of investments and become more a part of the community. And when they come up here for off-season camps or during the season, they've got their own places to call home. The competition is so fierce for every position that players have to take care of themselves year-round, and teams have added more programs and minicamps to maintain contact with them during the off-season.

A lot of guys still try to find off-season jobs here to get a head start on their post-football careers, even though, unlike the old days, they might not need to financially. If guys have an education in a particular area, the Packers find companies that would be willing to hire them on a part-time basis as a steppingstone toward post-NFL "real" life. A lot of guys volunteer their time for various causes as well. Running back Tony Fisher (2002–05), for example, was a high school track coach in the spring and got into a job in finance.

It's nice to see some of the players who've stayed in the area because they want to or because they've become part of the Packers' coaching staff. Running back Harry Sydney (1992) owns a nonprofit male mentoring business called My Brother's Keeper; Linebacker Bryce Paup (1990–94) moved back here after finishing his NFL career in Minnesota and is a high school football coach; linebacker Brian Noble (1985–93) co-owns the Green Bay Blizzard arena football team, and there are many others.

Center James Campen (1989–93) and running back Edgar Bennett (1992–96) are enjoying a lot of success as assistants on Mike McCarthy's coaching staff. You have to give Coach Sherman credit for giving some of these former players a chance to get back into the game. I got to know "Campy" well when I was a policeman in the early '90s and he was the Packers' starting center. Edgar, or EB, has always been one of the best-liked people in this organization and is in the Packers Hall of Fame. He married a woman from Green Bay and they have two children.

Assistant coaches work hard for very little recognition. I think safety LeRoy Butler (1990–2001) could've had a chance to be a coach, too. He's a good teacher, but it's hard for a lot of players to want to put in those kinds of hours.

Jerry Kramer (1958–68) was a guard who blocked for Bart Starr during the glory years of the '60s and has been a fan of his quarterback ever since. The Packers were so powerful at that time—many think the 1962 team was the best—that they didn't have to throw many deep passes. The game plan was to run the ball and overpower people, and keep the defense honest by throwing just a few passes. Jerry said the linemen would get mad at Bart because he refused to throw the ball away and they hated to see him get hit.

Jerry told me he learned early in their careers how tough a player Bart was. When they played the Bears, someone busted Bart in the face and split his lip wide-open, and then taunted him a little, too.

Bart said, "This (bleeping) game isn't over with yet."

"That's when we knew how tough he was," Jerry said. "Bart said, 'Get back in the huddle; we've got a play to call.' We knew this was one tough SOB we had as a quarterback, and that's when we knew he was our leader."

The quarterbacks called their own plays then, and Bart stayed in the game even though blood was squirting out of his face and he'd require stitches afterward. You don't hear Bart tell that story, but Jerry tells it.

Jerry was always very articulate and detail-oriented, and has written several books about his experiences in Green Bay and with Coach Lombardi. We all change with age, but back in the day, Jerry was a tough guy and played the game that way. He was one of the best guards the Packers ever had. It's a shame he's not in the Pro Football Hall of Fame.

Fuzzy Thurston (1959–67), another guard during the glory years, was very outgoing and very likable. He had a lot more people skills than most players and was a natural in the entertainment business. He became the proprietor of restaurants and taverns in town when his playing career ended, and he continues to be a diehard Packer fan. He's always willing to share stories with fans about his playing days, both the good and the bad.

Jim Carter (1970–75, 77–78) had the unenviable task of following Ray Nitschke as the Packers' middle linebacker. That was as difficult to accomplish as succeeding Vince Lombardi as head coach or Bart Starr as quarterback. Carter wasn't a bad player, but he never had a chance—he just couldn't do right by the fans. Off the field, Carter was a wild, crazy guy who was a really likable person. He was a personal friend of the Noels, and was one of the players Bob would invite to a party he held at his cottage every year. Carter became very successful with car dealerships after his football career.

Wide receiver James Lofton (1978–86) had a great following with his classy family from California. Bart Starr was head coach during part of Lofton's playing days in Green Bay, and the two became very close. When you have tremendous athletes like Lofton or Brett Favre in their prime, that's where the team gets its confidence. You've got to have a go-to guy like that who brings an ability to make plays. Lofton left the Packers in disgrace after a sexual-assault scandal. He went on to play for several other teams, including three Super Bowls with the Buffalo Bills. He was inducted into the Pro Football Hall of Fame in 2003 and is an assistant coach with the Oakland Raiders.

My first full-time season with the Packers was 1992, the same year Ron Wolf made Terrell Buckley (1992–94) the Packers' first-round draft choice. T-Buck, as he called himself, caused fits for the Packers. He went to Florida State along with Edgar Bennett, who was taken in the fourth round that year, and LeRoy Butler, who was drafted two years earlier.

Players can take a real financial beating around jewelry, and T-Buck loved his bling. It's nothing for some of these guys to spend $25,000 to $50,000 on a piece of jewelry, but if you don't have a reputable dealer, you can't be sure what you're getting. T-Buck found that out the hard way when he bought something in Milwaukee that turned out to be a fake. Green Bay vendors would never risk their business doing something like that because word would get out so fast.

T-Buck lived in Suamico, about fifteen minutes north of the stadium. He was late for a meeting one day and called in claiming car trouble. The following week, the same thing happened. Coach Holmgren grabbed me and asked if I knew where Buckley lived. He said, "Go over to his house, pick him up and bring him in." I drove up to Suamico and knocked on Buckley's door. When he answered, all I said was "I don't want to hear it, and neither does Coach. Let's go."

I didn't know much about Buckley's personal life, but he didn't cause me any problems. He hung out with the other Florida State guys, and I'd see them together on Saturdays watching college games on TV. I did a few little things behind the scenes for him, which was better than having to run damage control. Despite his immaturity, T-Buck was an amiable guy. I think I liked him because he was a little guy like me. He had great ability and anticipation — almost Deion Sanders talent — but the size discrepancy was too much. Michael Irvin, the great Cowboys receiver, just ate him up. There were times T-Buck probably shouldn't have been on the field; in fact defensive-backs coach Dick Jauron wanted to start someone else. Ron Wolf had drafted Buckley and wanted him on the field, and Dick wasn't real happy about having to play him.

T-Buck had a lot of confidence in his abilities and wasn't shy about saying how good he was, even comparing himself to Jim Thorpe, who was considered one of the greatest athletes of the twentieth century. After all the talk during his contract holdout following the draft, Buckley made Ron look very smart in his first game as a Packer by intercepting a pass and taking it back for a touchdown. Unfortunately, that was one of the few big plays he made during his three seasons in Green Bay.

Defensive end Reggie White (1993–98) was a very special person, and not just in his football ability. He brought a lot to the table in many ways. He was a leader and really had a way with people. Reggie's sudden death the day after Christmas 2004 left a hole in the hearts of everyone in the Packers organization as well as the rest of the NFL.

It was big news when Ron Wolf and Mike Holmgren persuaded Reggie to sign with the Packers as the first big-name player to switch teams in the new unrestricted free-agency era following the 1992 season. Things were happening fast for the Packers at that time. The team went 9-7 and just missed the playoffs in Holmgren's first season. Brett Favre had taken over for the injured Don Majkowski at QB, and things were really starting to come together. We lost the last game of the season at Minnesota, and it was obvious we didn't have "soldiers" on defense to compete with the best teams.

Reggie White's courtship by teams around the league was quite an event. Every day there was a story in the paper about Reggie visiting various teams and cities and receiving great gifts, like a fur coat, and we wondered what Green Bay would have to offer. Mark Schiefelbein and I were out running together when the story began to break that the Packers were going to make a pitch. If Reggie was interested in coming here, our front office was determined to find a way to get it done financially.

Reggie and his agent, Jimmy Sexton, flew in about six in the evening, and I was part of a group that picked them up in a Cadillac rented by Ron Wolf. We met them in a non-public part of the airport where we were able to keep the media away. It was very exciting.

In the end, the deciding factor behind Reggie's decision to join the Packers was the presence of Brett Favre. The Packers had beaten the Eagles 27-24 in Milwaukee during the 1992 season, and Reggie had put a hard lick on Brett during the game. He saw that young man get back up and play the rest of the game. No one saw the pain Brett was in until the drive home. It was the first of six victories in a row for Brett and the Packers, and that spoke volumes to Reggie.

I didn't analyze the team position by position, but I knew how much the possibility of getting Reggie to Green Bay meant to the people here. Now, with a young quarterback in Brett, and Reggie to lead the defense, everyone's spirits were up. We'd been through twenty-nine years since the Packers' last championship, and it always seemed like the season was over for us by Christmas. That was about to change.

The four-year contract Reggie signed for $17 million, including a $4.5 million signing bonus, was huge for that time. He brought great credentials with him, starting back in the USFL and then with the Eagles. We all knew how good a player he was, but we didn't yet know Reggie as a person. You don't really know him until you start spending some time with him.

Reggie was something of a motorcycle guy, and he used to call me "Dirty Jerry" after Clint Eastwood's character Dirty Harry. When he moved up to Green Bay, he brought his beautiful black Harley-Davidson with him. The bike only had about 350 miles on it, but Reggie knew how to ride it. You don't see a lot of black men on Harleys, but Reggie was even interested in becoming the first African American to get a Harley-Davidson dealership.

The Packers played an exhibition game in Japan in 1998, Reggie's last year here, and the prize for the game's most valuable player was a new motorcycle. Reggie wanted that bike, but he wasn't named the MVP. The following spring, Reggie decided he wanted to buy that kind of motorcycle, so we went over to McCoy's in Green Bay and he bought a brand-new bike.

He said, "Jerry, I can't bring it home. Sara won't like this." So we ended up storing the bike in my garage, and Reggie and I did a little riding together.

When Reggie's home church, the Inner City Church in Knoxville, Tennessee, was destroyed in an arson fire in 1996, he asked for my help in connecting with the FBI. He wanted to meet with Wisconsin agents, because he had no confidence in the law enforcement of the South.

"You don't know what it is to be a black man in the South," he said. "Jerry, I trust you and the FBI up here, but I don't trust them down there."

We set up a meeting with the Wisconsin-based FBI agents, especially since there was speculation that Reggie's co-minister might have been involved in setting the fire. Reggie had trusted the people there to run the church.

A controversy arose later when $250,000 was donated—a lot of it coming from Packer fans—to rebuild the church, but it never happened and the money disappeared. The arsonists were never found, but four years later a key church official was found guilty of cocaine trafficking and gun charges. He was never able to give a full accounting of what happened to the more than $900,000 in donations and insurance money that came in after the fire.

The day before losing to the Eagles in Philadelphia during Reggie's second season here, a number of kids came over to the hotel for a program Reggie had arranged. I helped escort some of them up to the floor so Reggie could meet and talk with them. Reggie was respected not just because of his football ability, but because of the person he was. It was impressive how he was able to handle those kids. He would correct them on how they were dressed or the way they were speaking, and he signed whatever they'd brought for him to sign. A number of kids went through that line, and I couldn't help thinking *this isn't right—we're not supposed to be doing this type of thing in the hotel.* Yet I was so impressed with Reggie that day.

Football teams seem to grow together during the course of a season or two. Chemistry often develops between players at certain positions, but to get the whole team's chemistry going in the right direction takes time and effort. It seems to grow stronger on the road when you're together all the time, eating meals and playing in a hostile environment. I could see this football team getting stronger with the players Ron was adding, putting the pieces of the puzzle in place to compete for the Super Bowl. Being a lifelong football fan, I was optimistic we were going to win every game. It was so much fun in those years to see the turnaround taking place. It takes a good organization with good coaches and great players like Reggie to get to the top.

What Reggie brought to the crowd was very special. Midway through his first season here, the Packers beat the Broncos and John Elway 30-27 in an exciting game at Lambeau Field. Reggie sacked John on back-to-back plays to end the game, and people didn't want to leave afterward. They just waited to see Reggie walk around the stadium and slap hands.

Reggie's passing was the end of a very difficult time for the Packers' family. In addition to Brett's family losses and Deanna's cancer diagnosis, we also lost Mark Hatley, our vice president for football operations, to a heart attack. A lot of people didn't know Mark, but I knew him well. He was a delightful person. We also lost long-time scout Red Cochran to complications from hip surgery. Bob Harlan fought off skin cancer, Nick Barnett lost his father after a long struggle with cancer, and I was still dealing with my own cancer issues.

Reggie's death really affected us. It was such a shock. The final regular-season game was the next weekend in Chicago. Red Batty, our equipment manager, set up a locker in Reggie's honor, complete with pads, jersey, everything. The team wanted to go out and win that game for Reggie. The Packers won 31-14 to finish 10-6 and qualify for the playoffs. I'm still surprised we didn't win more championships when Reggie White was a Green Bay Packer.

I got to know Bernardo Harris (1996–2001) during minicamp prior to his first season here. After getting off to a slow start Bernardo became a decent linebacker for the Packers for seven seasons. He wasn't drafted out of college, and signed as a free agent with Kansas City for his rookie season. He didn't make the team with the Chiefs, and he was nervous about making the roster with the Packers. He was married in college and now had a family to support.

Just before training camp got started that July, I happened to go into the training room and see Bernardo sitting on a bench with tears in his eyes. I asked him what was wrong.

"Jerry, they're going to cut me," he said. "I took something that I shouldn't have."

Bernardo had taken home some clothes that belonged to the team, sweatpants, or whatever. To me it was a very small item, and certainly something that lots of players had taken as souvenirs over the years. Red Batty is a very compassionate guy, but he must've said something to Bernardo about being fed up with players stealing stuff. I understood that the big picture wasn't that serious, but Red told Bernardo he was going to report the incident to Coach Holmgren, and that Coach wouldn't put up with it.

I went in and talked to Red, then told Bernardo to go to go in and apologize and return the gear or offer to pay for it. This meant the world to Bernardo, because he was facing a world in which he was worried about raising a family. Sometimes you don't see the big guys cry, but he was so fearful that Coach Holmgren would cut him. Bernardo went on to have a fine career, and eventually got a contract for over $1 million to play for the Baltimore Ravens after leaving the Packers. I was really happy for him.

Najeh Davenport (2002–05) was one of my all-time favorites. The Packers drafted him in the second round in 2002, and he proved to be an able ball carrier for three seasons. He then went on to play two seasons with the Pittsburgh Steelers until they released him in the summer of 2008. The players know I won't take care of traffic tickets for them, but near the end of his rookie season Najeh got a speeding ticket that I tried to help with.

I preach to these guys all the time about having respect for the law and taking the ticket even if they don't agree with it. Najeh had driven down to Sheboygan (about an hour south of Green Bay) to buy a leather jacket, and on the way back he was clocked doing 102 mph in a 65 zone. He claimed he thought the squad car was a fan trying to follow him.

Prior to his court appearance, Doug and I made some calls trying to justify Najeh's actions, explaining that he thought he was being followed. I was trying to keep a straight face, because I knew this was just a lame excuse. I figured the Sheboygan County people were going to tell me to jump in the lake, but instead they suggested that Najeh make an appearance and see what happened. Najeh figured he had nothing to lose and planned to go.

"You're kidding," I said. "They might throw you in jail. Don't drive down there if you're not valid to drive. Have somebody take you. You're not going to be disguised too much in Sheboygan."

Of course I knew they wouldn't throw him in jail, but I didn't think it was a good idea for him to go there. When we didn't hear anything from him, I figured he'd paid the fine. On the day of his court date, he called our office from the reception area at the Sheboygan County Courthouse. He told our receptionist to page Doug or me because he was in jail. He finally got through to Doug, and told him he'd been jailed.

Najeh said he had to hang up because they were taking him to a cell. Doug and I were sweating bullets, running around wondering what we could do. We swallowed Najeh's story hook, line, and sinker. Finally, he came clean and we could breathe a sigh of relief.

"I did really well," he told us. "The judge asked me if I was the Najeh Davenport that plays for the Packers, and I said, 'Yes, I am.' It cost me $500 and I got the points taken off."

Najeh is just a great guy. I don't know how responsible he is, but he's a great guy.

Donald Driver (1999–present) was the 213th selection of the 1999 draft when Ron Wolf chose him in the seventh round out of Alcorn State. I remember seeing him for the first time in the Don Hutson Center along with another receiver named Zola Davis, who went on to play one season in Cleveland. I got to like both of these guys because they were very humble. They would work and work at catching passes.

One of the reasons I liked "Drive" was because he was a track guy. He qualified for the US Olympic Trials in 1996 in the high jump with a leap of seven feet six and a half inches, and was ranked number one in the nation that year. He was a fantastic college athlete, winning conference track titles in the long jump, triple jump, and decathlon. Funny thing was he never won the conference high-jump title. You could tell right away that he had raw ability and tremendous speed.

He was built like Lofton—lean and long-legged, and with no body fat on him. He was one of those guys you could pull for.

It was great to see Brett call his number for the play that broke Dan Marino's all-time passing yardage record in a win over the St. Louis Rams on December 16, 2007. Drive's sure hands and bright smile had been on the receiving end of a lot of Brett's passes over their careers, and he was the object of many fireman's carries by Brett after scoring touchdowns.

Changing Ethnicity

When I worked as a policeman in the '60s, only one African American guy who wasn't a Packer was living in the whole city. Yorkie is what people called him, and he did maintenance jobs at a number of places. That poor man got killed in a hit-and-run while crossing Main Street. I don't know if that case was ever solved. How we've changed in the forty years since—Green Bay has become multicultural and ethnically diverse, especially with immigrants from Mexico and Southeast Asia. By the 1970s, more African Americans started getting transferred to Green Bay for work. Procter & Gamble had two big paper mills in town and was committed to affirmative-action recruiting. Amazingly, the Green Bay Police Department has never had an African American on the force.

The ethnic makeup of the Green Bay area lagged behind that of the Packers. We started hiring African American players in the 1950s, then more in the '60s, especially at the skill positions. There were certainly prejudices in town, just from the fact that if a person was African American, he almost certainly were part of the football team. People in the stores would see guys and immediately know they were players, especially if they were big. African Americans who weren't players had to put up with people asking them if they were. It wasn't a racial thing; there were just no African American people in our community until relatively recently.

Defensive tackle Bob Brown (1966–73) was an African American player who was quite a cook and even worked as a chef for a place on Washington Street. He used to make raccoon stew, and it was really good. Bars offered things like that back in those days. Big Bob told me one time that someone had stolen his car from the stadium parking lot, and he was upset because in the trunk there were two raccoons that he was going to cook up that night. We found his car later that afternoon and the raccoons were still in the trunk. I think Bob was even happier about that than about getting the car back.

We've never had a player come in and complain he was being mistreated by the team because of his race, but every once in a while we'll hear about some unfortunate situations players encounter. In the early 1990s, some contractors were working on the back side of the old administration building when linebacker Burnell Dent (1986–1992) overheard a conversation that bothered him so much that he came and told me about it. The workers were talking about another African American player's body, and used the N-word. I went out and talked to the foreman, and he took those guys right off the job. I got a lot of respect from the African American players for dealing with that situation, though that wasn't my motivation.

Racial profiling doesn't happen often, but it's unpleasant when it does. Earl Dotson was a big, quiet guy from Texas who rode a motorcycle during his time here as an offensive tackle (1993–2002). His younger brother and his brother's girlfriend went to a store in town to return some items for Earl and buy some movies. One of the employees started following them around. It was totally uncalled-for. Earl was so upset he called me at home. I contacted the store manager and got full cooperation from him. He said one of his employees used poor judgment, and the ended up giving the couple an apology along with their movies.

Probably the worst example of racial profiling happened to defensive lineman Cletidus Hunt (1999–2004). Cletidus was coming up to attend a minicamp in his gold Cadillac when he was stopped for speeding a few counties south of us by a state patrol officer. Cletidus claimed he wasn't speeding, and it got really ugly. The officer treated him like he was a dangerous person, even putting Cletidus on the ground and drawing his gun, then searching the car. We followed up with the district captain and made him aware of his officer's actions. If you've got a policeman who's a racist, you've got a problem—a big problem. We got a lawyer involved and eventually got the situation resolved.

Green Bay will always be a small town without a lot of the glamour and nightlife that some players want. But our Midwestern values and the friendliness of the people make it a nice place to live, and over the years, many players have found it a great place to raise a family after their playing careers were over.

Chapter 18
The Leaders of the Pack

I'VE WORKED WITH TEN different head coaches during my association with the Packers. As you'd expect, some have been more enjoyable than others. While the team's success depended in part on how fulfilling it was to work with each coach, that wasn't the only factor. Some of them were just plain nicer guys than others were, which made working for them more of an honor than a chore. Here are my thoughts, listed chronologically, about several coaches who aren't covered elsewhere in the book.

Dan Devine (1971–1974)

Dan Devine was head coach of the successful University of Missouri program when the Packers hired him to replace Phil Bengtson. The Packers were a team in decline as the great players of the 1960s aged or retired, and it was hoped that Devine could resurrect the team's fortunes. Bart Starr was in his final year as a part-time player in 1971, and the team struggled to a 4-8-2 record. The first game of the year was played in a driving rainstorm at Lambeau Field, and Devine suffered a severely broken leg on the sideline. The Packers lost to the New York Giants 42-40 that day, won their next two games, then managed only two more wins the rest of the season. At least they both came against the Bears.

I got along very well with Devine, who was an interesting man. He gave me my first opportunity to travel with the team. I really respected him for that, since I was just a policeman. I got the chance to go to Detroit in week 7 of the 1974 season for the last game the Packers would play in Tiger Stadium. We got lost going through the baseball dugouts to get to the field.

Detroit can be a tough city, especially compared with Green Bay, but we stayed in an old hotel called the Pontchartrain and I was awed by the place. Tom Miller was the Packers' travel coordinator, and he told me I could have my own room. I was excited about the whole weekend, going on an airplane with the team, and seeing Detroit for the first time. I ended up rooming with Dad Braisher, the equipment manager.

On the top floor of the hotel there was a bar from which you could see the Detroit River and Joe Louis Arena. I spent the evening before the game with two media guys, Cliff Christl of the *Green Bay Press-Gazette* and Mike McKenna of WBAY-TV. We went out to a few bars and didn't get in until very late. We didn't do anything wrong, but "Dad" was getting up at 3:00 a.m. morning for the noon game just as I was coming in. I was on pins and needles because I was afraid he was upset, but thankfully Dan was a good guy.

The players had the chance to wear white shoes for that game, but we didn't bring any with us. so the day before the game, one of my main jobs was to help the equipment guys paint the players' shoes white. The Lions' equipment people assigned to assist with the visiting locker room helped out. too. Nowadays, you wouldn't even think of doing such a thing; you could have shoes for an entire team shipped overnight if anything like that was needed.

Devine had a lot of personality, which I could see even in my part-time equipment position. I started working a lot of hours for the Packers about then, and we had a lot of transportation challenges because Devine was in a wheelchair. We did a lot of little things to move him around since his broken leg so limited what he was able to do. I got fairly close to him because I was helping the man do his job.

Devine was a very hands-on person who had to have his little comforts. Either Bob Noel, his brother, Jack, or I would make sure Dad got his sandwich, ice cream, or malt after practice. Jackie would come into the building and get that sandwich ready, and one of us would go over to Dean's Ice Cream to get the ice cream or malt.

Devine could be paranoid, too. Coaches didn't share game tapes like they do today, so they used a lot more human resources to scout opponents. All the coaches were concerned about spies at practice, and there was no full-time security person for the Packers until Al Stevens was hired in 1982. When I worked the practices, I was the default security guy and had to take care of those issues along with my equipment responsibilities. One day, some guys were working on the roof of the Brown County Arena, and Coach was concerned about them being spies. They were probably 200 yards away and not on Packers property, so there was nothing I could do.

The team really took off in Devine's second season, 1972. In what would prove to be the Packers' only playoff appearance until the 1982 strike season, the team won six of its last seven games to finish the season 10-4 and win the NFC Central. Scott Hunter was the quarterback, though the ground game of John Brockington and MacArthur Lane was the primary offensive weapon.

The Packers had a Christmas Eve playoff game in Washington against the Redskins, and the weather in Green Bay made it very difficult for the team to prepare. This was well before the Packers had an indoor practice facility. We had all kinds of snow that year; we got it early, and we got a lot of it. We had to plow the Oneida Street field just so the team could practice, and there were huge snow banks all around it. The cold wasn't as much of a problem as the amount of there was.

The Packers lost that game 16-3 and immediately retreated back into mediocrity the following season. This was Devine's first and only NFL job (he would go on to coach at Notre Dame after leaving the Green Bay), and a lot of the media viewed his record negatively. Dan had a good coaching staff that included a few guys from Michigan's Upper Peninsula.

There were also local connections with the players, highlighted by quarterback Jerry Tagge, who graduated from my former high school, Green Bay West, before starring at Nebraska. That was fun for me because I also knew his brother-in-law, Mike Mason, a policeman who was married to Tagge's sister. Mike's brother, Dave, a defensive back for Nebraska, had also played at West, and he and Tagge, along with Jerry Wied, an all-state player from Green Bay Premontre and my son-in-law's father, all attended Nebraska together.

The Packers drafted Tagge in the first round in 1972, and he started the last half of the 1973 and first half of the 1974 seasons. There was a lot of hype about him, but the expectations never panned out. He was a great athlete, but a lack of mobility probably hurt him. He finished those two seasons with just four touchdown passes against seventeen interceptions.

Devine then made a last-gasp trade to fix his quarterback problems, which would haunt the Packers for years to come. In 1974, as the Packers were struggling through their third season under his leadership, Devine traded the team's first-, second-, and third-round draft picks in the 1975 draft, along with the first- and third-round picks in the 1976 draft, for aging veteran John Hadl.

Hadl played out the rest of the 1974 season and all of the 1975 season, throwing just nine touchdowns against twenty-nine interceptions. That trade left the cupboard pretty bare for Devine's successor, Bart Starr, and it took the Packers years to recover.

Bart Starr (1975–1983)

Bart Starr might be the most popular player ever to put on a Packers jersey. He was the quarterback for the Packers' five championship teams of the 1960s and MVP of the first two Super Bowls. His number 15 is one of the five ever retired by the Packers, along with Tony Canadeo (3), Don Hutson (14), Ray Nitschke (66), and Reggie White (92) — all of whom are in the Hall of Fame. Bart has always been a gentleman, and he and his wife, Cherry, are wonderful ambassadors for the Green Bay Packers organization.

Bart was an overachiever as a player after being taken in the seventeenth round of the 1956 draft. He's a perfect example of how a player can come into a system like Vince Lombardi's and excel. Bart had a great ability to study the game and read defenses, and was always very disciplined.

I didn't know Bart well when he was a player, but he gave me respect as a policeman and I always heard good things about him and Cherry from my friends Al and Bernice Crispigna. The Crispignas owned Sammy's Pizza, which at the time was located across from the Orpheum Theater downtown. Al was one of the people who meant a lot to me in the '60s. When I worked downtown as a policeman, I always had a place to go in Sammy's. Al would ask about my family, and he went to more policemen's retirement parties than anyone. If Al thought Bart was a good man, then you can bet he was.

Upon retiring in 1971, Bart coached the team's quarterbacks under Dan Devine, then succeeded Devine as head coach. Everybody was really excited when Bart was hired. The general feeling was he was an outstanding leader and would bring that great success from the '60s with him. He was a vital cog in that championship run that the fans thought we couldn't miss when he became head coach. It put a lot of pressure on him.

Bart's honeymoon period with the fans and the media didn't last long, as the team went 4-10, 5-9, and 4-10 his first three seasons. Taking on the roles of both head coach and general manager was a huge responsibility, just as it is now. Once the wagon wheels start wobbling, the questions always start coming. No matter how tough things got, though, Bart's personal pride didn't waver and he took on every battle. It was a sign of the kind of person he was. I know Bart felt anger and disgust, but he never stopped treating people respectfully. Whether we were winning or not, he worked to maintain the image of the Green Bay Packers.

Family and friends meant everything to Bart, and I was in a position to really know his character and values. I had duties as a policeman for all the home games, but missed one in 1977 because of a kidney biopsy. I had to stay home for a few days to keep an eye on any possible bleeding. I was sitting in my living room a couple hours before the game when the phone rang. It was Bart, saying he hoped I was feeling well and that I'd be missed at the game. He said he hoped I'd be able to come back to work soon, because I was a part of the team.

What could I say to that? For someone just working part-time for the Packers, that was really something. I was so proud that he thought enough of me to make that call. I was here for the love of the game, and felt honored just to be part of the organization. When he was coach, Bart even bought Christmas presents for the staff, including me. From the City, my main employer, I got a Christmas card.

The Packers finally got their own indoor practice facility while Bart was coach. He was proud of that barn, and he wanted us to keep the carpet in there looking sharp. We had vacuums all over the place because Bart wanted us to keep it clean. I remember vacuuming the locker room, too, because Bart wanted everything looking sharp. Bart's dad, Ben, was a career military man, and Bart had grown up in a very structured environment. He told me he'd also picked up some of that tendency from legendary coach George Allen. All

I knew was that when Bart and the team would come down to the barn, the crew would have it spotless.

To this day, every time you see Coach Starr he's neat and his cars are always clean inside and out. He takes pride in his appearance, and that carries over to how people see him. That's just part of Bart's character.

Bart's only winning season was at 8-7-1, in 1978, but that was a disappointment after getting off to a 6-1 start. There were some great players on those teams, but not enough of them. James Lofton was a gazelle at wide receiver, and John Jefferson had the softest hands of any receiver I've ever seen. "JJ" kept to himself off the field, but I was just awed by his abilities.

I was working practice one day when Bart got annoyed with a writer from Milwaukee. We'd kicked the media out of practice, but this guy would stand on top of his car to look over the canvas tarps that covered the fences. I had to get in his face a couple of times. He had a right to be there because he was on a city street, not on Packers property, but he was just trying to aggravate us. Bart's relationship with the media went downhill from there.

Bart was always the ultimate gentleman, even when things were rough. The situation with the public late in his coaching career was tough on me because I admired him so much. One of the things that hurt the most was a campaign to honk your horn while going past the practice field if you wanted Bart fired. Those horns would come right through the canvas, and would continue all through practice. I thought it was vicious. How could Bart even work through that?

We'd park his car inside the gates of the stadium on game days, and if we lost, we didn't know what the wrath of the fans would be. Sometimes they'd yell terrible things. I bet a lot of those fans look back now and wish they hadn't done some of the things they did. They got caught up in thinking the team had to get rid of him as coach. I'm not going to get into what was right for the Packers or not, as I was just a part-time equipment and security guy, but the whole situation was just so painful.

The last game of an 8-8 season in 1983 was a 23-21 loss at Chicago on a very cold Sunday. My routine was to come in the next day and clean or paint the players' shoes. "I think this is going to be a bad day around here," Bob Noel said when I arrived on Monday following my police shift. "I've got a bad feeling."

A while later, Bart called Bob upstairs, and twenty minutes later he returned to tell me Bart had been fired. I didn't know what to say. To make matters worse, the man who'd fired him was my cousin, team president Judge Robert Parins. I always wondered whether Bart knew that the judge was only a cousin of mine and not my dad. The judge and I would meet at family functions, and our relationship was good, but he was always very professional.

Was the judge right in firing Bart? As a football decision, maybe. I'm sure he felt he was doing the right thing. I just knew what this organization meant to Bart, and time has shown that he ranks among the top five people in the team's history.

We continued working after the news broke, and it wasn't long before Bob took a call: Coach Starr wanted to see me. The upstairs was foreign territory to me unless I had to carry something up there, like toilet paper. Bart had tears in his eyes. He just wanted to make sure I knew he'd been relieved of his duties. We didn't say much, but his professionalism was obvious. He just stood tall. There was no anger in his voice. He felt sorry that he had let the organization down and wasn't able to mold us into a winning team. It was a very emotional moment and I'll never forget it.

After the turmoil of his coaching career had subsided, Bart regained his status as one of the most revered players in Packers history. That's never more obvious than at Fan Fest every spring. The Packers began hosting this annual event in the Lambeau Field Atrium in March 2005. It's a two-day affair, and nearly 3,000 fans from around the world pay an admission fee to meet some of their favorite current and former players and coaches, hear them speak, and get autographs. Bart is one of the former stars who attends every year.

Fan Fest begins on a Friday, and that first year someone from Italy had already arrived on Wednesday morning. He bought so many things in the Packers Pro Shop that he had to go out and buy some more suitcases to bring it all back home. Bob Harlan even came downstairs to meet him.

The passion our fans have for the team is truly remarkable. Lots of people come to Fan Fest who've never attended a game here, and the atmosphere for the event's opening is really exciting. It's set up so fans know when certain people will be signing autographs or making appearances, with drawings held to get an autograph from a big star. People paid $200 for a ticket to get a Brett Favre autograph that first year. Brett was in town to do a Nike ad, and stayed through Saturday for Fan Fest.

We didn't really know how big a deal Fan Fest would turn out to be. We opened at 9:00 a.m. the first day, and people were already waiting outside to get in. I had the best job of anyone because I got to spend six hours with Bart. He's really something special, and not just because he was a great player. He's the class act of the National Football League. He won't even let us pick him up at the airport, choosing instead to get his own rental car.

Bart came into town on Thursday night and I picked him up at the hotel the next morning. He said, "Jerry, I want to go over to a nursing home. Could you take me there?" He wanted to stop at Grancare Nursing Home, which happened to be the same facility my father was in at the end of his life. We visited a ninety-eight-year-old woman who was Bart and Cherry's housekeeper when they lived in Allouez. She was a delightful woman, and Bart told me how good she was to them when they lived in town. She was a part of their lives and he never forgot her.

We drove to Lambeau Field afterward, where Bart had some time to relax with Bob Harlan and Mark Schiefelbein. Meanwhile, I was busy dealing with something that had come up a few hours earlier: Gary Knafelc's son had committed suicide. Gary was a wide receiver for the team from 1954–62, the longtime public address announcer, and a good friend of Bart's. Gary was down in Florida, and Bart was going to meet him the next day for a charity golf outing. We didn't tell Bart anything right away, because we didn't yet know the details.

Bart and Cherry had lost the younger of their two sons in tragic circumstances. Bret died of a drug overdose well after Bart's coaching career had ended. There had been allegations of Bret dealing and using drugs with players, but I never knew that to be true. Bob Noel would give my three daughters five dollars each to clean the players' lockers while the team was on the road. I'd be there to oversee the girls and help out, too. Obviously, we didn't violate anyone's rights, but still I was asked if I ever saw any drugs in the lockers. I could honestly tell Coach Starr I didn't see anything, and that was the end of it.

A little later that day, Bart attended an event in one of the restaurants on the atrium level for the VIP honorees and the Packers' board of directors. The restaurant wasn't open for business except for this group, which allowed them to sit around and chat in a relaxed setting. Lynn Dickey, Don Majkowski, and Jerry Kramer were some of the former players in the room.

Some of the fans had seen us go into the restaurant, and Bart asked me if we could do a quick autograph-signing session. We had time before his scheduled appearance, so I said, "Sure." I found a hostess table outside the restaurant and asked the twenty people waiting there to get in line. People had brought pictures with them that had been taken of Bart over the years, and presented them for him to autograph. Bart's very meticulous about autographs. Every time he signs an autograph, he takes his time so you can read his name. He doesn't just scribble down anything; he even stops to ask the people if blue or black ink would work better for them.

This autograph session wasn't in the plan for the day, just something extra Bart offered to do for the fans. The next thing we knew, we had a hundred people standing in line. Bart became concerned. I told him we'd have to curtail it because of his appearance commitment, but he didn't want to disappoint anyone. He told the people that if they'd make a donation to Rawhide Boys Ranch — Bart's favorite charity — and send the item they wanted autographed to his office in Birmingham, Alabama, he'd sign it and send it back to them. He even walked down the line to tell people that personally. He's just the ultimate professional, so respectful to people.

After a short break, Bart met with the media and then his formal autograph session began. His assignment was to do 150 autographs for people who'd won the raffle drawing for the opportunity. Additionally, people were able to take Bart's picture when it was their turn. Combined with the personalized autographs he gives, the session took considerable time.

A woman from New Jersey named Annette Wells was there and had a special picture of Bart she hoped to get signed. She wasn't in the drawing, however, and I felt bad for her because she had just missed the cutoff at the earlier impromptu session. I told her that maybe I could get her in afterward. Every time I turned around for the next couple of hours, she was there. The soft part of me then took over.

We had a private jet ready to fly Bart out, and it was snowing, so we wanted to get him on his way. There was a mob of people standing outside the elevator, and I grabbed Annette to join us for the ride so she could get her autograph. That made her whole trip. She called me later to say that someone in her family was sick with cancer, and she wanted to make a donation to my Cruise for Cancer in their honor.

While riding to the airport in Sandy's car, Bart said, "Jerry, this is wonderful. I just love coming back to Green Bay. It's always going to be part of my life. I tell Cherry that, and she says she just can't figure it out. But look at how beautiful the snow is."

We talked about his dad and a little about our country. Ben Starr was a historian and a very disciplined man. He always had a big cigar in his mouth, but he quit smoking just to prove he could. Ben was a regular in Green Bay during Bart's playing days. He was a member of the old Martha's Coffee Club that started in the '60s at a Broadway restaurant.

Bart's dad wasn't the only parent who made an impression on me over the years. Larry McCarren's parents came up from Illinois all the time during his playing days, and John Anderson's family came up from Waukesha. It isn't just parents of Packers who make the trip to Green Bay, either. Lambeau Field draws family members from the visiting teams as well, and the host team usually has an area where the immediate family of the players and coaches can meet after the game.

People go out of their way to see special players like Bart, even after their playing careers are long over. You can't believe the people who turn out for Fan Fest. Bart draws almost as much interest at Brett Favre, which is a tribute to Bart's personality and the fact that he comes back for these special events. Diehard fans will always remember the leaders of the team.

Forrest Gregg (1984–1987)

I worked part-time for the Packers during Forrest Gregg's tenure because I was consumed with police work and the Margaret Anderson murder case in particular. It's probably just as well—the Packers weren't a good team then, and the roster was filled with thugs.

Forrest was very supportive of his players. As maybe the best offensive tackle who ever played the game, he had a player's mentality, but he was a tyrant in his own way, and that was reflected in how he dealt with people.

Forrest had taken the Cincinnati Bengals to Super Bowl XVI following the 1982 season, where they lost 26-21 to the San Francisco 49ers. He went to Southern Methodist University after he left Green Bay to try to resurrect a program that the NCAA had given the "death penalty" for numerous rules violations.

I got off on a bad note with Forrest, but the main issue was that he just wasn't a pleasant person. I had been working for the Packers for years—doing a lot of gofer-type jobs—and he didn't even take the time to even meet me when he came onboard. Bob Noel relied on me and I was part of the organization. All I knew was that Coach Lombardi had said Forrest was the greatest offensive lineman who ever lived and was our new head coach.

The first thing I said to him was "Good morning, Coach. I'm Jerry Parins, and I've been helping out here for a long time."

He looked at me, and I asked him about a simple procedural thing, saying, "I take it for granted you'd like this checked, too?" I thought this was a positive conversation, but I should've been more careful, considering the way he looked at me.

"You don't take anything for granted," he growled back at me.

Whoa, was I set in my place! I'd been working here when Forrest was a player, but I don't know if he remembered me from that time or if he knew I was a policeman. That was my first impression of Forrest Gregg, and I never forgot it. I don't think our relationship ever got much better.

Ron Wolf, General Manager (1992–2001)

Ron Wolf wasn't a coach, but he was the first general manager I knew as a full-time member of the organization. Working under Ron was interesting. He made his own decisions and most of the time he was right. What you saw was what you got with Ron.

Ron's best trait was his ability to be the big man sitting on top of the football organization. He was the closest thing we had to Vince Lombardi as far as personality was concerned, though he had his soft spots, too. While he was tough and could easily fire a coach, he couldn't bring himself to fire a secretary.

Things really changed around here when Ron took over near the end of the 1991 season. He let Lindy Infante play out his final games, then immediately fired him, and hired Mike Holmgren from the 49ers' staff for 1992. Things also changed from a security standpoint, as Ron wanted to deal with issues internally if possible. I was used to that type of philosophy in my internal affairs role with the police department.

One year, Ron told me he wanted to get a pistol and asked if I could help. I hooked him up with the widow of a retired police officer, who still had the gun that the police department had issued her husband. Ron agreed to buy it for $500, and peeled off the hundreds from his money clip to have me pay for it.

I had learned to shoot with the old revolvers, so this 9-mm semiautomatic was different for me. I took Ron out to the sheriff's department shooting range and was amazed at how well he could shoot. He didn't want to have the gun at home, so I kept it under my control and just brought it out when he wanted to go shooting.

Ron's also the guy who got me involved in following NASCAR. He'd request a few extra game credentials and invite some NASCAR people to watch a game on our sidelines. Ron had his own network of people in that sport, which he followed closely. I had thought Ron was just a football guy, but he has a number of varied interests. His real love is history, and he's visited the battlefields of Europe.

Three years after Ron stepped down as general manager, he and his wife, Edie, had a situation with their older son, Jonathon, in which they asked for my help. Paul Craven, the manager of Southern Motors in Savannah, Georgia, had called Ron to report that Jonathon hadn't shown up for work in two days. Craven had gone to the two places Jonathon could have been, and he wasn't at either. Ron and Edie knew he'd gone to a college reunion in Williamsburg, Virginia, over the weekend, so now the question was whether he had returned.

Edie had spoken with Jonathon on Sunday afternoon, and he told her he'd be flying out of Newport News, Virginia on Delta Airlines. Privacy laws kept Delta from telling Edie whether or not her son had boarded the plane. They told her that only the police could get the information. I told Edie I would help, since she and Ron didn't know what else to do, and I could sense her anxiety building. Part of why they'd called me was because of my connections to the police department.

The first thing that flashed through my mind was what had happened with Bart, who had gone to Tampa to find his son and learned that Bret had died of a drug overdose. I hoped this wasn't going to be a similar situation.

I called Mr. Craven, telling him who I was and why I was inquiring. Ron Wolf was a very special person in the history of the Green Bay Packers, and I was trying to help him out. He said he didn't realize Ron was *that* Ron Wolf, and our conversation helped him get more comfortable talking to me.

"I'm not his mom or dad," I said. "Is there anything you could tell me that you wouldn't tell them? Does he have any problems that would indicate why he hasn't called?"

"No," he replied, "but I know he had a cyst on his back and was taking medication for it."

Edie had mentioned that, too, and it didn't appear to be anything major.

Jim Arts arrived from the Green Bay PD a little before 2:00. Jim, Doug, and I put our heads together about how we could handle this. Jim went back downtown to work on confirming that Jonathon was on the Delta flight. Doug called Tim Decker, who heads up the TSA operations at Austin Straubel in Green Bay and helps the Packers with their movements in the airport. Tim got on the horn to the Savannah airport to have their security department check for Jonathon's car. He also had the authority to request information from Delta.

At 4:15 he called back to say that had Jonathon never boarded the flight out of Newport News. Where to start looking next? I called Edie back to give her the update, which just raised their anxiety level that much more.

We found out a short time later that the Savannah security people had checked flights from Green Bay to Savannah instead of from Newport News to Savannah. Jim called back to report that Jonathon's flight had never left Newport News Sunday because of bad weather, and that the young man had left on an Atlantic Southeast flight on Monday instead. That was great news, because we now knew he'd gotten out of the Northeast.

I called Edie, and she said she had just received an e-mail from her son telling her he was okay. That episode taught all of us a lesson about the value of checking in, and I was very proud of the information we were able to get because of our good contacts. We were very happy that this story had a happy ending.

Ray Rhodes (1999)

After Mike Holmgren left the Packers to take the Seahawks job, there was a lot of pressure on the organization to hire an African American head coach. Race can be an issue in the NFL, but I think the media plays it up too much. Good players and good systems are what take you to the Super Bowl, not the color of anyone's skin.

Ray Rhodes and Sherman Lewis, two African Americans, soon became the front-runners to succeed Holmgren. Ray had been Holmgren's defensive coordinator in 1992 and '93 before leaving to become defensive coordinator for San Francisco. A year later he was hired as head coach of the Philadelphia Eagles. After two solid 10-6 seasons — including the '95 season when he was named NFL Coach of the Year — the Eagles fell on hard times. Ray was fired after his team struggled to a 3-13 mark in 1998. He was replaced by Andy Reid, who had been the Packers' quarterbacks coach.

Sherm Lewis was the Packers' offensive coordinator from 1992–99, a period of great success for the team as Brett Favre developed into a Hall of Fame quarterback. While there was no doubt that Sherm was a great assistant coach, I think his social reputation might have hurt his chances at getting the top job. The Packers have a forty-five-person board of directors, and you can't believe how much information comes from the community and makes its way through the board members. They were hearing things about Sherm that I'm sure made them uneasy. It was well known that Sherm spent a lot of time socializing in the clubs. He enjoyed being around people and was one of the funniest and most likable people I've met in this business.

I don't know how much of what the board was hearing was factual, but within the organization it generated questions as to whether they wanted to risk a potential public relations problem. Sometimes you have to take a look at your position and where you'd like to be, as well as the culture of the organization you're working for. I was getting a lot of feedback, even from policemen, and I'm sure Ron Wolf and Bob Harlan were as well. In the end, I think maybe Ron was scared to put Sherm in that position, and he hired Ray instead.

Ray was a lot more laid-back than Holmgren, so there was a big difference in the team. Ray's a fantastic defensive coordinator, but I don't know if he was meant to be a head coach. Discipline quickly deteriorated, and some of the players and assistant coaches took advantage of Ray's soft approach. The team was treading water at 5-5 when we had an incident in San Francisco that illustrated the breakdown in discipline. Some of the players had women up in the hotel, which isn't the best thing for staying focused on the road. I was upset because our whole security team and off-duty police officers had to deal with it. Even so, the team went out and beat the 49ers the next day, 20-3. I don't know how we did that. Distractions like we had on that trip usually show up on the football field the next day.

Holmgren had been very disciplined, and everybody from the equipment managers to assistant coaches knew what was expected of them. Coach did that with every department that made up the football program, and there was no doubt he was in charge. Holmgren's system was the only way I knew to do things; I didn't know how to be less structured. Coach Mike brought in that San Francisco 49ers mindset, and it worked. How we did everything was very structured, from meals to when the buses left, and we never had a losing season under him. If you didn't fall in line you got fined—and that didn't apply only to players; it went all the way down the system.

Ray was the opposite. He didn't spend a lot of time in his office, and he wasn't really a hands-on type of guy. He let people do their jobs, which didn't always work out. His coaching staff was very talented—in fact, Mike McCarthy was on that staff as a young quarterbacks coach—but the team underachieved nonetheless We lost three of our last four games to finish 8-8 and missed the playoffs. That was hard coming off the success of the Holmgren years.

Brett Favre was in the prime of his career, and he helped pull out a few close wins early in the season; otherwise it could've been more disastrous than it was. That's probably why Ron dismissed Ray after only one year—he was concerned about the direction the franchise was headed. Had the team finished under .500, firing Ray would've been easier for Ron.

I don't believe race played any role in Ray's dismissal. Ron saw things happening with the team that weren't good. He knew we were loose, which was a big change from how we'd been under Coach Holmgren, and he was concerned about non-football issues, too.

THE LEADERS OF THE PACK

There were reports that Ray was often at the local Oneida Casino, and that on one occasion he was so drunk he fell off a stool. I had to go out to the casino and talk to the people working that night. They told me Ray hadn't been drunk; rather, he was tired and hadn't had enough to eat. I have no reason to think the casino staff lied to me, and I never got any confirmation of heavy drinking that night, but those were the types of reports that were feeding back into the organization, and we had to deal with them.

The Packers beat the Arizona Cardinals 49-24 at Lambeau to wrap up the season. I was sitting in my kitchen not more than three hours after the game when Ron called and said, "Jerry, come back to work. I'm getting rid of the head coach."

That was a difficult time for me because I loved Ray. He's a great guy, very warm and very easy to approach. I had a one-on-one with him back at the stadium, and I cried after that.

Even though Ray was fired by the Eagles and Packers, he's a good football coach, no doubt about it. He's one of the league's great coaches of defense, and has continued to prove it as an assistant, first with Coach Holmgren in Seattle and then with the Houston Texans.

Mike Sherman (2000–2005)

Mike Sherman left with Mike Holmgren to become offensive coordinator for the Seahawks following two seasons as the Packers' tight ends coach. After firing Ray Rhodes, Ron Wolf wanted go back to what had been working for the Packers, so other former assistants with ties to Holmgren became the logical candidates.

Sherman was a much more structured coach than Ray was, and his strength was the offensive side of the ball. He came from the same type of professional background as Holmgren. Having been an English teacher, he was very articulate. He was also very humble when he was hired, and fully appreciative of what he was getting into. He's a very confident man with no doubt in his abilities. Knowing Mike's family, I'd say he developed his strong faith during childhood.

When Mike took over as the Packers' head coach, we got better right away. He went right back to Holmgren's system and we followed the same rules. It was like we took the 1999 season and wiped it off the board. Everything went back to how it had been in '98, only under Mike Sherman's personality rather than Mike Holmgren's.

After a slow start his rookie season, we won five of the last six games to finish 9-7 and just miss the playoffs. We then went 12-4 in 2001 and '02, with both seasons ending in early playoff losses. Some people in the organization thought Mike was the second coming of Lombardi because he had a good won-lost record, but that was just stupid talk.

I began to notice a change in Coach Sherman's demeanor with his added responsibilities as general manager in 2001. He grew a lot more difficult to deal with and became unapproachable on the football field. He didn't want anyone talking to him. In the security part of the business, you're only as good as your head coach in dealing with issues. I was comfortable with Mike in the beginning. When he was hired, he asked me to be a team member, and I was always there to help out and do anything asked of me. It wasn't long, though, before we had to go through his assistant just to talk to him. I can understand that to some extent, especially when he succeeded Wolf as GM prior to the 2001 season. The man spent a lot of time here and was a hardworking coach. Still, I think you have to deal with the people you've got on your team. I finally got in to see him one day, and about half the time I was talking, he was looking the other way. His body language said he didn't care what I had to say.

"Coach, you're a very difficult man to talk to," I said.

He looked at me and said, "Jerry, why do you say that?"

He'd put the ball right back in my court, and that exchange bothered me for weeks. After that, my relationship with him was never the

THE LEADERS OF THE PACK

same. He put me on the back burner, so to speak, and it seemed like he didn't want my help. He probably felt that I'd offended him.

Holmgren respected my ability to evaluate a player. He always encouraged the player to tell the truth, because he didn't want any surprises down the line. I never had that kind of cooperation and support from Sherman. I can't remember one issue that he wanted my opinion about, other than the few times he asked if I thought a player was lying.

Sherman started to become obsessed with details and control, even putting in a dress code for the people working in football operations. They were required to wear dress slacks in the Lambeau third-floor offices — no jeans were allowed. There was an incident in late January 2003, when I went to the football level to talk to someone. I had on a new sweater over a dress shirt, polished shoes, and a nice pair of jeans. I got off the elevator as Coach Sherman was coming through the area.

"Good morning, Coach," I said.

He didn't respond. Instead, he just looked me up and down. I was deeply insulted. I have a lot of respect for everyone, no matter what his or her job, and I felt he had no respect for me at all. I was devastated by that encounter, and it burned on me so bad that I went and talked to Bob Harlan the next day. Bob's a great listener and he knew I was upset. I forget exactly what I said to him, but I had to vent. I even shared it with my whole family, Doug Collins, and Pepper Burruss.

Within a couple weeks of that incident, my whole world collapsed when I found out I had cancer. After the news hit back at Lambeau, I began to receive support from a number of people. I was getting ready to fight this illness and was very emotional. There was a knock on our door, and it was Coach Sherman. I immediately forgot about all those things that had aggravated and hurt me. I was very humbled that he would come to my house. That shows his underlying character, too. He had some very warm and special words for me. "This is going to be a battle, Jerry, but go after it. Let me know what I can do to help."

I had my differences with Coach Sherman, but he's still a fine man. It was just very difficult for me to work for him.

Mike McCarthy (2006–present)

Mike McCarthy was a young quarterbacks coach on Ray Rhodes's staff during the 1999 season, so he was familiar with the Packers organization when Ted Thompson hired him to be head man in 2006. I didn't get to know Mike personally when he was here the first time, but he had a good relationship with Brett Favre even then, and the two worked together very well.

The biggest change from the way Holmgren and Sherman conducted business was in how very detailed they were in talking to players and how much time they spent in meetings. Coach McCarthy gives players the substance of what he wants them to know, then gets them out of meetings a lot quicker. He doesn't say as much, but what he says is very meaningful. It's just a different approach from the other two guys'.

Mike's father was a policeman and fireman in Pennsylvania, and Mike obviously learned something from him about how to be a leader and deal with men. He's got a lot of people skills, and everybody in the organization became much more relaxed when he took over. I feel that's very important.

Ted and Mike came to the conclusion that our team wasn't physical enough under the previous leadership, and correcting that starts in the weight room. Mike hired Rock Gullickson as the strength and conditioning coordinator, and the team spent about $200,000 redoing the weight room. Rock is a Harley rider and has become a close friend of mine.

The success of the 2007 season actually started at the end of the

2006 season, when the team won its last four games to finish 8-8. That was a lot of fun, and that team felt as close as the ones in the 1990s had. It was quite an accomplishment for that team to win five games on the road. For some reason, though, we struggled at home. I saw Coach lose his temper twice, which wasn't bad considering the team was 4-8 at one point. He's very good at handling losses, and he doesn't let his emotions control him. Coach Holmgren was one of the best coaches I've ever been around, but I've seen him become irate at halftime.

The enjoyment that came with those four season-ending wins—especially the last one in Chicago—is probably what brought Brett back for the 2007 season. I saw his tears of emotion when he gave that post-game TV interview, and I thought he was saying goodbye. Sandy kept telling me I was wrong. She was right.

The way Coach McCarthy deals with Brett and his fame is very important to the Packers' success. Some coaches would have a real problem with that. The night before that game, Brett had dinner in a back room at the Westin Hotel with Deanna, their daughter, Brittany, and Deanna's sister. After we were done, we had to walk Brett through the restaurant and over to a private service elevator to keep him away from the public. Brett wore jeans, a T-shirt, and flip-flops, and it was so funny watching the domino effect as people in the restaurant realized who was walking past them. Before they could react we were gone. I'm there to make sure things go smoothly and no one bothers Brett, because he can draw a lot of attention real fast.

Brett always gets more attention than the coach, but Mike understands that it's not all about him. He doesn't care that he's overshadowed by one of his players. When you have a player of Brett's magnitude it can be difficult to handle because you've got the rest of the team to deal with as well. But you can't treat every player the same. Cameramen are all over Brett after the games. In my field, it's important how Mike handles that.

Right from the start, Mike would go to both church services with the players. He comes from a very strong Irish-Catholic family and attends Mass, but he also attends the chapel service. We made a change to the schedule so he could attend both, and the players appreciated that. It's another little thing that I think is important, and it shows his character and the personality he brings to this team.

After every home game, everyone is invited over to Coach's house to hang out and have a beverage and something to eat. It's not just the players and coaches — but the whole staff, including trainers, equipment people, security team, and others. That sends a great message, and it's really nice of him to do that.

From a security perspective, Mike is very approachable and makes you feel like he's on your side. He's sensitive to players' issues and makes sure guys get their rest. He puts a lot of faith in us to do our jobs, and the 2007 season went relatively smoothly despite the increasing pressure. I didn't notice it affecting him at all. In fact, I saw him become more confident in his ability and the team's ability to perform on Sunday. Mike Sherman wouldn't be comfortable with things right up until kickoff, where Coach McCarthy is done with any changes by Friday's practice.

McCarthy did a remarkable job getting the team ready for the 2007 season. As soon as the draft was over, he told the players he was going to work them hard in May and June so training camp could be a little easier. His goal was to get them ready to play a sixteen-game regular season and the playoffs. It made for the most relaxed atmosphere by far since I've been here. The players believe in Mike and they had fun. Going 13-3 and making it all the way to the NFC Championship Game also made it a fun year for Brett, because winning is his biggest concern. So many things have to go your way to get that far. Some teams are better than others, but part of it depends on when in the season you play them and on turnovers and other mistakes.

We won some big games early in the season despite the fact that our running game was weak. Coach put in a five-receiver set that featured Brett and the passing game, then Ryan Grant started running the ball terrifically about halfway through the season and we started to dominate. We even won back-to-back games at Denver and Kansas City, and we never win there.

After losing at Dallas late in the season, everyone figured we'd have to win a playoff game on the road to make it to the Super Bowl. We earned a first-round bye as the second seed in the NFC, and beat Seattle easily in a snowy divisional playoff game at Lambeau. Our guys didn't care whom they played next. I think they were geared up to go back down to Dallas and beat the Cowboys, but when the New York Giants eliminated Dallas and gave us home-field advantage for the NFC Championship Game, I think there may have been a letdown.

The Giants came into Lambeau and played a great game. The difference was Eli Manning; nobody expected him to become the quarterback he has, and he's going to be one tough customer from now on. The Giants were more physical than we were that day, and two weeks later they were more physical against the New England Patriots in the Super Bowl. The tough part for me was losing that game at home. We got our nose bloodied, and it hurt.

Everyone was really down the next day, so it was nice to see the great memo Ted Thompson wrote to the whole organization:

> I want to say thank you for all the hard work and sacrifice you have made throughout the year. This organization is made up of wonderful people who care about each other and work very hard to do their part in lifting up the Packers as an example of how people can come together to form something special. We are all hurting a bit today, but you are to be congratulated. Most of you do your work in the background, but know that your efforts are

> appreciated. I am personally indebted for all that you do and proud to work alongside you. go pack.

You only get so many chances to get to the Super Bowl, and that was a great opportunity; however, I have a feeling we'll get there again as long as Ted and Mike are at the helm.

Epilogue

WHEN I STEPPED DOWN from the security director's position right after my Cruise for Cancer ride in June 2007, it had been more than four years since my diagnosis. Some things are just a blur for me during that period. When I was down, Doug Collins did an excellent job with the Packers' security team as we moved the organization into a full-time, round-the-clock security service. He directed that transition and did my administrative job when I was too sick to work full-time.

Now we've kind of reversed roles. I'm here to support Doug and deal with issues in my new role as senior security advisor. Officially, I'm a part-time employee, but I'm probably still at Lambeau Field just as much as I was before. The Packers are very good to me; they don't make me punch a clock, and I'm very happy with what I'm doing. The biggest difference is that I spend less time on the phone now and less time dealing with internal issues.

I still have a passion for football, and my cancer ride remains a major focus for me in my dealings with the organization. I hear all sorts of nice stories regarding the ride. That really sustains me. Prior to our September 2007 game in Minneapolis, the guy who plays Ragnar, the Minnesota Vikings' mascot, told me how much he enjoyed coming over to Green Bay for the ride. It seems to be growing its own identity, and it means everything that we can help people who aren't as fortunate as I was in my cancer journey.

Doug counts on me to help take care of things at practice, which gives him some space to take care of other things. Coach McCarthy relies on Doug to do a lot, so if I'm needed to take care of some of the rest, that's fine with me. I travel with the team for the most part, and Doug and I still do bed checks together. I'm very involved with the team, and that makes me feel good.

The 2007 season was my first full season outside the security director's role. It was a wonderful surprise to see the team so successful. Coach McCarthy and his staff did a great job and Brett played as well as he ever has. His arm strength remains fantastic, and just being around him is fun. He treats me almost like a father, and I'm honored by that. It's easy to be friends with such a spectacular player, but our relationship is more than just that.

Brett still has a lot of fun on the field, and Doug helps keep him busy off the field. Brett got away from golf over the past several years, but he loves to hunt. He and Doug go out in the woods often during deer bow season, but Brett's a loner, too. He can sit up in a tree stand for hours and wait for a deer to walk by. It's his time to just be.

I'm proud of the fact that Doug has continued to do virtually everything regarding security the way I did. The players are very respectful of me, and I'm honored by that, too. If I didn't feel I was of value to this football team, I would give it all up. I have too much pride to just stay here for health insurance or for just having a job. I don't want to be a hanger-on. I know I could derive a lot of satisfaction from just helping people in the cancer field. It's not a limelight situation like working for the Packers, but it's got true meaning.

Regardless of whether I continue to work for the organization or not, I've truly enjoyed my association with the Green Bay Packers over the past five decades, and I hope I've had a positive impact on one of the greatest sports organizations in the world.

Go Pack!

A Word to My Readers

I WAS LUCKY.

A colonoscopy isn't something that ranks high on my list of fun things to do or even talk about. In fact I never seriously considered having one until blood began showing up in my stools when I was sixty-four years old. Colonoscopy, a simple, painless screening procedure, could have detected the cancer growing in my colon much earlier and given me a better chance of survival.

I was lucky the cancer didn't kill me. I'm grateful that my medical team succeeded, using every tool at its disposal—surgery, chemotherapy, and radiation—to rid my body of this awful disease. As of this writing, I'm happy to report that the doctors have given me a five-year clean bill of health. Every year, however, thousands of men and women aren't so lucky. Colon cancer is the second leading cause of cancer-related death in the United States.

The good news is that colorectal cancer (cancer of the colon or rectum) is highly curable when it's caught early. The five-year survival rate for stage 1 patients is better than 90 percent. That plunges to only about 10 percent for people in the advanced stages of the disease.

My doctors told me my cancer was at least stage 2 and possibly stage 3 by the time I'd begun to notice symptoms. That's why I needed chemotherapy before and after surgery, along with thirty-three radiation treatments.

Screening is the most important tool for catching colorectal cancer early, yet about 40 percent of Americans age fifty or older haven't had a colonoscopy in the past ten years. That's a national statistic we need to improve upon. If I could choose one benefit for you to derive from reading this book, it would be to increase your awareness of the need to get screened.

Because such wonderful work is done to promote the benefits of breast exams, women are much better at understanding the need for screening than men are. It's a different story for us guys. Typically, cancer screening—especially for colorectal cancer—isn't a subject we want to talk about. But we have to, not just for our own sake, but for the welfare of our families and others who are important to us. We have to get past the idea that discussing this topic is embarrassing and that getting screened is somehow a sign of weakness. It's not.

I'm thankful that I was able to talk about it with my friends and coworkers in the Packers organization, who were a tremendous source of support to me. In the process, we all learned a lot about the vital importance of screening and early diagnosis.

I wrote *Bodyguard* with the intention of bringing you inside the Packers; however, it's my hope that those who read this book—men in particular—will learn to be bodyguards to their own health. There's nothing heroic or athletic about putting off health screenings or ignoring physical symptoms. Women have learned to go in for regular examinations. We men can learn, too. If you're a woman reading this book, please pass it to a man in your life and create the discussion.

Guys, talk to your doctor today. Screening takes just a few hours of your time, and it can literally save your life. Don't roll the dice like I did. Your life is too important to leave to chance.

I was just lucky.

Jerry